Business & Marketing Across Cultures

Sara Miller McCune founded SAGE Publishing in 1965 to support the dissemination of usable knowledge and educate a global community. SAGE publishes more than 1000 journals and over 800 new books each year, spanning a wide range of subject areas. Our growing selection of library products includes archives, data, case studies and video. SAGE remains majority owned by our founder and after her lifetime will become owned by a charitable trust that secures the company's continued independence.

Los Angeles | London | New Delhi | Singapore | Washington DC | Melbourne

Julie Anne Lee, Jean-Claude Usunier & Vasyl Taras

Business & Marketing Across Cultures

Los Angeles | London | New Delhi
Singapore | Washington DC | Melbourne

Los Angeles | London | New Delhi
Singapore | Washington DC | Melbourne

SAGE Publications Ltd
1 Oliver's Yard
55 City Road
London EC1Y 1SP

SAGE Publications Inc.
2455 Teller Road
Thousand Oaks, California 91320

SAGE Publications India Pvt Ltd
B 1/I 1 Mohan Cooperative Industrial Area
Mathura Road
New Delhi 110 044

SAGE Publications Asia-Pacific Pte Ltd
3 Church Street
#10-04 Samsung Hub
Singapore 049483

Editor: Matthew Waters
Assistant editor: Charlotte Hanson
Production editor: Sarah Sewell
Copyeditor: Clare Weaver
Proofreader: Bryan Campbell
Marketing manager: Lucia Sweet
Cover design: Francis Kenny
Typeset by: C&M Digitals (P), Ltd, Chennai, India
Printed in the UK

Library of Congress Control Number: 2022947629

British Library Cataloguing in Publication data

A catalogue record for this book is available from the British Library

ISBN 978-1-5297-5438-4
ISBN 978-1-5297-5437-7 (pbk)

At SAGE we take sustainability seriously. Most of our products are printed in the UK using responsibly sourced papers and boards. When we print overseas we ensure sustainable papers are used as measured by the Book Chain Project grading system. We undertake an annual audit to monitor our sustainability.

BRIEF CONTENTS

CONTENTS

ABOUT THE AUTHORS

Julie Anne Lee is a Winthrop Professor in Marketing and the Director of Research and Research Training in the Business School at The University of Western Australia. She is the Founding Director of the Centre for Human and Cultural Values, established in 2018. She holds a PhD degree from the University of Illinois at Urbana-Champaign, and previously worked at the University of Hawaii and University of Miami, Florida, USA. Her research interests are in cross-cultural consumer behaviour, in particular, in human values and how they are expressed in consumer behaviour. Her publications have appeared in many prestigious journals, such as the *Journal of Personality and Social Psychology*, *Social Psychological and Personality Science*, *Journal of Consumer Psychology*, *Journal of International Marketing*, *Tourism Management*, and the *Journal of Travel Research* (winning the Charles R. Goeldner Article of Excellence Award in 2020). Her recent books include *International and Cross-Cultural Business Research* (Sage, 2017, with Jean-Claude Usunier and Hester van Herk) and *Marketing Across Cultures* (Pearson, 2013; with Jean-Claude Usunier). Before embarking on her academic career, she worked in management and tourism, including the position of Regional Manager for Tourism in the Kimberly region of Western Australia.

Jean-Claude Usunier is an Emeritus Professor from the Faculty of Business and Economics at the University of Lausanne, Switzerland. His research interests are in cross-cultural consumer behaviour, and cultural and linguistic aspects of international marketing and management. He has served on the editorial boards of several international business and marketing journals. His publications have appeared in prestigious journals, such as the *European Journal of Marketing*, *International Journal of Research in Marketing*, *Journal of International Marketing*, and *International Marketing Review*. His recent books include *Intercultural Business Negotiations: Deal-Making or Relationship Building?* (Routledge, 2019), *International and Cross-Cultural Business Research* (Sage, 2017, with Julie Lee and Hester van Herk) and *Marketing Across Cultures* (Pearson, 6th edn, 2013; with Julie Lee).

Vasyl Taras is a Professor in the Bryan School of Business and Economics, University of North Carolina at Greensboro, USA. He is the X-Culture Founder and Project Director (www.X-Culture.org). He holds a PhD from the University of Calgary, Canada. His research interests are in cross-cultural and global virtual teams and crowd-based business problem solving, and experiential learning. He is an Associate Editor of the *International Journal of Cross-Cultural Management*, and an Editorial Board member of *Journal of International Business Studies, Journal of International Management*, and *Management Research Review*. His publications have appeared in many prestigious journals, including the *Journal of Applied Psychology, Journal of International Business Studies, Journal of International Management*, and *Organizational Dynamics*. He is a recipient of numerous research and teaching awards for his work in International Business. Vas has lived, worked and studied in half a dozen countries and has experience as a manager, businessman, and business consultant.

PREFACE

The idea for this book came from a passion for working collaboratively across cultures and a desire to facilitate deeper learning and the development of life-skills through the X-Culture project. As a real-life global collaboration, the X-Culture project offers a safe space for students and professionals to gain experience and insight into the complexity of working with globally dispersed teams, and all the challenges of managing time zones, teams, and personalities, where individuals have deeply held and very different assumptions of how things should be based on their own experiences and culture. Our aim was to develop a concise and insightful text to support students, and anyone, grappling with the complexities of cross-cultural collaboration and/or the development of a well-crafted and insightful international business plan. While cross-cultural collaboration can be challenging, it can also be a wonderful opportunity for growth, introspection, and creativity.

The world of international business, and how we prepare for it, has changed dramatically in recent years, and with it the broad *global,* and sometimes *ethnocentric,* perspective portrayed in many global and international business texts is no longer tenable. Businesses need to move beyond replicating past practices, and students need to gain real-life, guided, international experience to help them develop the necessary skills in dealing with highly diverse cultural environments before they are involved in international business decision making. We aim to do this by delivering state-of-the-art cross-cultural insight to help businesses and individuals recognise that a greater understanding of cultural differences will improve their performance.

Unlike most other international business and international marketing texts, this text recognises and demonstrates diversity in world markets, in local consumer knowledge, and in marketing practices. This text uses a two-pronged cross-cultural approach to learning. First, we provide a ***comparative cross-cultural approach*** to investigate what is country specific and what is universal. Then, we take an ***intercultural approach***, which focuses on interactions between business people, buyers and sellers, and consumers, with different national/cultural backgrounds. This intercultural view also extends to the interaction between products (their physical and symbolic attributes, as well as the messages surrounding them) that are from a definite nation-culture and consumers who are from a different nation-culture. This two-pronged approach helps to make sense of cultural insight in the preparation and implementation of effective business strategies for different international contexts. Throughout this text, we encourage the reader to engage in cultural self-reflection with the aim of changing their worldview and enhancing their ability to make effective decisions in cross-cultural environments. We promote experiential learning by providing activities, examples and links to the X-Culture project which builds multicultural collaborative virtual teams who are tasked with solving real-world international business problems. We also support the learning process by providing practical recommendations to manage team interactions and improve the business planning process.

This text aims, in just six chapters, to provide deep and meaningful insight into cross-cultural collaboration and to the development of sound strategies for successfully entering new international markets. It starts in Part 1 with a focus on understanding the self and others in cross-cultural and international contexts. In Chapter 1, we discuss broad cultural frameworks that can be used to scaffold deeper cultural knowledge. In Chapter 2, we discuss communication and language differences and provide recommendations for successful intercultural communication, as well as advice on how to write in English for non-native English speakers. In Chapter 3, we discuss the process of intercultural interactions and provide recommendations for effective intercultural teamwork, including how to deal with communication misunderstandings. Then, in Part 2, we consider the international environment and how cross-cultural differences may impact the success of business decisions, especially when entering new international markets. In Chapter 4, we explore international business strategy, including the selection of new target markets and modes of entry, as well as how to deal with foreign partners and control foreign operations. In Chapter 5, we examine cross-cultural marketing strategy and implementation, including international product and branding decisions, distribution and pricing under different market conditions, and the influence of culture on communication strategies. Finally, in Chapter 6, we provide practical advice on how to develop a well-crafted, culturally sensitive business plan, including the conceptualisation of clear aims, the utilisation of appropriate analysis tools, concepts, and theories, and the development and communication of clear recommendations.

This book is intended as a primary text for international and global marketing units and as a supplemental text for international business units, especially units that incorporate the X-Culture or similar cross-cultural projects. It is targeted at advanced undergraduate or masters' students, as well as managers involved in international business decision making.

INTRODUCING X-CULTURE

Add a real-life global collaboration exercise to your International Business Course.

X-Culture is an experiential learning project managed by over 200 International Business professors.

Over 6,000 MBA and undergraduate students from 50+ countries on 6 continents participate in X-Culture every semester (90,000+ have participated in X-Culture so far).

We put our students in global virtual teams (GVTs). About 6 students per team, each in a different country.

The students work on real-life international business challenges presented by real companies. The students basically serve as IB consultants, while also learning how to work with people from other cultures.

Separate tracks for Undergraduate, Master's, and EMBA students, as well as for non-student professionals.

Step-by-step

1. Students are enrolled by their teachers (entire class) or parents (one child).
2. Students receive age-appropriate training on online collaboration tools, teamwork, problem-solving, and report writing.
3. Students work in international teams, 6 per team, each from a different country.
4. All communication online and in English.
5. Real companies submit real business challenges. The teams develop solutions.
6. We monitor student performance and provide support as needed.

7. When done, the students present their reports to their client companies.
8. The students and teachers receive X-Culture International Business Certificates and recommendation letters.
9. The best students are invited to the X-Culture Symposium.

Research

Research is a big part of X-Culture. We collect immense amounts of data suitable for studying just about any aspect of global virtual teams, as well as organisational behaviour and international business in general. Dozens of papers have been published, and half a dozen doctoral dissertations have been defended based on the X-Culture data. We are always open to collaboration with researchers who might be interested in using our data.

More info

- How it works: x-culture.org
- What you gain as an instructor: x-culture.org/for-instructors
- What your students gain: x-culture.org/for-students

PART 1
UNDERSTANDING THE SELF AND OTHERS IN CROSS-CULTURAL AND INTERNATIONAL CONTEXTS

International business and marketing give a prominent place to culture, but not everything is culturally driven. Individual behaviour is influenced, but not exclusively determined, by culture. Understanding what is influenced by culture is often more complicated than initially expected. Culture is complex, multifaceted, and sometimes fuzzy. Our understanding of other cultures is often limited, forcing us to rely on rather shallow or stereotypical ideas about other cultures.

Culture is difficult to isolate. International business often resorts to using country or nation-states as primary segmentation bases, because borders are easily definable. Yet, there are few nations whose ethnic, linguistic, and religious groups are homogeneous. Throughout Part 1 of the book, we strive at giving a balanced view of what is cultural and what is related to purely individual characteristics such as personality, gender, and age.

- In Chapter 1, we discuss the seminal definitions and major aspects of culture, including values, beliefs, language, and social institutions. We examine what culture is and what it is not, and how individuals are embedded in their societal culture. We integrate two main cultural frameworks, those of Hofstede and Schwartz, to describe how they provide solutions to problems that all societies face. These frameworks provide a scaffolding that can be used to integrate more detailed cultural knowledge. Finally, we describe critical incidents that can be used to diminish the effect of our cultural conditioning.

- In Chapter 2, we discuss language differences, how language influences worldviews and mindsets, and communication styles and context. We explain a number of key concepts of intercultural communication: low-context/ explicit messages versus high-context/implicit messages, direct versus indirect communication, and instrumental versus representative communication. We also discuss how cross-cultural communication channels, whether face-to-face or online, based on speech or written materials, influence the quality and efficiency of information exchange at different stages in the collaborative process. A set of recommendations for successful intercultural communication is provided, including advice for non-native English speakers on how to write in English.

- In Chapter 3, we examine the process of intercultural interactions, which will be of paramount importance for cross-cultural teams (e.g., in the X-Culture project). A series of key issues are developed to answer questions, such as the role of task versus non-task orientations in intercultural interactions, how to learn about foreign partners, and how to avoid the pitfalls of ethnocentrism and stereotypes. We explain how to deal with communication misunderstandings and conflict escalation. The basics of negotiating and cooperating across cultures are discussed, including how emotional and cultural intelligence can be used to foster intercultural interaction skills. We offer different paths towards adjustment in intercultural interactions, based on alternative sequences of awareness, knowledge, and adjustment stages. Finally, we provide a set of recommendations for effective intercultural teamwork.

1
SIMILARITIES AND DIFFERENCES ACROSS AND WITHIN CULTURES

Learning objectives

After reading this chapter and completing the activities, you should be able to:

- Define culture and understand how culture influences individuals.
- Understand the differences between etic and emic views and how they lead to different conclusions about cultural similarities and differences.
- Know and describe the broad cultural patterns that reflect differences in the preferred solutions to the problems all societies face, including (1) boundaries between people and the group, (2) equality or inequality between people, (3) whether people should act with or for others, (4) dealing with uncertainty, and (5) dealing with time.
- Analyse cultural differences between countries and explain how they are likely to relate to patterns of consumer behaviour.
- Critically discuss the concept of cultural distance.
- Recognise conditions that lead to cultural clashes and deal with prejudices.
- Learn how to isolate self-reference criteria to eliminate it from intercultural interactions.

Introduction

The major factor that distinguishes international and cross-cultural business from its main disciplines is the context. Within this context, *culture* is one of the most important and complex environmental factors to understand and effectively deal with in international and cross-cultural business. Given that there are almost 200 countries in the world today, and few can be considered to be truly homogeneous in terms of language, ethnicity, religion, etc., it is well beyond any one person's capacity to gain a deep and meaningful understanding of all the world's cultures. However, it is within our capacity to learn enough about broad cultural similarities and differences to build a scaffold or structure upon which deeper cultural knowledge about specific cultures can be integrated to effectively inform international and cross-cultural business decisions.

While it is possible to develop cultural awareness from reading materials written from a culturally alien perspective, it takes conscious, deliberative, and reflective thinking to examine and understand both your own and the other culture's perspectives. Cultural assumptions are not completely in the realm of unbewußtsein (unconsciousness, deep-seated and inaccessible); they are rather in the realm of unterbewußtsein, which is located at a subconscious level, where interaction and self-questioning can reveal them. As such, exposure to different cultural solutions, along with a concerted effort to understand, compare, and contrast them in a non-evaluative manner, can lead to a deeper level of cultural understanding.

To assist with your journey, we invite you to complete a series of activities designed to help you engage in deeper learning. For readers who are not currently working in international and cross-cultural business settings, we suggest you explore participation in the X-Culture project[1].

The X-Culture project offers students and professionals the opportunity to work in a virtual intercultural team to solve a current, real-world international business expansion problem. This provides the opportunity to employ and test your insights into real-world international challenges in a 'safe' environment. However, before we begin, we need to understand what culture is.

What is the X-Culture project? It is where students and professionals learn business through a global virtual team experience. They work on real international business challenges, presented by real companies, in teams where each team member is in a different country.

X-Culture = Students + Professors + Business + Research

- Businesses ask for help.
- Students help businesses while gaining international business experience.
- Professors help their students learn from experience.
- Researchers use the data for research.

At the end of the project, teams present their business plans to be evaluated by 6 or 7 independent experts. So far, over 66,000 students, in more than 12,500 teams, from over 100 countries have successfully participated in the project, and received peer evaluations, performance records, a personalised letter of recommendation, and an X-Culture Global Collaboration Experience Certificate. The best reports are uploaded to the X-Culture website and the authors receive Best Student Awards. But the most valuable part of the project is the intercultural experience gained.

Chapter Overview

We discuss the seminal definitions and major aspects of culture, including values, beliefs, language, and social institutions. We examine what culture is and what it is not, and how individuals are embedded in their societal culture. We integrate two main cultural frameworks, those of Hofstede and Schwartz, to describe how they provide solutions to problems that all societies face. These frameworks provide a scaffolding that can be used to integrate more detailed cultural knowledge. Finally, we describe critical incidents that can be used to diminish the effect of our cultural conditioning.

In this chapter, we focus on the concept of culture in broad, etic terms as a practical starting point into which deeper cultural knowledge can be integrated. In the following sections, we describe the main cultural orientations in business studies and discuss how culture influences, but does not determine, individuals' behaviour:

- **Section 1** explains what **culture** is and how it links to the individual through the institutions and groups they are exposed to on a daily basis. We also explain that some cultures (i.e., tight cultures) place more situational constraints on everyday behaviour than others (i.e., loose cultures), where people have more freedom.
- **Section 2** describes how different perspectives can lead to a different understanding of the world: an etic view that looks from the outside to reveal generalities versus an emic view that looks from the inside to reveal what is unique. We integrate two main etic cultural frameworks that are commonly used in international business (i.e., Hofstede's and Schwartz's), forming a scaffold upon which more specific cultural knowledge can be integrated.
- **Section 3** discusses cultural comparisons and cultural distance. We also distinguish culture from nationality and discuss different types of homogeneity that can lead to more or less cohesiveness within a nation-state.

- **Section 4** explains that an individual's personal values are distinct from cultural values. However, since values reflect what is important in life, people tend to think what they value should be important to everyone. But this is not the case. We outline a set of steps to help diminish the decisional bias related to self-referencing.
- **Section 5** highlights the need to adjust in intercultural interactions. It describes different types of critical incidents that are used to train people in intercultural interactions.

1.1 What is culture?

In an ideal world, we would begin with a simple definition of culture; however, culture is one of the most complicated words in the English language. It is used to describe different concepts in different fields of study:

- In anthropology, culture is primarily related to material productions (e.g., art, music, and physical productions). Cultures may also differ in the strength, in addition to the content, of social norms.
- In history, it is primarily related to symbolic systems (e.g., religious and moral beliefs); and
- In psychology, it is primarily related to values and norms that exist in the minds of individuals.

At its broadest, Williams defined culture as 'a whole way of life, material, intellectual and spiritual.'[2].

Culture is often described by normative systems that indicate preferred solutions to a set of universal problems that all societies face (e.g., how to best promote cooperative and productive behaviour; how to best regulate individual and group relations). While various solutions to each of these societal problems are present in some form in each society, specific solutions are preferred, leading to a dominant preferred solution and numerous alternative or substitute solutions[3]. Together, the combination of preferred solutions forms a coherent and complex culture that works for that society.

It is useful to think of culture as a hypothetical, latent, or *concealed* concept to which individuals are exposed, to a greater or lesser extent, in their daily lives[4]. In this way, those who grow up in a particular culture implicitly 'know' culturally normative beliefs, values, behaviours, and styles of thinking that sojourners might find difficult to recognise and understand. Individuals living in a culture are exposed to cultural stimuli (e.g., symbols and material productions) and reward contingencies that promote (approval) or demote (disapproval) specific goals, understandings, and preferences within a culture[5]. Based on their experience of these cultural exposures, people will internalise aspects of culture that make sense to them as individuals. This view highlights the idea that the way in which individuals within a society experience their culture depends on the groups they belong to (e.g., age, gender, religious, occupational, and family groups). Given this, it is entirely reasonable that cultures will differ both within and across countries.

Cultures may also differ in the strength, in addition to the content, of social norms. Even when two cultures endorse similar norms, they may differ in the expected compliance to those norms. Some cultures (i.e., tight cultures) have strong norms and a low tolerance for deviant behaviour, whereas others (i.e., loose cultures) have weaker norms and a higher tolerance for deviant behaviour[6]. Gelfand and colleagues[7] explained that tight, as opposed to loose, cultures are more likely to be religious, have more laws and regulations, have more controls on the media, and also have less access to and use of communication technologies, fewer political rights and civil liberties, and lower crime rates. They describe Pakistan, Malaysia, India, Singapore, South Korea, and Turkey as relatively tight cultures, where people have more situational constraints on everyday behaviour (e.g., in restaurants, workplaces, and banks), whereas Ukraine, Estonia, Hungary, the Netherlands, Brazil, New Zealand, and Australia are relatively loose cultures, where people have more freedom and there is a high tolerance for deviant behaviours. The strength of social norms also has important implications for understanding the drivers of an individual's behaviour. In tight cultural contexts, people are more likely to follow social norms rather than their own personal values, whereas in loose cultural contexts, people are more likely to ignore what others do and follow their own personal values[8].

Finally, in order to persist, culture must be carried from one generation to the next. Of course, a common language may be important for the communication of culture (as discussed in Chapter 2), but culture is also embedded in and communicated through social institutions and systems, as well as the symbolic productions (e.g., religious and moral beliefs) and material productions (e.g., art, music, products, and services) within a society. Differences in exposure to these elements of culture lead to variations in the content and distribution of beliefs, values, styles of thinking and behaviours between and within societies[9].

How culture links the individual to society

If we accept that culture is external to individuals, but embedded in social institutions and their policies and practices, we need to understand how people *internalise their culture and subculture* (see **Figure 1.1**). People are exposed to culture at different levels of society (i.e., macro, meso, and micro levels). At a **macro level**, the dominant normative systems in a culture are important to the smooth functioning of a society. They are expressed in and through social institutions (e.g., political, economic, legal, and educational systems) that link the individual to mainstream society. As previously mentioned, how strongly these cultural normative systems influence behaviour depends on the strength of norms that constrain the range of acceptable behaviour in society (i.e., tightness-looseness)[10]. The tighter the norms, the stronger the macro-mainstream influence will be on individuals. However, in many societies, **meso or mid-level** groups and social categories act as a mechanism that integrates and socialises individuals into the larger societal structure[11]. Groups (e.g., religion, profession) and social categories (e.g., age, gender) are meaningful subcultures that can have a profound impact on individuals. People who grew up in different religious communities, or were educated in different schooling systems, or work in different occupations, will be exposed to subcultures that emphasise different norms, despite the need to 'fit' within the mainstream culture to function effectively[12]. Even at the **micro level**, smaller social or family groups that individuals interact with on a continual basis impact how people internalise the culture in which they live. While all individuals will belong to different subcultures within society (e.g., a specific social class, a religious and/or ethnic group, or an occupational category), we still expect they will share a similar and profound knowledge of the pervasive cultural norms in society.

When people operate in more than one subculture (e.g., immigrants, bilinguals, international business professionals, and even teenagers who switch between their parent and peer cultures), they may need to develop different social representations that help to categorise and interpret circumstances, phenomena, and the behaviour of others, to guide their own behaviour in a specific context. These social representations, which can be viewed as schema or aspects of operational culture, are less profound than macro-mainstream cultural norms, as they alter within shorter time spans (10 to 20 years versus centuries), but they do provide insight as to why individuals within a country might behave differently in different situations.

A nice example of the fluid nature of social representations can be seen in the way bilingual and bicultural individuals (e.g., those who have lived in different countries) react to environmental cues that seem to elicit a subconscious switch in their operational culture. Researchers have found culturally consistent differences in the way bilinguals respond to the same survey written in different languages (e.g., Mandarin versus English). Similar differences in response have been found in bicultural individuals (e.g., those who have lived in different countries), when different cues are presented that prime one particular country (i.e., making it more salient), such as culturally common symbols (e.g., American flag versus Chinese dragon), pictures of famous people (e.g., Marilyn Monroe versus a Chinese opera singer), landmarks (e.g., the Capitol Building versus the Great Wall), and even popular cartoons (e.g., Superman versus Stone Monkey)[13]. This illustrates the importance of an operational culture in the interpretation of what is right for a given situation.

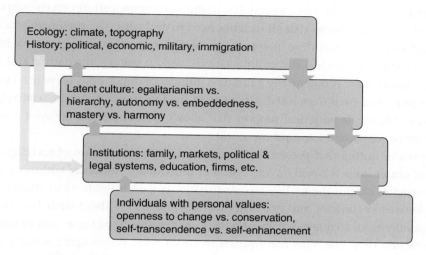

Ecology: climate, topography
History: political, economic, military, immigration

Latent culture: egalitarianism vs. hierarchy, autonomy vs. embeddedness, mastery vs. harmony

Institutions: family, markets, political & legal systems, education, firms, etc.

Individuals with personal values: openness to change vs. conservation, self-transcendence vs. self-enhancement

Figure 1.1 Relations between latent societal cultural values, emphases, institutions and individuals' values. Source: Adapted from Schwartz, S. H. (2014). Rethinking the concept and measurement of societal culture in light of empirical findings. *Journal of Cross-Cultural Psychology*, 45(1), 5–13.

1.2 Understanding similarities and differences between cultures

Etic versus emic research

A practical starting point from which to understand the influence of culture is to scaffold it onto research that examines broad similarities and differences that emerge when comparing cultures. This type of research comes from a more etic than emic perspective. Etic research looks from the outside, seeking relatively universal frameworks to compare similarities and differences across cultures, whereas emic research looks from the inside, seeking culture-specific information to uncover what is unique about a culture. Both etic and emic views are valid perspectives that are used to answer very different questions, and naturally they uncover very different information, leading to very different decisions. For instance, a business seeking to standardise globally is likely to take an etic approach in search of a universal concept that can be similarly applied in all its international markets, whereas a business looking to optimise its strategy for each market is likely to take an emic approach, developing concepts locally to best fit each culture. In this way, different *truths* about a culture will be uncovered, depending on the research paradigm applied.

Etic investigation, as a view from the outside, is naturally much more superficial than emic investigation. Nonetheless, it is useful to compare cultures on the ways they respond to basic problems that all societies need to deal with (i.e., their preferences for different solutions), including how to (1) promote cooperative and productive behaviour, (2) regulate individual and group relations, and (3) manage the natural and social world[14]. While there is potentially a limitless number of dimensions on which cultures can be compared (well over 100 distinct sets in the literature!), there are relatively few that have large-scale empirical support that allows for comparison between a significant number of societies around the world.

It is worth noting that the empirical support for the comparison of societies along cultural dimensions is based on aggregates of individuals' responses within a society, since societies cannot themselves answer surveys. To gain insights into cultural differences between countries, surveys either focus on questions about what is important to respondents, or to questions about what they perceive to be important to the society in which they live. This corresponds to either what respondents actually desire (e.g., the Schwartz Value Survey asks how important each value is to you as a guiding principle in YOUR life), in the first case, or what respondents think those in their society should desire (e.g., the GLOBE survey asks questions about society, such as whether the economic system in their society is designed to maximise individual interests versus collective interests[15]), in the second case. Both are valid approaches. However, in the first case, there is no expectation that respondents will prioritise the same values; rather, the average scores at the societal level capture normative differences. In the second case, there is an expectation of consensus across individuals, as perceptions of the pervasive norms in society should be shared.

In this section, we highlight two main cultural frameworks that are commonly used in international business. Both have large-scale empirical support (based on what people actually desire) and published societal level scores on each relevant dimension that allow the comparison between a wide range of societies (see end of chapter website links[16]). Specifically, we describe how these frameworks (i.e., Hofstede's and Schwartz's frameworks) relate to different preferred solutions to a range of important problems that all societies face:

- Hofstede's cultural dimensions were originally empirically derived from data collected around the 1970s from over 100,000 IBM employees in 40 countries[17].
- Schwartz's cultural values were empirically supported by data originally collected from 1988–2000 from around 40,000 teachers and students from 70 cultural groups in 67 nations[18], and later with representative samples from the European Social Survey[19].

Both have received subsequent support more recently. However, each framework has its own strengths and weaknesses. Hofstede's seminal work in developing his cultural dimensions provided ground-breaking insight, as the first major framework that allowed for easy comparison across a large number of countries. Hofstede's dimensions remain the most commonly used in international business, despite criticisms that they are overly simplified, empirically derived, based only on IBM employees, and are out-dated[20]. In contrast, Schwartz's cultural value orientations emerged from his study of personal values with a view to explaining differences between values at the societal level. His orientations were derived from *a priori* theorising about the problems that societies face, and then by testing their fit to empirical data. Interest in these orientations in the field of international business is growing, at least in part because they do not suffer the same criticisms as those of Hofstede, due to their theoretical basis.

A major advantage of examining two cultural frameworks, rather than one, is that both commonalities and unique aspects of cultures can be revealed. It is important to understand that there is no one truth or one set of true cultural dimensions, given that cultural frameworks are designed to reduce and describe complex cultural phenomena that are measured using individuals' subjective responses[21]. The number and nature of dimensions revealed depend on the variables studied, as well as the countries, time-period, methodology, and interpretation of the researchers[22]. Despite this, these frameworks are useful in understanding differences in the preferred solutions to the problems all societies face, such as

1. boundaries between people and the group,
2. equality or inequality between people,
3. whether people should act with or for others,
4. dealing with uncertainty, and
5. dealing with time.

Problem 1: Boundaries between people and the group

The first problem is the nature of relations between people and the boundaries between the person and the group. Solutions to this problem are described by the dimensions of Hofstede's individualism and collectivism, and Schwartz's autonomy-embeddedness dimensions.

●   *Individualism* describes societies where the ties are looser between individuals and their groups and people are expected to look after themselves and their immediate family, whereas *collectivism* describes societies where people are integrated into strong and cohesive in-groups that they are expected to be loyal to[23].

- *Autonomy* describes societies where people are encouraged to find meaning in uniqueness and express their own preferences, feelings, ideas, and abilities, whereas *embeddedness* describes societies where people are encouraged to find meaning in life through their social relationships, to identify with the group, and to strive for shared goals[24].

In more *individualist* societies, the norm is for people to take care of their own and their immediate family's needs, and relationships are expected to be reciprocal, where individuals who give something to others expect some sort of return within a reasonable time span. In contrast, in *collectivist* societies, the social structure is stronger, with the norm being that people clearly distinguish between members of their in-group and members of an out-group. In relationships, people normally expect their group to care for them in exchange for unwavering loyalty.

Schwartz describes two types of *autonomy*[25], where people in societies that emphasise *intellectual autonomy* are encouraged to value broadmindedness, curiosity, and creativity and people in societies that emphasise *affective autonomy* are encouraged to value pleasure, excitement, and variety in life. This contrasts with societies that emphasise embeddedness, where people are encouraged to value social order, security, respect for tradition, obedience, and wisdom.

Problem 2: Equality or inequality between people

The second problem relates to the legitimacy of inequality, in terms of the unequal distribution of power, which is reflected in Hofstede's *power distance* and Schwartz's *hierarchy-egalitarianism*. The legitimacy of inequality is shown as much by the behaviour of superiors who display and exercise their power, as by subordinates who expect this and feel uncomfortable if superiors do not display their authority[26].

- *Power distance* describes societies where less powerful members expect power to be unequally distributed[27].
- *Hierarchy* describes societies where people rely on vertically structured systems that ascribe roles to people to ensure productive and responsible behaviour, whereas *egalitarianism* describes societies where people are encouraged to see each other as moral equals, to cooperate, and to feel concerned for everyone's welfare[28].

In *high power distance* societies[29], the norm is for people to accept that everybody has a place in the hierarchical order. Families in *high power distance* societies tend to encourage children to be obedient and respectful to parents and elders, and organisations normally separate superiors and subordinates, where it is not easy to meet or talk with higher-ranking people, and power is likely to be concentrated at the top. In contrast, in *low power distance* societies, the norm is to equalise the distribution of power. Families in *low power distance* societies tend to treat children as equals, and organisations normally delegate power, with employees tending to feel equal and close to each other in their daily work relations.

While Schwartz's *hierarchy-egalitarianism* dimension[30] also focuses on (un)equal distribution of power, it is less fear-based, and the concept of *egalitarianism* is broader, as it stresses a greater recognition of all humans as moral equals, which leads to a concern for the welfare of all. In societies that emphasise *hierarchy*, the norm is for individuals to adhere to rigid roles designed to ensure smooth societal function, and people are encouraged to value social power, authority, humility, and wealth. This contrasts with societies that emphasise *egalitarianism*, where the norm is for people to acknowledge the importance of cooperation to ensure individual and collective success, and people are encouraged to value equality, social justice, responsibility, help, and honesty.

Problem 3: Interacting with others or for others

The third problem relates to whether we interact *with* or *for* others. That is, should we help people (at the risk of their being weakened by a lack of personal effort) or should we not (at the risk, for them, of being even worse off)? This is reflected in Hofstede's *masculinity-femininity* and Schwartz's *mastery-harmony* dimensions, which relate to assertiveness and ambition, in contrast to femininity and harmony.

- *Masculinity* describes societies where there is a preference for assertiveness, competitiveness, and material reward for success, whereas *femininity* describes societies where there is a preference for cooperation, caring for the weak, and quality of life[31].
- *Mastery* describes societies where people are encouraged to master, direct, and change the natural and social environment to attain group or personal goals, whereas *harmony* describes societies where people are encouraged to fit into the social and natural world and appreciate, rather than change or exploit it[32].

In *masculine* societies[33], there is stronger gender role differentiation between males and females, but both learn to be assertive and ambitious, showing off possessions and caring less about the welfare of others. Generally, the norm is for people to be more possession-oriented, where achievement is demonstrated by status brands and expensive jewellery[34]. People tend to admire the strong, depicted by male/assertiveness and female/nurturing roles. In contrast, in *feminine* societies, there is less gender role differentiation, and both learn to be modest and sympathise with the underdog. Generally, the norm is to be caring and nurturing. The welfare system is usually highly developed, education is largely free and accessible and there is openness about admitting to having problems. People are also more likely to share decisions.

Schwartz's *mastery* dimension[35] also emphasises assertiveness and ambition, but contrasts this to *harmony* with the social and natural environment, rather than femininity. *Mastery-harmony* regulates how individuals relate to others and their environment. In societies that emphasise *mastery*, there is an emphasis on skill development and directing and changing the environment to attain personal and group goals. People are encouraged to value ambition, success, daring, and competence. In contrast, in societies that emphasise *harmony*, there is an emphasis on understanding and appreciating the environment in its current state. People are encouraged to value unity with nature, protecting the environment, and a world at peace.

Problem 4: Dealing with uncertainty

The fourth problem relates to how we deal with uncertainty. In Hofstede's conceptualisation, societies differ in their tolerance for uncertainty. High *uncertainty avoidance* assumes that uncertainty is bad, and society must aim to reduce it.

- *Uncertainty* avoidance describes societies where there is a preference for certainty.
- Organisations in *high uncertainty avoidance* societies normally promote stable careers and produce rules and procedures to reduce ambiguity. People in these societies tend to be better groomed, as a way of organising their world, and prefer purity in food, as evidenced by higher consumption of mineral water[36]. In contrast, *low uncertainty avoidance* societies assume that people have to deal with uncertainty because it is inevitable. The future is by definition unknown, but can be speculated upon, and people and institutions can deal with likely outcomes. People in these cultures tend to be more innovative and entrepreneurs tend to take more risks[37].

While there is no parallel concept to uncertainty avoidance in the Schwartz cultural orientations, some items capture aspects of *uncertainty avoidance*. Specifically, the more conservative items of *embeddedness* emphasise maintaining the status quo, which may be aligned with uncertainty avoidance, and the more adventurous items of *affective autonomy* emphasise having an exciting and varied life, which may be aligned with uncertainty acceptance[38].

Problem 5: Dealing with time

The fifth problem relates to how we deal with time. The fact that we share a common clock does not mean that assumptions around the concept and importance of time are similar across cultures. Cultural attitudes towards time shape the way people structure their actions. This pervasive influence is reflected in punctuality in everyday behaviour, which is a visible consequence. Yet differences in time orientations, especially toward the future, are more important as they affect long-range issues, such as the strategic framework of decision making or the trade-offs made by organisations between long-term company values and short-term profitability. There are differences in the nature and degree of temporal orientations to the past, present, and future, and the preferred ways to schedule activities according to time or relationships.

● *Long-term orientation* describes societies where there is a focus on long-term virtues as a way to prepare for the future, whereas short-term orientation describes societies where there is a focus on the past or present.

Important differences in time orientations were found in the Chinese Values Survey (CVS), which purposefully introduced an Eastern bias to counter the historical Western bias in values surveys[39]. The CVS proposed the dimension of *Confucian Work Dynamism*, which corresponds to a future orientation on the one hand and a past and present orientation on the other[40]. Later, Hofstede referred to this as *Long Term Orientation (LTO)*, emphasising long-term virtues such as frugality, perseverance, saving, and investment, in contrast to *Short Term Orientation (STO)*, emphasising virtues related to the past (respect for tradition, preservation of 'face' and fulfilling social obligations) or present (immediate gratification, including social consumption and spending)[41]. *LTO* is related to economic growth and has been used to explain the dramatic growth of East Asian economies[42]. Many Asian countries (e.g., Japan and South Korea) score high on *LTO*, whereas most Western countries and developing nations (e.g., Pakistan and countries in West Africa) score much lower.

1.3 Comparing countries
and regions across dimensions

One of the major advantages to comparative cultural frameworks like those of Hofstede and Schwartz is that they not only reveal aspects of culture that differ across societies, but they also provide scores as to the *degree* to which societies differ on these aspects. These scores can help identify how societies differ on one or more dimensions, in order to understand where potential cultural clashes in assumptions about what is commonly accepted may occur. However, it is also important to remember that cultural norms serve as constraints and opportunities, as opposed to dictating how individuals act. Culture is normative, rather than deterministic. As such, cultural frameworks and theories provide a valuable starting point for understanding the impact of culture as a cohesive whole. This information can then be modified, based on additional information about specific individuals and situations, which may interact to influence behaviour.

As a first step, Hofstede's cultural dimension scores can be downloaded from the end of chapter website[43], and compared as we do in **Figure 1.2**. From this figure, we can see that Australia has large cultural differences from China and Venezuela on long-term orientation and a new dimension, termed indulgence, which represents the extent to which societies emphasise control of desires and impulses. It is also interesting to note that Switzerland shows quite large cultural differences between its German and French-speaking citizens on power distance, consistent with Germany being lower and France being higher on this dimension. This illustrates the danger in using national cultural scores; the assumption of homogeneity within countries is rarely a tenable one.

Activity 1.1

Understanding culture and the individual

If you were preparing to work with a team from each of the cultures depicted in Figure 1.2 (i.e., someone from Australia, China, Venezuela, and Switzerland, but you are unsure of whether they are German or French speaking), you might compare these societies to see where team members might have different assumptions about how people should (a) prioritise group versus individual goals, (b) organise the structure, (c) cooperate, (d) deal with the unknown, and (e) deal with time. This comparison provides initial information about potential clashes between group members. However, it must be remembered that individuals internalise their culture to a greater or lesser extent, based on their experiences and their own personal characteristics.

What questions would you ask team members to better understand how interactions with macro, meso, and micro level groups and institutions influence their operational culture in this setting? Remember that cultural frameworks capture normative differences across societies, rather than specific information about individuals.

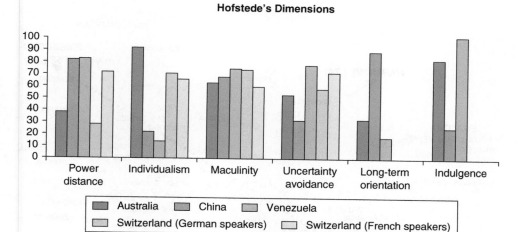

Figure 1.2 Selected country scores on Hofstede's six dimensions (where available)

Activity 1.2

Cultural groupings

Rather than compare countries on each cultural dimension separately, Schwartz[44] combined his cultural value orientations into an integrated system on which societies can be located on a two-dimensional map for comparative purposes. In Figure 1.3, each cultural dimension is revealed as a vector or line, where nations are located to reflect their relative position on all cultural value orientations. On this map, countries that appear near each other share similar cultural orientations. Schwartz identified seven cultural groupings that are co-located on the map: West European, English-speaking, Latin American, Eastern European, South Asian, Confucian-influenced, and African and Middle Eastern. *Investigate which cultural value orientations each of these seven cultural groupings share.*

Both of these frameworks provide broad brushstrokes of knowledge that reveal an etic view, a view *from the outside*. The comparison of two major, empirically tested cultural frameworks shows that different frameworks often pick up on similarities in the cultural assumptions that various societies emphasise, as well as adding some interesting, unique aspects. Importantly, they also offer a system of scaffolding upon which deeper and richer cultural knowledge can be integrated.

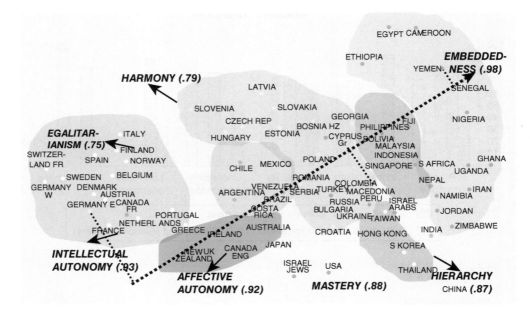

Figure 1.3　Co-Ploy Map of 76 national groups on seven cultural orientations Adapted from Schwartz, S. H. (2013). Culture matters: National value cultures, sources, and consequences. In *Understanding Culture* (pp. 137–160). Psychology Press. Printed with permission of Taylor and Francis.

Can we reduce the number of cultural dimensions to distil the essential information?

As indicated earlier in the chapter, there is a potentially limitless number of dimensions on which cultures can be compared. This has led researchers to search for more and more parsimonious systems that highlight cultural differences, using a simpler structure.

Several researchers have proposed a reduced set of characteristics which include superfactors that conflate many different dimensions into just one or two. For example, Fog[45] found a superfactor that reflects countries' level of development and modernisation, as well as cultural values, including collectivism, regality (i.e., cultural and psychological reactions to collective danger), and tightness, as well as a second factor reflecting characteristics of East Asian countries, including long-term orientation, thrift, shame, and possibly differences in response styles. **Figure 1.4** shows the relative positions of different societies on just these two dimensions. However, there is some danger in a reductionist viewpoint, as it may in fact make it more, rather than less, difficult to understand cultural similarities and differences in any meaningful way. Despite this, it seems that in most cases, when researchers map differences between societies, they find similar sets of cultural regions.

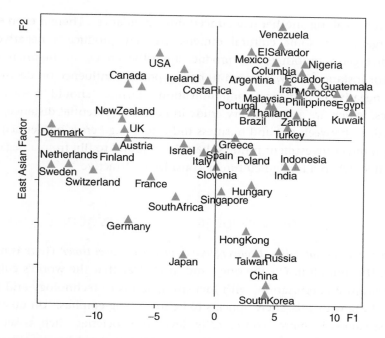

Figure 1.4 Mapping countries on two superfactors. Source: Fog, A. (2021). A test of the reproducibility of the clustering of cultural variables. *Cross-Cultural Research*, 55(1), 29–57.

Cultural distance

In business, an even more reductionist approach is often sought, as there is an emphasis on distilling essential information to provide high-level insight, before delving deeper into the detail needed for decision making. This emphasis, coupled with a rather superficial understanding of culture, can lead businesses to begin with a construct that summarises the *distance* between cultures, rather than focusing on what the differences are.

Cultural distance (CD) indices have been extensively used in international business[46]. Most CD indices simply aggregate the absolute difference between country-level scores on each of a set of cultural dimensions (often the four main Hofstede dimensions) for pairs of countries, as a proxy for cultural differences. At its most simplistic level, the use of a CD index is justified by the assumption that the greater the cultural distance between two countries, the higher the transaction cost in terms of doing business. But this is not necessarily the case.

Despite their ongoing popularity, CD indices have been deeply criticised as ignoring the potential importance of differences along specific cultural dimensions[47]. That is, differences along one dimension (e.g., hierarchy) may be more important than differences along another (e.g., uncertainty avoidance). There is even evidence that divergence on some cultural dimensions may produce a negative effect, whereas divergence on others may produce a positive effect, on the phenomena of interest. For instance, CD was found to have a positive influence on decision making, but a negative influence on communication[48]. Business should be wary of using CD indices, which are at best a very crude indicator of potential distance, in isolation. Relations between CD and business indicators (e.g., cross-border acquisitions and foreign direct investment inflows) have been found to flip from a negative to a positive effect when a foreign culture is considered attractive[49].

Cultural convergence or divergence

Is there more evidence of cultural convergence or divergence over time? There is no simple answer to this question. On the one hand, it is clear that the world's cultures are moving toward modernisation, with increasing access to technology and financial markets. Along with this, there appears to be increasing emphasis on qualities that tend to be valued in more economically developed societies, such as self-reliance and creativity, and decreasing emphasis on qualities that tend to be valued in less economically developed societies, such as faith and obedience[50]. The gap between these societies appears to be narrowing. On the other hand, the trend toward a greater acceptance of morally debatable behaviours, which allows people the freedom to live as they wish, is stronger in more economically developed societies, leading to a widening gap[51].

The question is, whether these changes are changes in degree or in the nature of the concept. Since the cultural dimensions commonly examined in international business were revealed through an etic paradigm, focusing on universals, differences are likely to be in the degree of preference for different cultural assumptions. However, these differences may also point to potential differences in the nature of cultural assumptions that require an emic paradigm to gain a deeper understanding of the structure and content of these changes. There is some evidence that Hofstede's dimensions (based on data collected around the 1970s) have become less predictive over time[52]. Research has also found that some of these dimensions seem to have changed in their structure and become less coherent[53]. This may be a more general trend, indicating a change in the nature of cultural dimensions; however, in terms of degree, there is little evidence of convergence in the preferred solutions to different problems.

Culture and nationality

When comparing similarities and differences across cultures, we purposefully refer to societies, rather than nations. Societies refer to an aggregate of people living together in a more or less ordered community, whereas nations are defined by the borders of a country or territory. Nationality is a relatively easy way to divide individuals into larger groups. However, the relationship between nationality and culture is unclear. While a commonly shared culture is important in building modern nation-states, it is more fundamental at the community level. As soon as nation-states began to emerge, they struggled against local particularisms, such as dialects and customs. Conflicts in large countries are often based on conflicts between cultural subgroups, such as the Civil War in the United States, the rivalry between the English and the Scots in the United Kingdom, and today's struggles between different religious groups in the Middle East and other Asian countries. Each of these conflicts relates to distinctive differences in cultural elements within a nation, including language, values, religion, and concepts of freedom.

Businesses must be especially wary of equating culture directly with a nation-state, as effective communication is crucial to the marketing process. There is a long list of very good reasons to avoid this, including the following:

1. A country's culture can only be defined by reference to other countries' cultures. India's culture can be compared with Italian or German culture, but the Indian subcontinent is made up of highly diversified ethnic and religious groups, including Muslims, Hindus, and Sikhs, and has over 20 principal languages, leading to many subcultures.

2. Many nation-states are explicitly multicultural. For instance, Switzerland has four official languages, German, French, Italian, and Romansch, which are spoken to various extents in different regions of the country. The Swiss political system, established more than seven centuries ago, helps people to successfully manage the complex trade-off between compliance with local cultural peculiarities and a common attitude toward anything that is not Swiss.

3. Political decisions, especially during the last century, have imposed the formation of new nation-states, particularly through the processes of colonisation and decolonisation. The borders of these nation-states, sometimes straight lines on a map, were often set with little regard for cultural realities. Many significant national cultures, such as that of the Kurds (split between the Iraqis, the Syrians, the Turks, and the Iranians) have never been accorded the right to a territory or state.

While homogeneity clearly favours the emergence of a coherent culture in a nation-state, few countries are truly homogeneous, especially when different types of homogeneity are considered, such as:

1. Linguistic homogeneity;
2. Religious homogeneity;
3. Ethnic homogeneity;
4. Climatic homogeneity;
5. Geographical homogeneity;
6. Institutional and political homogeneity; and
7. Social/income homogeneity.

From this, it is easy to see that global homogenisation is unlikely. It is also easy to see why international market segmentation is so challenging for firms.

1.4 Understanding similarities and differences between people

In the previous sections, we discussed cultural similarities and differences in normative systems that indicate preferred solutions to a set of universal problems that all societies face. These normative systems are embedded in the social institutions that individuals are exposed to in their daily lives, producing common knowledge that is implicitly understood, especially by those who grew up in that society. In this way, cultural norms serve as guides to behaviour through constraints and opportunities, rather than dictating how individuals act. People internalise their culture, to a greater or lesser extent, in ways that make sense to them as individuals, based on their experiences and socialisation, as well as their genetics, personality, health, etc[54]. In this way, people can share a common understanding of what society values, but they do not all have to value the same thing.

The normative systems we discussed in the previous section were revealed through aggregated individual responses from within a society, with the aim of producing a set of scores for each society, rather than each individual. Through aggregation, the unique aspects of different people in society largely neutralise each other, with the mean sample scores reflecting aspects of culture that have influenced all, or at least most, individuals in the society. The observed differences between societies on these aggregate scores reflect cultural differences, whereas the variance of individuals within a society indicates the heterogeneity associated with personal values.

In the previous sections, we examined two main frameworks that relied on aggregates of individuals' responses in society to reveal similarities and differences between societies. In the case of Schwartz's cultural value orientations, societal level aggregates of responses to his values survey were used as an indicator of cultural values across 70 countries. From this, Schwartz found support for seven cultural values that reflect different preferences for solutions to the problems that all societies face (i.e., intellectual and affective autonomy-embeddedness, egalitarianism-hierarchy, and mastery-harmony), as well as the expected structure of interrelations or trade-offs between them[55]. On face value, we might expect that a similar structure of interrelations among values might appear when examining how values relate to each other using responses at the individual level. However, this is not always the case. Aggregate and individual level scores reflect different concepts that reveal different things. For instance, at the societal level, values like social power, wealth, and authority are closely associated with humility. This makes sense for society, where it is important to have both those who want authority and those who are willing to accept it, but it would not make sense at the individual or personal level for people to ascribe high importance on both personal authority and humility as guiding principles in life.

To better understand the similarities and differences between cultures and the individuals who live in them, we compare Schwartz's personal and cultural value orientations. Cultural values, as a central feature of culture, emphasise common knowledge of what is worthy and desirable in society. They influence, but don't determine individuals' values, as individuals experience mainstream culture in different ways (e.g., through different school or religious systems), and each of us has unique characteristics (e.g., genes, temperament, personality and health) that have been linked to differences in value priorities[56].

An understanding of differences in value priorities between people in society can help avoid the ecological fallacy or fundamental attribution error where people attribute country characteristics to individuals[57]. Stereotypes and limited observations of the behaviour of individuals from different countries can lead us to believe that people in different countries will value different things. If we remember that cultural dimensions are broad normative patterns across individuals, we can then accept that individuals within any society are likely to differ in their views of what is important in life, and depending on the tightness or looseness of society, they will be more or less free to act according to their personal preferences[58].

Personal values

Personal values are broad motivational goals that reflect what is important to people in life. While all values are at least somewhat desirable to most people, individuals in society are likely to differ in the importance they place on specific values[59].

For instance, younger people and males tend to ascribe higher importance than older people to personal-focused values, such as stimulation and hedonism, and women tend to ascribe higher importance than men to social-focus values, such as benevolence and conformity.

It is important to understand how people differ in their value priorities, as values that are highly important provide strong guides for beliefs, attitudes, and behaviour[60]. And they do this even when people are not consciously aware of their values. So, how do we know what our own and other people's values are?

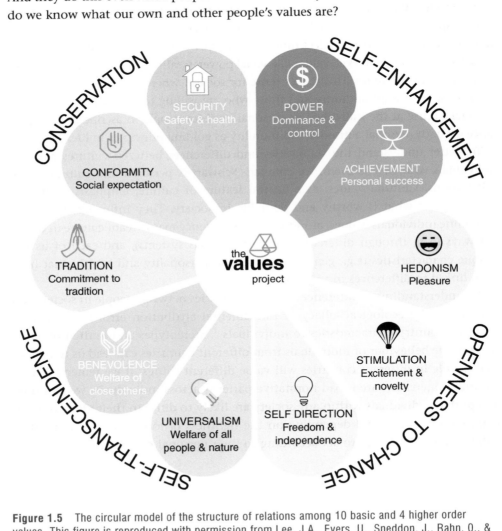

Figure 1.5 The circular model of the structure of relations among 10 basic and 4 higher order values. This figure is reproduced with permission from Lee, J.A., Evers, U., Sneddon, J., Rahn, O., & Schwartz, S. (2019) *What do we value? How our values influence everyday behaviours*. The University of Western Australia[61].

Figure 1.5 illustrates the Schwartz personal values theory, which posits a near-universal set of basic values, arranged in a circular structure that reflects a motivational continuum. These values and their structure in this theory have been empirically supported in more than 80 countries[62]. Personal values that are neighbouring in the circle share compatible motivations that can be satisfied in similar ways. For instance, *benevolence* and *universalism* values both emphasise caring for the welfare of others, close others in the case of *benevolence* and all others and nature in the case of *universalism*. People who attribute a high importance to these values are motivated to promote the welfare of others, which is why these values are labelled *self-transcendence values*. In contrast, people who attribute high importance to the opposing *achievement* and *power* values are motivated to seek social superiority and esteem. To do this, they need to put their own status ahead of others, which is why these values are labelled *self-enhancement values*.

Opposing values in the circle (see Figure 1.5) have conflicting motivations that cannot be satisfied in the same way. For instance, *tradition* values emphasise acceptance and maintenance of cultural and/or religious customs and ideas. On the opposite side of the circle, *stimulation* values emphasise novelty, variety, and adventure. It is difficult to pursue *tradition* and *stimulation*, or any set of opposing values, at the same time. It is also quite difficult to understand someone who is motivated by values that oppose your own. For instance, people who attribute high importance to caring for the welfare of others will find it difficult to understand the choices of people who seek personal status and power, and vice versa. However, knowing that other people are likely to prioritise different values to your own can help you understand why their choices may be different from yours.

Given that the aggregate values of individuals differ between societies, people will, on average, be more likely to place higher importance on values that are endorsed in their society. However, this may be masked by what is termed pancultural values[63], where *benevolence* is almost always the most important and *power* the least important to individuals across societies. Since *benevolence* emphasises caring for close others, like family and friends, most people will endorse this value regardless of their culture.

Since values reflect what is important in life, people tend to think what they value should be important to everyone. Research shows that people elevate the importance of their most important value when they are thinking about what others value[64]. For instance, people who highly value *achievement* or *tradition* tend to think most others also value *achievement* or *tradition* highly, even though these values are less commonly endorsed by society. This is an example of self-referencing, which relates to a spontaneous and unconscious tendency to refer to our own thought framework to interpret situations and evaluate people.

Self-Reference Criterion and ethnocentrism

The *Self-Reference Criterion* (SRC) refers to our spontaneous and unconscious tendency to refer to our own thought framework – mainly tied to our culture, which, in general, we did not choose – to interpret situations, evaluate others, communicate, negotiate, or decide which attitude or choice to take. As such, this type of spontaneous self-referencing is heavily influenced by the norms of our society and related to our level of ethnocentrism.

The term ethnocentrism was introduced more than a century ago to distinguish between in-groups (those groups with which an individual identifies) and out-groups (those regarded as antithetical to the in-group). Sumner defined ethnocentrism as a tendency for people to perceive their own group as the centre, and to scale and rate out-groups with reference to their own group[65].

In its most extreme form, ethnocentrism relates to beliefs about the superiority of one's own culture, which may lead to disinterest in, and even contempt for, the culture of other groups[66]. However, ethnocentrism should not be regarded too negatively as a cognitive and/or affective defect, drawback, imperfection, or shortcoming; rather it is a fact of life. Nevertheless, it does act as a limitation to understanding people who have a different ethnocentric background. Since it is difficult to put oneself in 'their shoes', most people do not even try.

For those who are willing and motivated, the following steps outline a way forward in attempting to eliminate the decisional bias related to the SRC in intercultural interactions[67]:

1. Define the problem according to your own behavioural standards and ways of thinking.
2. Similarly, define the problem according to (what you know and/or can guess from) your foreign partner's behavioural standards and ways of thinking.
3. Isolate the influence of the SRC on the problem as you perceive it, and identify the gap with how your foreign partner perceives it.
4. Redefine the problem (and often the objectives) by removing the bias related to the SRC, and then try to find joint solutions and make decisions which fit with both cultural contexts.

Activity 1.3

Try to follow the steps to eliminate the SRC in a situation where you are confronted with an uncomfortable intercultural interaction. You might think about how you would feel if you are waiting to be served and someone pushes in front of you. How you feel is likely to be related to the norms in your society, as to who and how people should wait. For instance, when people wait in line at Disneyland in the USA, discipline with respect to queues is strong. Waiting lines are well organised with corridors and information on waiting times. In other cultural contexts, where there is a sense of 'free-for-all' and waiting lines are *not* organised, the free-riding problem will be stronger and more difficult to tackle. *Is there a way to find a joint solution that fits with both cultural contexts?*

Despite sincere efforts, bias removal may prove insufficient, since it assumes that it is possible, at least partly, to penetrate the intricacies of a particular culture without being a native. However, it is likely to be worth the effort.

1.5 The process of intercultural interaction

The process of intercultural encounters is one in which people play by different rule books. There is a great deal of adaptation that needs to take place to develop a common understanding. However, people tend to adjust to the other party's behaviour in ways that derive significantly from what is normal or stereotypical in their own native culture. It is naturally difficult to step away from one's own cultural norms in order to see the situation in a new light.

In business interactions, which are often complex and dense in the exchange of information, the aim is usually focused on the goals of the interaction, rather than aiming to understand the beliefs and attitudes of the other party. However, it is important to work towards at least some mutual adjustment with a view toward maximising outcomes. People tend to adapt their behaviour to that of the other party, at least to the extent that they perceive will be useful for smoothing the process and improving the outcomes. Cultural adaptation, provided that it is done properly (without naïve imitation), is often positively experienced by the other side.

Clashes in intercultural interactions are likely to be experienced more strongly at first, when people expect behaviour from the other side to normatively correspond to what they are used to, as well as to what they consider as the most appropriate for effective teamwork. In business, cultural adaptation is not necessarily symmetrical. For instance, Japanese negotiators tend to adjust to their American counterparts by using more direct information sharing and less indirect communication than in interactions with their countrymen, whereas Americans tend to adapt less to their Japanese counterparts [68]. However, adaptation may be less necessary, where there is a common professional operational culture that helps overcome the barriers related to cross-cultural understanding. That is why culture sometimes appears as a relatively poor predictor of the intercultural interaction process and outcomes in business.

There are several ways of adjusting in intercultural interactions. No one way is the best. They are based on which step is prioritised first, in successive steps in the interaction: *Awareness, Knowledge, or Adjustment*. However, these aspects of intercultural adjustment can follow different paths. For instance, people adapt and adjust first, without being really aware of the intercultural interaction process, and later search for cultural knowledge which will help them debrief the experience (*Adjustment-Knowledge-Awareness*). Academically, the best linear route should be *Knowledge-Awareness-Adjustment*, with the formal acquisition of knowledge and learning first, followed by an awareness of problematic issues in the intercultural encounter, and finally, adjustment based on the assumed ability to apply knowledge as solutions to perceived problems. However, a third sequence, *Awareness-Knowledge-Adjustment* is often found in the real world of intercultural interactions, which starts with awareness, followed by the acquisition of knowledge, which finally leads to adjustment.

How to deal with prejudices and recognise cultural clashes

Cultural clashes are often surprising and elicit strong emotional feelings, but fore-warning about common culture clashes can help to prepare for them. Richard Brislin assessed a wide range of intercultural interactions and identified 18 different themes in which culture clashes occur, in three broad categories, as follows[69]:

1. **Emotional experiences from cross-cultural encounters**

    1.1 Anxiety – about whether or not a behaviour is appropriate

    1.2 Disconfirmed expectancies – situations differ from what is expected

    1.3 Belonging – feeling less accepted as an outsider

    1.4 Ambiguity – unclear messages that are difficult to understand

    1.5 Confrontation with one's prejudices and the realisation that beliefs and attitudes learned in one's own culture are no longer useful

2. **Cross-cultural differences in knowledge or norms**

    2.1 Work – attitudes toward the creative effort, relationships, and tasks differ

    2.2 Time and space – attitudes to the importance of being on time and the proper social distance for interactions differ

    2.3 Language – language differences and attitudes toward language use differ

    2.4 Roles – who can occupy various roles and how they are enacted differ

2.5 Importance of group vs individual – emphasis on individual and group allegiances differ

2.6 Rituals and superstitions – activities that help people cope with everyday demands can easily be misinterpreted and attributed as superstitions

2.7 Hierarchies – class and status distinctions and markers differ

2.8 Values – understanding differences in internalised values is critical

3. **Cross-cultural differences in how people think about and evaluate information**

3.1 Categorisation – confusion caused by different information being allocated to different categories

3.2 Differentiation – differences in the importance of information leading to new categories

3.3 In-group-out-group – out-group members will be excluded from participation in some behaviours

3.4 Change and growth – learning styles may differ

3.5 Attribution – judgements about the cause of behaviour can differ

Cultural assimilators

Richard Brislin used these themes to design a culture-general assimilator that uses critical incidents to train people in intercultural interactions. One of these critical incidents is in **Activity 1.4**. *Read the scenario and pick which of the four alternatives best describes the situation.*

Activity 1.4

Learning the ropes

Helen Connor had been working in a Japanese company involved in marketing cameras. She has been there for two years and was well-respected by her colleagues. In fact, she was so respected that she often was asked to work with new employees of the firm as these younger employees "learned the ropes." One recent and young employee, Hideo Tanaka, was assigned to develop a marketing scheme for a new model of camera. He worked quite hard on it, but the scheme was not accepted by his superiors because of industry-wide economic conditions. Helen Connor and Hideo Tanaka happened to be working at nearby desks when the news of the nonacceptance was transmitted from company executives. Hideo Tanaka said very little at that point. That evening, however, Helen and Hideo happened to be at the same bar. Hideo had been drinking and vigorously criticized his superiors at work. Helen concluded that Hideo was a very aggressive Japanese male and that she would have difficulty working with him again in the future.

Which alternative provides an accurate statement about Helen's conclusion?

1. Helen was making an inappropriate judgment about Hideo's traits based on behavior that she observed.
2. Since, in Japan, decorum in public is highly valued, Helen reasonably concluded that Hideo's vigorous criticism in the bar marks him as a difficult coworker.
3. Company executives had failed to tell Helen and Hideo about economic conditions, and consequently, Helen should be upset with the executives, not Hideo.
4. Helen felt that Hideo was attacking her personality.

Rationales:

1. For Alternative 1, trainees would read:

This is the best answer. When observing the behavior of others, a very common error is to make conclusions about the traits or qualities of those others. Here, those judgments (called attributions) are that Hideo is aggressive and hard to work with. There is much less a tendency to take into account the immediate factors in the situation which could also cause the behavior, such as the frustration upon hearing bad news. Interestingly, if Helen had been asked to interpret *her own* behavior had *she* gotten angry, she would undoubtedly have said something like, "Well, wouldn't you be angry if a plan you had worked hard on ended up being rejected." In addition, vigorous behavior in bars is an acceptable outlet in Japan. People are not supposed to make permanent conclusions about others based on the "bar behavior" they see. But in analysing the behavior of others, there is much less tendency to take into account such immediate factors of the situation or social context. This error – making trait judgments about others and not taking situational factors into account – has been called the fundamental attribution error (see Ross, 1977) and is probably more prevalent in cross-cultural encounters since there is so much behavior that is new and different to sojourners. When abroad, sojourners often make more attributions about people and events than they would in their own countries. Even though Helen has been in Japan for two years, there will still be many new experiences that demand judgments or attributions from her.

2. For Alternative 2, trainees would read:

Certainly a common observation about Japan is that decorum is highly valued. Yet people do become angry and upset. Rather than jumping to a conclusion, it is usually better to go beyond the common observation (in this case the frequently noted value placed on proper decorum) and to analyze in more detail the specific instance. If a person has been exposed only to the common observation, then he/she is ill prepared for behaviors (which will inevitably be encountered on a long sojourn) which are at odds with the general observation. An important point is that vigorous behavior in bars is an acceptable outlet in Japan. Permanent conclusions should not be made based on "bar behavior," Japanese hosts tell us. Please choose again.

3. For Alternative 3, trainees would read:

Helen and Hideo, if they are capable professionals, should know about industry-wide conditions on their own. While Hideo might be expected to take into account these conditions before his reaction to the nonacceptance of his plan, a highly abstract and nonimmediate thought like "industry-wide conditions" rarely wipes out the frustration of seeing hard work leading to no visible reward. Please choose again.

4. For Alternative 4, trainees would read:

This could be part of the interpretation. There is a strong tendency on the part of people, upon seeing the negative behavior of others, to wonder if they somehow were involved. Since Helen had been working with Hideo, such feelings would be natural. During cross-cultural experiences, this tendency is probably stronger. Since Helen and Hideo have not worked together for a long time and are still learning things about each other, Helen is not going to be able to readily interpret all of Hideo's actions. Since she is not intimately knowledgeable about Japanese culture after two years there, she will be motivated to wonder even more if she somehow is personally involved. Because of felt personal involvement, any of Helen's final conclusions will be even more intense. There is another explanation that focuses on a mistake Helen could be making in her thinking. Please choose again.

Reprinted with permission from pages 220–222. Brislin, R. W. (1986). A culture general assimilator: Preparation for various types of sojourns. *International Journal of Intercultural Relations, 10*(2), 215–234.

This critical incident was designed as a general cultural assimilator to describe behaviour that might occur in any country. Rather than focusing on an interaction between citizens of two specific countries, general assimilators offer the opportunity to try to figure out the problem and discover reasons for the communication difficulties when you do not have specific cultural knowledge.

Cultural assimilators describe critical incidents that usually include a potentially confusing cross-cultural interaction and ask the reader to think about what the source of misunderstanding is likely to be. After choosing one of the four or five plausible alternatives, which usually include different perspectives from the host and home countries, readers are offered an explanation of each alternative for reflection. Cultural assimilators help individuals to identify behaviours that are appropriate in their own but not the other culture, and to learn from this to make attributions similarly to people in another culture[70]. This is a process called isomorphic attributions, where individuals no longer use their own cultural framework alone, but also use the frameworks of other cultures to interpret behaviour in a similar manner to members of those cultures.

There are many different types of cultural assimilators, from culture-specific assimilators that are grounded in a specific cultural context, to general assimilators, to theory-based assimilators[71]. For instance, Bhawuk identified 44 theory-based themes that identify potential culture clashes between people from more individualist and more collectivist cultures[72]. These themes capture critical work and social situations in intercultural interactions that can serve as a guide for flashpoints where cultural differences should be considered. In cross-cultural training, it is important to consider both work and social contexts, as managers often return from overseas posts due to difficulties in social rather than work contexts. Selected themes are shown in Tables 1.1–1.5, below, with brief descriptions of the issue that may generate the clash.

Critical incidents focusing on the Concept of Self

Table 1.1 focuses on differences in the concept of the self that tends to be more interdependent (view themselves as connected) in collectivist cultures and more independent (view themselves as separate and distinct from others) in individualist cultures[73]. This aspect helps us understand differences in social behaviours in the workplace and in interpersonal relationships. For example, in a more collectivist culture, missing a deadline is less likely to be seen as an individual failing and more likely to be seen as due to unforeseen circumstances that are beyond the control of any individual (acceptance rather than controlling nature).

Table 1.1　Contexts and self-concept: independent (more likely in individualist cultures) or interdependent (more likely in collectivist cultures)

Settings	Independent	Interdependent
Work		
1. Missing a deadline or failing to follow a schedule	Negative consequences	Acceptable
2. Valued skills	Technical	Interpersonal
3. Being direct and forthright	Favoured	Avoided
4. Hiring a friend's relative	Not acceptable	May be acceptable
Social		
5. Sharing resources or skills	Not necessary	Necessary
6. A friend's friend is a friend	Not applicable	Applicable

Adapted from Bhawuk, D. P. (2001). Evolution of culture assimilators: toward theory-based assimilators. *International Journal of Intercultural Relations*, 25(2), 141–163. Printed with permission of Elsevier

Critical incidents focusing on goal prioritisation

Table 1.2 (below) focuses on differences in the prioritisation of goals, where people from individualist cultures are more likely to prioritise personal goals, whereas people from collectivist cultures are more likely to prioritise group goals, when they are in conflict. This aspect helps us understand motivational differences. For example, people from individualist cultures are more likely to be motivated by individual gains, whereas people from collectivist cultures are more likely to be motivated by in-group responsibility, if these two motivations clash.

Table 1.2 Contexts and goal prioritisation: personal goals (more likely in individualist cultures) or group goals (more likely in collectivist cultures)

Settings	Prioritise personal goals	Prioritise group goals
Work		
1. Individual gain versus group responsibility	Individual gain	Group responsibility
2. Reward allocation	Equity	Equality
3. Social loafing	Likely in groups	Less likely in groups
4. Selection & Promotion	Based on merit	Favours in-group members
Social		
5. Reward allocation for in-group versus out-group	Always equity rule	Equality versus equity
6. Career versus family	Career	Family
7. Pleasure versus in-group	Pleasure	Sacrifice pleasure for in-group

Adapted from Bhawuk, D. P. (2001). Evolution of culture assimilators: toward theory-based assimilators. *International Journal of Intercultural Relations, 25*(2), 141–163. Printed with permission of Elsevier

Critical incidents focusing on motivation for behaviours

Table 1.3 (below) focuses on differences in the motivations for behaviour, where people from individualist cultures are more likely to act according to their own beliefs and attitudes, whereas people from collectivist cultures are more likely to follow norms and do what is considered 'right' for the situation.

Table 1.3 Contexts and motivation: internal motivation (more likely in individualist cultures) or norms (more likely in collectivist cultures)

Settings	Internal motivation	Normative motivation
Work		
1. Workplace behaviours and interactions with superiors	Less normative	Formal norms
2. Work orientation	Task focused	Social focused
3. Problem-solving	Results oriented	Procedure oriented

(Continued)

Table 1.3 (Continued)

Settings	Internal motivation	Normative motivation
Social		
4. Social gathering (party)	Informal/few norms	Norms are clear
5. Gender differences	Less clear	Clear
6. Role differentiation	A lot of variation	Little variation
7. Demographic characteristics	Not relevant	Relevant

Adapted from Bhawuk, D. P. (2001). Evolution of culture assimilators: toward theory-based assimilators. *International Journal of Intercultural Relations, 25*(2), 141–163. Printed with permission of Elsevier

Critical incidents focusing on rational and relational orientations

Table 1.4 (below) focuses on differences in orientation to relationships, where people from individualist cultures are more likely to view relationships as an exchange, whereas people from collectivist cultures are more likely to view most interactions as leading toward a longer-term relationship. For example, managers from collectivist cultures may be reluctant to lay off employees, or not charge a friend for a service, than people from individualist cultures.

Table 1.4 Contexts and rational (more likely in individualist cultures) or relational (more likely in collectivist cultures) orientations

Settings	Rational – short term	Relational – long term
Work		
1. Retrenchments	Rational	Relational
2. Relationship versus task	Task focused	Relationship focused
3. Work relationship	Short term	Long term
Social		
4. A service from or to a friend	Pay or charge a fee	Return a favour
5. Social relationship	Short term, based on common interests	Long term

Adapted from Bhawuk, D. P. (2001). Evolution of culture assimilators: toward theory-based assimilators. *International Journal of Intercultural Relations, 25*(2), 141–163. Printed with permission of Elsevier

Critical incidents focusing on vertical and horizontal individualism and collectivism

Table 1.5 (below) focuses on differences in vertical versus horizontal individualism and collectivism[74]. Some collectivist cultures are more vertical in terms of their hierarchy (e.g., South Korea, Japan, and India), whereas others are more horizontal (e.g., Brazil and the Israeli Kibbutz). In vertical collectivist societies, people tend to be more concerned with enhancing the cohesion and status of their in-group and complying with authorities, in contrast to those from horizontal collectivist societies, who tend to be concerned with sociability and interdependence. Similarly, some individualist cultures are more vertical (e.g., the USA and France), whereas others are more horizontal (e.g., Sweden, Denmark, and Australia). In vertical individualist societies, people tend to be more concerned with distinguishing themselves from others to improve their standing, in contrast to those from horizontal individualist societies, who tend to be more concerned with expressing uniqueness and self-reliance. This categorisation helps to explain differences in superior-subordinate relations.

Table 1.5 Contexts and vertical-horizontal dimensions of individualism and collectivism

Settings	Horizonal-individualist	Vertical-collectivist
Work		
1. Decision making	Independent	Check with superior
2. Interaction with superior	As an equal	Hierarchical
3. Reward allocation and privileges	Equity rule	Status, favours superiors
Social		
4. Social interaction	Informal	Formal rules
5. Language	One for all	Many layers
6. Greetings and apologies	Informal	Formal and nuanced

Adapted from Bhawuk, D. P. (2001). Evolution of culture assimilators: toward theory-based assimilators. *International Journal of Intercultural Relations*, 25(2), 141–163. Printed with permission of Elsevier

1.6 Chapter summary

In this chapter, we discuss what culture is, and how countries and regions can be compared with the broad brushstrokes of cultural value orientations, derived from the average of citizens' values. We argue that culture is external to individuals, but still influences them through societal institutions that, in part, shape their beliefs, values, and behaviours. Finally, we illustrate how critical incidents can be used to help reduce the impact of our own cultural conditioning.

References

1. The X-Culture Project website: www.x-culture.org
2. Raymond Williams (1960, p. 20) – seminal figures in cultural studies
3. Hills, M. D. (2002). Kluckhohn and Strodtbeck's values orientation theory. *Online Readings in Psychology and Culture*, 4(4).

4. Schwartz, S. H. (2014). Rethinking the concept and measurement of societal culture in light of empirical findings. *Journal of Cross-Cultural Psychology*, *45*(1), 5–13.

5. Schwartz, S. H. (2014). Rethinking the concept and measurement of societal culture in light of empirical findings. *Journal of Cross-Cultural Psychology*, *45*(1), 5–13.

6. Gelfand, M. J., Raver, J. L., Nishii, L., Leslie, L. M., Lun, J., Lim, B. C., ... & Yamaguchi, S. (2011). Differences between tight and loose cultures: A 33-nation study. *Science*, *332*(6033), 1100–1104.

7. Gelfand, M. J., Raver, J. L., Nishii, L., Leslie, L. M., Lun, J., Lim, B. C., ... & Yamaguchi, S. (2011). Differences between tight and loose cultures: A 33-nation study. *Science*, *332*(6033), 1100–1104.

8. Elster, A., & Gelfand, M. J. (2021). When guiding principles do not guide: The moderating effects of cultural tightness on value-behavior links. *Journal of Personality*, *89*(2), 325–337.

9. Schwartz, S. H. (2014). Rethinking the concept and measurement of societal culture in light of empirical findings. *Journal of Cross-Cultural Psychology*, *45*(1), 5–13.

10. Gelfand, M. J., Raver, J. L., Nishii, L., Leslie, L. M., Lun, J., Lim, B. C., ... & Yamaguchi, S. (2011). Differences between tight and loose cultures: A 33-nation study. *Science*, *332*(6033), 1100–1104.

11. Fine, G. A. (2012). Group culture and the interaction order: Local sociology on the meso-level. *Annual Review of Sociology*, *38*(1), 159–179.

12. Schwartz, S. H. (2014). Rethinking the concept and measurement of societal culture in light of empirical findings. *Journal of Cross-Cultural Psychology*, *45*(1), 5-13.

13. Hong, Y.-y., Morris, M. W., Chiu, C.-y., & Benet-Martínez, V. 2000. Multicultural minds: A dynamic constructivist approach to culture and cognition. *American Psychologist*, *55*(7): 709–720.

14. Schwartz, S. (2006). A theory of cultural value orientations: Explication and applications. *Comparative Sociology*, *5*(2–3), 137–182.

15. The Globe Project website: https://globeproject.com/

16. Hofstede's value scores: https://geerthofstede.com and Schwartz value scores: www.researchgate.net/publication/304715744_The_7_Schwartz_cultural_value_orientation_scores_for_80_countries for societal scores

17. Hofstede, G. (2011). Dimensionalizing cultures: The Hofstede Model in context. *Online Readings in Psychology and Culture, 2*(1). https://doi.org/10.9707/2307-0919.1014

18. Schwartz, S. (2006). A theory of cultural value orientations: Explication and applications. *Comparative Sociology*, *5*(2–3), 137–182.

19. Schwartz, S. H. (2009). Culture matters: National value cultures, sources and consequences. In C.- Y. Chiu, Y. Y. Hong, S. Shavitt, & R. S. Wyer, Jr. (Eds.), *Understanding Culture: Theory, research and application* (pp. 127–150). New York: Psychology Press.

20. Minkov, M., & Kaasa, A. (2020). A test of Hofstede's model of culture following his own approach. *Cross Cultural & Strategic Management*.

21. Tuleja, E. A., & Schachner, M. (2020). From shared values to cultural dimensions: A comparative review. *The Cambridge Handbook of Intercultural Communication*, 96–119.

22. Kaasa, A. (2021). Merging Hofstede, Schwartz, and Inglehart into a single system. *Journal of Cross-Cultural Psychology*, *52*(4), 339–353.

23. Hofstede, G. (2001). Culture's Consequences: Comparing values, behaviors, institutions and organizations across nations. London: Sage Publications.

24. Schwartz, S. (2006). A theory of cultural value orientations: Explication and applications. *Comparative Sociology*, *5*(2–3), 137–182.

25. Schwartz, S. (2006). A theory of cultural value orientations: Explication and applications. *Comparative Sociology*, *5*(2–3), 137–182.

26. Hofstede, G. (2001). Culture's Consequences: Comparing values, behaviors, institutions and organizations across nations. London: Sage Publications.

27. Hofstede, G. (2001). Culture's Consequences: Comparing values, behaviors, institutions and organizations across nations. London: Sage Publications

28. Schwartz, S. (2006). A theory of cultural value orientations: Explication and applications. *Comparative Sociology*, *5*(2–3), 137–182.

29. Hofstede, G. (2001). Culture's Consequences: Comparing values, behaviors, institutions and organizations across nations. London: Sage Publications.

30. Schwartz, S. (2006). A theory of cultural value orientations: Explication and applications. Comparative Sociology, 5(2–3), 137–182.

31. Hofstede, G. (2001). Culture's Consequences: Comparing values, behaviors, institutions and organizations across nations. London: Sage Publications.

32. Schwartz, S. (2006). A theory of cultural value orientations: Explication and applications. *Comparative Sociology*, *5*(2–3), 137–182.

33. Hofstede, G. (2001). Culture's Consequences: Comparing values, behaviors, institutions and organizations across nations. London: Sage Publications.

34. De Mooij, M., & Hofstede, G. (2011). Cross-cultural consumer behavior: A review of research findings. Journal of International Consumer Marketing, *23*(3–4), 181–192.

35. Schwartz, S. (2006). A theory of cultural value orientations: Explication and applications. *Comparative Sociology, 5*(2–3), 137–182.

36. De Mooij, M., & Hofstede, G. (2011). Cross-cultural consumer behavior: A review of research findings. *Journal of International Consumer Marketing, 23*(3–4), 181–192.

37. Kreiser, P. M., Marino, L. D., Dickson, P., & Weaver, K. M. (2010). Cultural influences on entrepreneurial orientation: The impact of national culture on risk taking and proactiveness in SMEs. *Entrepreneurship Theory and Practice, 34*(5), 959–984.

38. Kaasa, A. (2021). Merging Hofstede, Schwartz, and Inglehart into a single system. *Journal of Cross-Cultural Psychology, 52*(4), 339–353.

39. Chinese Culture Connection. (1987). Chinese values and the search for culture-free dimensions of culture. *Journal of Cross-Cultural Psychology, 18*(2), 143–164.

40. Chinese Culture Connection. (1987). Chinese values and the search for culture-free dimensions of culture. *Journal of Cross-Cultural Psychology, 18*(2), 143–164.

41. Hofstede, G. (2001). Culture's Consequences: Comparing values, behaviors, institutions and organizations across nations. London: Sage Publications.

42. Hofstede, G. (2001). Culture's Consequences: Comparing values, behaviors, institutions and organizations across nations. London: Sage Publications.

43. Hofstede website: https://geerthofstede.com

44. Schwartz, S. (2006). A theory of cultural value orientations: Explication and applications. *Comparative Sociology, 5*(2–3), 137–182.

45. Fog, A. (2021). A test of the reproducibility of the clustering of cultural variables. *Cross-Cultural Research, 55*(1), 29–57.

46. Shenkar, O., Tallman, S. B., Wang, H., & Wu, J. (2020). National culture and international business: A path forward. *Journal of International Business Studies, 53*, 516–533.

47. Shenkar, O., Tallman, S. B., Wang, H., & Wu, J. (2020). National culture and international business: A path forward. *Journal of International Business Studies, 53*, 516–533.

48. Shachaf, P. (2008). Cultural diversity and information and communication technology impacts on global virtual teams: An exploratory study. *Information & Management, 45*(2), 131–142.

49. Shenkar, O., Tallman, S. B., Wang, H., & Wu, J. (2020). National culture and international business: A path forward. *Journal of International Business Studies, 53*, 516–533.

50. Kaasa, A., & Minkov, M. (2020). Are the world's national cultures becoming more similar?. *Journal of Cross-Cultural Psychology, 51*(7–8), 531–550.

51. Kaasa, A., & Minkov, M. (2020). Are the world's national cultures becoming more similar?. *Journal of Cross-Cultural Psychology, 51*(7–8), 531–550.

52. Taras, V., Steel, P., & Kirkman, B. L. (2012). Improving national cultural indices using a longitudinal meta-analysis of Hofstede's dimensions. *Journal of World Business, 47*(3), 329–341.

53. Minkov, M. (2017). A revision of Hofstede's model of national culture: Old evidence and new data from 56 countries. *Cross Cultural & Strategic Management.*

54. Schwartz, S. H. (2014). Rethinking the concept and measurement of societal culture in light of empirical findings. *Journal of Cross-Cultural Psychology, 45*(1), 5–13.

55. Schwartz, S. (2006). A theory of cultural value orientations: Explication and applications. *Comparative Sociology, 5*(2–3), 137–182.

56. Schwartz, S. H. (2014). Rethinking the concept and measurement of societal culture in light of empirical findings. *Journal of Cross-Cultural Psychology, 45*(1), 5–13.

57. Winzar, H. (2015). The ecological fallacy: How to spot one and tips on how to use one to your advantage. *Australasian Marketing Journal, 23*(1), 86–92.

58. Gelfand, M. J., Raver, J. L., Nishii, L., Leslie, L. M., Lun, J., Lim, B. C., ... & Yamaguchi, S. (2011). Differences between tight and loose cultures: A 33-nation study. *Science, 332*(6033), 1100–1104.

59. Sagiv, L., Roccas, S., Cieciuch, J., & Schwartz, S. H. (2017). Personal values in human life. *Nature Human Behaviour, 1*(9), 630–639.

60. Lee, J. A., Bardi, A., Gerrans, P., Sneddon, J., Van Herk, H., Evers, U., & Schwartz, S. (2022). Are value–behavior relations stronger than previously thought? It depends on value importance. *European Journal of Personality, 36*(2), 133–148.

61. Lee, J. A., Evers, U., Sneddon, J., Rahn, O., & Schwartz, S. (2019). What do we value?: How our values influence everyday behaviours. The University of Western Australia.

62. Sagiv, L., Roccas, S., Cieciuch, J., & Schwartz, S. H. (2017). Personal values in human life. *Nature Human Behaviour, 1*(9), 630–639.

63. Schwartz, S. H., & Bardi, A. (2001). Value hierarchies across cultures: Taking a similarities perspective. *Journal of Cross-Cultural Psychology, 32*(3), 268–290.

64. Lee, J. A., Evers, U., Sneddon, J., Rahn, O., & Schwartz, S. (2019). What do we value?: How our values influence everyday behaviours. The University of Western Australia.

65. Sumner, G.A. (1906), *Folk Ways.* New York: Ginn Custom Publishing.

66. LeVine, R. A., & Campbell, D. T. (1972). *Ethnocentrism: Theories of conflict, ethnic attitudes, and group behavior.* Hoboken, NJ: John Wiley & Sons.

67. Lee, J. A. (1966). Cultural analysis in overseas operations. *The International Executive (pre-1986)*, *8*(3), 5.

68. Adler, N. J., & Aycan, Z. (2018). Cross-cultural interaction: What we know and what we need to know. *Annual Review of Organizational Psychology and Organizational Behavior*, *5*, 307–333.

69. Brislin, R. W. (1986). A culture general assimilator: Preparation for various types of sojourns. *International Journal of Intercultural Relations*, *10*(2), 215–234.

70. Bhawuk, D. P. (2001). Evolution of culture assimilators: Toward theory-based assimilators. *International Journal of Intercultural Relations*, *25*(2), 141–163.

71. Bhawuk, D. P. (2001). Evolution of culture assimilators: Toward theory-based assimilators. *International Journal of Intercultural Relations*, *25*(2), 141–163.

72. Bhawuk, D. P. (2001). Evolution of culture assimilators: Toward theory-based assimilators. *International Journal of Intercultural Relations*, *25*(2), 141–163.

73. Singelis, T. M. (1994). The measurement of independent and interdependent self-construals. *Personality and Social Psychology Bulletin*, *20*(5), 580–591.

74. Singelis, T. M., Triandis, H. C., Bhawuk, D. P., & Gelfand, M. J. (1995). Horizontal and vertical dimensions of individualism and collectivism: A theoretical and measurement refinement. *Cross-Cultural Research*, *29*(3), 240–275.

2
COMMUNICATION AND LANGUAGE

As we have no immediate experience of what other men feel, we can form no idea of the manner in which they are affected, but by conceiving what we ourselves should feel in the like situation. (Adam Smith, 1790, p. 4)

Learning objectives

After reading this chapter and completing the activities, you should be able to:

- Explain differences in communication styles across cultures, especially those between low-context/explicit and high-context/implicit communication styles.
- Understand translation issues and strategies to overcome problems with equivalence.
- Better manage misunderstandings in intercultural communication.
- Understand the difficulties and potential strategies that will help non-native English speakers to communicate and write effectively in English.

Introduction

When we think about communicating, we first think of the verbal mode of communication. Phrases and words in a single language have – more or less – a precise meaning, or at least this is the assumption necessary to believe that a listener can receive a clear message from a speaker. This assumption allows us to avoid the time-consuming task of constantly verifying that the message received is the same message that was sent. However, effective communication incorporates several elements:

1. **Non-verbal elements.** Even in an exchange that is primarily verbal, part of the message is non-verbal, including gestures, gesticulations, and attitudes. It is important to know the extent that non-verbal/implicit messages *mix* with verbal/explicit messages.

2. **Feedback mechanisms.** Communication integrates feedback mechanisms to verify or improve the clarity of messages. In many cultures, it is important to check the accuracy of communication by multiple means, including repetition, paraphrases, questions, and interruptions.

3. **Contextual factors.** In most cases, communication is dependent on its context, including who says it and where and when it is said. The same words can mean different things in different contexts.

HOW CONTEXT CAN CHANGE THE LITERAL MEANING OF WORDS

In his collection *The Snows of Kilimanjaro*, Ernest Hemingway tells a story entitled 'A Day's Wait', in which a young boy is told that he has a fever of 102° Fahrenheit (approximately 38.9° Celsius), though he does not know that the temperature was measured on this scale. Since he had previously been in France, he thinks of the temperature as being on the Celsius temperature scale, and asks: 'About how long will it be before I die?' His mother does not understand his interpretation and explains that people do not die of a fever of 102°. The young boy goes on arguing: 'I know they do. At school in France, the boys told me you can't live with 44 degrees. I've got 102.' Finally, his mother understands that he has been waiting all day to die and she explains that, like kilometres and miles, temperature can be measured on different scales, and what is 37 degrees on one thermometer is 98 on another.

The concept of context brings together the sum of mechanisms that allow the message to be understood in relation to the beliefs or standards shared by a group of people within a given culture. While almost all verbal messages involve some element of contextual information, cultures differ in the extent to which this information is central to understanding the message.

Successful international and cross-cultural business requires those involved to be able to communicate effectively, despite significant differences in language and communication styles. Awareness of how your own cultural background influences your communication preferences and style, combined with knowledge of how others may be influenced by *their* cultural background, is an essential first step in effective communication.

Chapter Overview

In this chapter, we discuss communication, which is never language-free. In the following sections, we describe different communication styles that relate to particular assumptions and experiences of the world, and explain how to avoid cultural misunderstandings and improve communication effectiveness in international business:

- **Section 1** deals with communication **styles and context**. Western linear and low-context communication style tends to fit better with explicit, precise, and digital communication, especially for online communication, emails, and web sites. In low-context communication, almost all, if not all, of the meaning is conveyed in the words used. These messages are delivered in a manner largely deemed to be organised and accessible. In this section, we contrast low-context/explicit with high-context/implicit communication, as well as direct versus indirect speech styles. We compare face-to-face communication with online communication, showing their complementarity at successive steps of the interaction process, from the first encounter to the final delivery of a collaborative task (e.g., a contract or joint report).
- **Section 2** presents **language issues** in cross-cultural marketing, and more generally, in international business. We examine the interface between language and high-context/low-context communication styles, and discuss the implications of the special place of English as the language of business. However, it cannot be assumed in international and cross-cultural environments that everything is understood in exactly the same way when interacting with business partners, drafting joint projects, writing contracts, preparing advertising campaigns, creating brand names, designing web pages, dealing with consumer complaints, adapting survey instruments for market research, etc. This creates a special duty for native English speakers to adjust their language to improve the effectiveness of cross-cultural communication with non-native English speakers. The proficiency gap cannot be ignored. Most people in international business are expected to effectively interact in a language that is not their native tongue; this rather bold assumption is often challenging in the real world. We also discuss language in different channels

of communication, from speech to reading and writing, and their implication for spontaneity, clarity, commitment, and therefore trust between business partners. This section concludes by examining the use of local language in implementing marketing strategies cross-culturally, and the translation issues and solutions involved in navigating across languages for market surveys, research instruments, slogans, and other language-bound marketing tools.

- **Section 3** examines **how language influences worldviews and mindsets**. We discuss the Sapir-Whorf hypothesis, which proposes that native language shapes how people perceive, categorise, and construct their realities. We illustrate the difference between the *big-picture worldview*, whereby people start from broad principles and derive consequences for more precise issues at hand versus the down-to-earth, *pragmatist mindset* in which concrete topics are dealt with directly, precisely, and in an action-oriented manner. We then discuss instrumental versus representative communication. *Instrumental communication* uses language to influence or manipulate listeners, whereas *representative communication* merely exchanges neutral information. Although this distinction exists in *all* communication styles, certain languages and cultures are more familiar with instrumental communication, while others are more inclined towards representative and unbiased, non-manipulative communication.

- **Section 4** provides **recommendations for successful intercultural communication**. We start with the thorny issue of writing collaboratively in English in situations where co-authors are a mix of native and non-native English speakers, and there is likely to be a significant proficiency gap. Written communication is key, not only to online communication such as emails, but also when jointly preparing a business plan. We provide solutions for non-native speakers to usefully participate in the joint drafting of a report. This section also proposes solutions for managing language misunderstandings and associated negative emotions.

2.1 Communication styles and context

There are four areas where communication styles are strongly bound by language and culture:

1. *Communication styles reflect variations in self-concept.* In cultures where the *independent* self-concept is more dominant (i.e., in individualist cultures), we may expect communication to be based on self-assertion. In contrast, in cultures where the *interdependent* self-concept (i.e., in collectivist cultures) is dominant,

self-suppression might be expected, as well as a more modest listening style, all other things being equal.

2. *Communication styles reflect a view of what is appropriate interaction.* The Latin style of interruption can be a way to show interest. Latins often find themselves speaking when others have not finished their sentences. In contrast, individuals with Anglo-Saxon, Germanic or Nordic communication styles may feel uncomfortable about what could seem an impolite overlap or a rude interruption, even though it is well intended. In Latin cultures, interruption and overlap show a shared interest in the topic, and empathy with the other speaker. Furthermore, Latins are, or they believe they are, able to speak and listen at the same time.

3. *Communication styles also reflect the appropriate emphasis on talking versus listening, according to cultural norms.* Whereas Latin cultures tend toward a *two speakers* communication style, the Japanese tend toward a *two listeners* communication style. Japanese top executives are expected to listen more than they speak and, with some exceptions, often display a mediocre talent for making public speeches. In Japan, silence is, in fact, valued as a full element of communication. It conveys messages which, although implicit, may be interpreted through contextual factors.

4. *Silent communication can convey important meaning through what remains unsaid.* In *general*, European and most Anglo negotiators tend to fear tacit or unspoken messages much more than Asians. Understanding the communication behaviour of the other side is important, irrespective of whether the value-judgement made is positive or negative, because it facilitates sharing meaning. Silence may be experienced positively, as a moment for listening or observing (especially for what is unsaid), or negatively, as a sign of possible damage in the interaction flow, as wasted time, or even as a sign of potential hostility. In the same way, conversational overlaps may be seen as reducing the clarity of exchange, as impoliteness, or as a lack of interest in what is said. In contrast, they may be seen as a sign of empathy, a quick time-saving feedback, or even a necessary sign for continuing the conversation.

Communication and context: Low-context/explicit versus high-context/implicit communication

In most cases, communication is dependent on its context: who says it, where, when, and how they say it. Contextual factors may change what seems to be the meaning of literal words. Edward Hall, the originator of the high-/low-context divide, explained that 'a high-context (HC) communication or message is one in which most of the information is either in the physical context or internalized in the person, while very little is in the coded, explicit, transmitted part of the message. A low-context (LC) communication is just the opposite; i.e., the mass of the information is vested in the explicit code' (p.91)[2].

At a minimum, the communication context includes the people involved (e.g., their age, sex, dress, and social standing) and the setting for the interaction (e.g., at the workplace, in a showroom, during a round of labour negotiations, or during a sales visit). Each element of the context needs to be examined, including:

- The **personal side of context**, which relate *to age, respect, ways of addressing others, as well as to one's own position in the implicit hierarchy including gender, profession, status, and role*[3]. Many of these cues are easier to access in face-to-face communication, but are also evident in online video communication.
- The **social side of context** relates to the *other person's position, based on their own view of the implicit hierarchy, including their status and role*, which influences what should and should not be said and what is for them an appropriate communication style (i.e., who should talk first, who should listen in a modest and humble way, rather than openly express personal opinions, etc.). Even with online written communication (e.g., emails), which are largely asynchronous and discrete, people need to be careful not to generate misunderstandings.
- The spatial and temporal side of context relates to ***where*** (i.e., the place or location of both parties, such as in an office or hospital, and whether it is neutral or considered non-situated, which may be the case in online or email exchanges) and ***when*** (i.e., the time, punctuality, task scheduling as monochronic-task oriented [one thing at a time on a set schedule] versus polychronic-relationship oriented [multiple things on a flexible schedule]).

Context brings together the sum of interpretation mechanisms that originate within a culture and allow the message to be clear. **In HC communication (common in Latin America, the Middle East, China, and Japan),** messages are often implicit and need to include context-specific knowledge particular to a definite culture, country, and language, in order to be effectively decoded by the receiver. As described above, key interpretive information is derived from both the physical (e.g., place, setting) and the social (i.e., peoples' status, age, gender, etc.) context. People in HC cultures generally address broader issues and consider their counterpart more holistically (e.g., as a private person, as a buyer, and as a potential friend). HC communication tends to be more indirect, ambiguous, and understated than LC communication, which rather openly and precisely expresses facts and intentions[4].

In LC communication (common in Germanic, Scandinavian and Anglo cultures), messages are explicit, containing information which, at the extreme, could be assigned a binary, digital value (Yes = 1, No = 0). LC communication cultures favour context-free messages, which can be more easily coded in an unequivocal manner than in HC communication. In LC cultures, people tend to focus on specific issues and consider their counterpart in a specific role (as a buyer, for instance), with a precise view of what the person in front of them has to *do*. The risk is that LC communicators will appear naïve and far too ready to disclose key information.

A diffuse HC communication style should not be thought of as confused, but it may seem complicated and confusing to people from LC cultures. For instance, in Japan, context plays a significant role. How others are addressed changes subtly between different forms, according to the age, sex, and social position of the conversation partner, as well as the speakers' relative positions in the social hierarchy (pupil/teacher, buyer/seller, employee/employer). Further, the word *no* is almost non-existent in the Japanese vocabulary, and a *yes*, in certain circumstances, can actually mean *no*. Keiko Ueda[5] distinguishes 16 ways to avoid saying *no* in Japanese. The range of possible solutions varies from a vague *no*, to a vague and ambiguous *yes*, a mere silence, a counter-question, a tangential response, exiting, making an excuse such as sickness or a previous obligation, criticising or refusing the question itself, saying 'No, but…' or 'Yes, but…', delaying answers ('We will write you a letter') and making apologies.

The virtual absence of no in Japan also manifests itself in email communication. A German manager comments:

'I know that Japanese people are very, very polite and never say "No"…So, I encourage them to say "No" when they mean no. And I double-check with them to make sure when they say "Yes," they mean yes.' Nuances in the tone of voice are lost in emails, so when dealing with important issues with Japanese associates, the German manager always follows up with a phone call[6].

—Activity 2.1—

Closing the loop

A Japanese counterpart seemed positive about your proposition. Write an email to confirm whether or not the proposition is going to be acceptable.

Context influences communication without the participants even being aware of it. Subconsciously, we may decide that a person does or does not deserve trust, based on both explicit and implicit information. For instance, the correlation between age and credibility differs according to culture. In some cultures, older people are seen as more credible than younger people, whereas in other cultures, the reverse is either true or age is unrelated to credibility. This influences the information exchange. It can affect how we perceive the *other*, including what we expect them to do, as well as how we interpret the message being communicated.

A major element of context is the knowledge of, and familiarity with, the people on the other side, and whether or not a personal relationship is a condition for working together effectively. This means that personalisation (i.e., what a person can *do* depends on who the person *is*) is largely required in HC cultures, especially in East Asia and the Middle East, whereas depersonalisation (i.e., who a person *is* is less important than what they *do)* it is often perceived as better in Western cultures.

Overcoming problems in communication between High- and Low-context team members

It has been argued that HC communication is more sophisticated and allows more complex information processing. According to Edward Hall, it is the ability to *understand and process context* that makes it possible for humans to automatically correct distortions and omissions in messages. In contrast, LC communication focuses on eliminating distortions and omissions in sent messages as much as possible, making messages linear, articulated, explicit, simplified, and easy to understand in the absence of contextual cues. LC communication provides the lowest common denominator for intercultural communication in a way that may not always be fully satisfactory, because it often looks 'minimal'. It does, however, provide a more secure basis for, and an easier path towards, mutual understanding. This largely explains the dominance of English as the typical LC business language.

English as the *lingua franca* of international business is both a significant apparent advantage for native English speakers and a significant responsibility for them vis-à-vis non-native English speakers. Tolerance on the part of native English speakers towards those less proficient in English (i.e., who may have poor pronunciation, broken grammar, and limited vocabulary) is an asset for cross-cultural communication in English. Differences in language competence can lead to unnoticed misunderstandings that may backfire later, sometimes too late to be corrected. For non-native English speakers, it can be a challenge to adjust to the English communication style, which is task-oriented, explicit, and direct.

However, there is a *shared* responsibility. If one side does not put in any effort for adjustment and the other side puts in a great deal of effort, the end result is a lack of mutual comprehension. It must be acknowledged and accepted that there is interdependence in communication between native and non-native English speakers. On the one hand, native English speakers need to slow down the pace of speech and avoid colloquial language. On the other hand, non-native English speakers need to ask for explanations and/or ask the speaker to rephrase when they are not sure of the meaning. And both parties need to regularly check that they are being properly understood. Spontaneity may suffer a little; however, it is the price to be paid for communication efficacy.

THE IMPORTANCE OF TAKING INTO CONSIDERATION COMMUNICATION STYLES IN INTERCULTURAL TEAMS

The communication styles of people involved in intercultural teamwork need to be assessed first, based on nationality, culture, and language. If all team members belong to a LC culture, communication can be assumed to be precise and explicit. If some team members are more comfortable using a LC style but others have a HC style, the LC individuals should ask precise questions, verify interpretation, and validate joint understanding. If all team members use HC communication but come from different areas of the world (e.g., Japan and the Middle East), people have to be aware that contextual codes are culture-bound and, therefore, not shared. Preparation and adaptation are needed, at least from one party. Communication may, at times, be uncomfortable and unclear. Patience, courtesy, and empathy can help achieve smoother and more accurate information flows. A selection of countries are classified according to their degree of Low- to High-Context communication style in **Table 2.1.**

Table 2.1 Classification of countries according to their degree of Low- to High-Context communication style

Low	Low-Medium	Medium	Medium-High	High
Denmark	Australia	Croatia, Cyprus	Algeria	China, Hong Kong
Finland	Austria	Czech Rep., Estonia	Bolivia	India, Indonesia, Iran
Germany	Belgium	France, Greece	Brazil	Japan, Kuwait, Lebanon
Luxembourg	Canada	Italy, Lithuania	Egypt	Macau, Malaysia, Nigeria

(Continued)

Table 2.1 (Continued)

Low	Low-Medium	Medium	Medium-High	High
Netherlands	Israel	Poland, Romania	Morocco	Pakistan, Philippines
Norway	US	Slovenia	Peru, Russia	Singapore, South Korea
Sweden		South Africa	Saudi Arabia	Syria, Taiwan, Thailand
Switzerland		Spain, UK	Turkey	U A Emirates, Vietnam

Source: Usunier, J. C., & Roulin, N. (2010). The influence of high- and low-context communication styles on the design, content, and language of business-to-business web sites. *The Journal of Business Communication (1973)*, *47*(2), 189–227.

WORKING WITH TEAM MEMBERS ACROSS CULTURES

Cross-cultural team members use many different types of communication media to work together, including face-to-face meetings, email, phone, Skype, WhatsApp, etc. It is important for team members to be aware that cross-cultural communication differs according to the media used to interact. As a rule, face-to-face communication is much richer in context than online communication, with online video chats being richer in contexts than pure email-based communication, which are almost context-free, especially between strangers.

LC communication, being context-free, is easier to use, especially in less personalised forms of communication (e.g., email). Context is also less important when people on both sides share common characteristics (e.g., same age, same profession, same religion, etc.), especially when they are peers in an egalitarian setting (such as collaborative teams like the X-Culture project). What remains is a rather context-free environment, especially when there is no prior face-to-face interaction to build a strong relationship and communication is mostly limited to online, digital, and electronic forms. However, a number of digital communication tools can be used to bridge the gap between electronic communication and face-to-face interaction (Skype, FaceTime, WhatsApp, etc.)

Direct versus indirect speech styles

Communication styles differ according to whether messages are sent in a *direct* versus *indirect* manner and whether individuals are *talkers* or *listeners*. This involves choosing what is considered as relevant information, as well as the best way to communicate this information to ensure that the message is neither too broad nor too narrow, whether it is largely context-bound or context-free, and whether it should be based on hard facts or general principles. Similarly, the tendency to disclose information, and the preference for asking questions as opposed to providing answers, are all embedded in communication styles.

Indirect styles, which are more common in HC cultures, often involve involuntary messages conveyed by personal characteristics of age, size, weight, sex, dress, and so on. These characteristics are *encoded* in the speaker, and *decoded* by the listener, using their own cultural frameworks. Cues for interpretation are provided by the circumstances of the conversation, including where and when it takes place, the meeting atmosphere, etc. Indirect elements of communication can be viewed negatively by LC people, who prefer to use a more direct communication style. Here, LC communicators must display patience and prudence, politely inviting the partner to be more straight-forward, avoid unnecessary digression, repetitive illustrations, and to speed up the process of getting to the point; remember that courtesy requires a certain amount of indirectness in all languages and cultures, such as when being asked an embarrassing question.

Reluctance (or apparent reluctance) to be direct has several culture- and language-related motives, all of which are perfectly understandable:

1. A fear of conflict or breach of harmony can lead to individuals, who are too direct, being perceived as being too assertive or confrontational, and resented.
2. A more holistic mindset can lead to the need to establish the *big picture* and the context first. Those who prefer an indirect communication style may need to understand or discuss general principles, past experiences, and events first and get to the point only later (i.e., be more direct at the end of a long speech).
3. A need to feel comfortable within a structure or hierarchy can lead to indirectness in communication, especially in the preliminaries, where directness may be perceived as disrespectful, especially in vertical interactions and in hierarchical, high power distance societies.

When such motives are present, the cultural habit of expressing oneself through indirect language forms is deeply ingrained, for fear of being perceived as impolite and/or quarrelsome.

Verbal communication styles involve not only the words, but also other elements, such as tone of voice, frequency and nature of conversational overlap, the pace of speech, degree of apparent involvement in what one says, emphasis on talking versus listening, direct or indirect speech styles, etc. These elements of style are influenced by cultural norms which implicitly define what is, supposedly, *good* communication (*good* meaning appropriate between members of the cultural community insofar as they share the same code).

Figure 2.1 below distinguishes four speech styles based on language structure, the logical sequence of thoughts, grammar, and rhetoric. Speech styles range from direct (common in Northern European and Anglo cultures), to semi-direct (common in Latin cultures), to semi-indirect (common in Arabic-Middle Eastern cultures), to indirect (common in East Asian cultures). These styles privilege either (a) linear or circular communication patterns, (b) single or parallel thought development, and (c) staying on or digressing from the topic. All these different styles communicate the point through different *speech routes*.

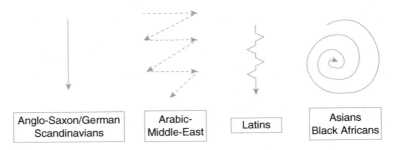

Figure 2.1   Direct and indirect speech style

Source: Adapted from Kaplan, Roger B. (1966). Cultural thought patterns in inter-cultural education. *Language Learning*, 16, 1–20. Printed with permission of John Wiley and Sons.

Steps in effective communication across cultures

Any time cross-cultural teams are brought together to solve a problem, all elements within the communication environment need to be considered. The communication environment is a *context* in itself, including the native languages of participants, their proficiency in English or English as a Second Language (ESL), the communication channels being used, and the tasks to be performed at each step of the collaborative process. This environment, including the content and channels, should be considered at each successive step of the interaction process, from first encounter to final delivery of a collaborative project. These successive steps include:

1. First contact between team members, including getting to know each other and the task,
2. Exchanging basic information, culture, and language adjustment,
3. Distributing tasks and roles,
4. Collecting and organising information,
5. Joint development of key ideas and preparing a draft document,

6. Writing and editing a joint report, and
7. Constant interpersonal (team) communication over the whole project duration.

Communication channels can be more or less conducive to efficient communication at different steps in the process, depending on how *context-rich* they are. Using a context-rich communication medium at the first encounter generally has a positive influence on subsequent encounters. Even if further email interactions are context-free, emails suddenly become richer in context when they follow a personal context-rich face-to-face encounter at the very start of the relationship.

In physical, face-to-face encounters, communication involves full personal presence (i.e., body, face, eye-contact, gesture, and body language, as well as natural voice), and often starts with getting personally acquainted. However, the costs of travelling often restrict the opportunity for personal contact, especially early in the communication, even though face-to-face communication is ideal for initiating a relationship. This can be at least somewhat mitigated through the use of virtual meetings that include interactive visual and oral synchronous communication (e.g., via Skype, Zoom, FaceTime). This gives a sense of actual live communication by including physical elements (i.e., face and body), gestures and natural voices. Today's technology allows for a wide variety of interactive modes of communication that are largely culture-free, but not context-free.

Other forms of interactive communication are less visual (e.g., phone, WhatsApp), most of which rely on pure voice communication through a conversation with personal presence. However, people still imagine what kind of person (e.g., what they look like, their gender and age, ethnicity, etc.) is on the other end of the line, based on cues from the sound of their voice. Even written sources (e.g., via email) provide a partial, and sometimes misleading, sense of who the person really is. This can be complemented by static images; however, dynamic cues related to body language and/or non-verbal gestures are lacking. These cues are important in cultures where people's identity is largely defined by their relationships and position in society.

Pure written email interaction with no physical cues results in an almost context-free, LC communication. It can be most useful at later steps in the interaction, as it allows for clarity when explicitness is required and precision when task commitments must be set among several people.

2.2 Language issues in cross-cultural marketing

In this section, we first explore the relationship between language and HC/LC Communication styles. Edward Hall assumed there was no relationship. Our view, however, is that certain languages are better tools than others for LC communication.

Language and HC/LC communication styles

Hall's theory of LC/HC communication cultures is based on his background as a cultural anthropologist, on his field studies of Indian cultures, and on his pioneering work with US diplomatic services. Hall seems to view language as being unrelated to HC/LC communication styles, when he emphasises the importance of context over language in *Beyond Culture* (1976, p. 86): 'The problem lies not in the linguistic code, but in the context, which carries varying proportions of the meaning. Without context, the code is incomplete since it encompasses only part of the message.' However, he writes about the linearity of language (with the English language implicitly in mind) and gives many examples related to the US context-free legal system (e.g., in US courts: 'Answer the question, Yes or No', p. 107). He also gives high-context examples based on the Chinese language and writing system as an art form, as well as on the way French courts tend to contextualise trials, adding that French culture is a HC/LC mélange (Hall's terminology). Being a cultural anthropologist rather than a linguist, Hall seems to overlook how deeply language structure is related to the HC/LC divide.

In our view, HC/LC communication styles are at least partly related to language structure. Many Asian languages use no gender, few or no personal pronouns, do not conjugate verbs, and provide speakers with a relatively under-signified text, which requires information from the context for the message to be understood by the receiver, as is the case for Chinese and Japanese. Similarly, a medium-context language, such as French, avoids repetitions of the same word for the sake of elegance and therefore uses synonyms or pronouns at the direct expense of precision and clarity. The meaning is supposed to be, at least in part, understood from the context. French people communicating in English must forget the sacred rule they have learned, not to repeat words, especially in writing. The *supposed* synonyms are misunderstood by English speakers (readers), who do not understand why different words are used, and often assume that their purpose is to add new information.

In very high-context languages like Japanese and Chinese, gender and number, as well as person, are often understood from the context. The subject, especially 'I', will often be omitted in Japanese. In Chinese, verbal forms will not change with time, gender, or person. Conversely, very low-context languages are often over-coded to make messages even more explicit. When a German speaker says 'Ich mache', the first-person singular is both in the personal pronoun Ich (I) and in the ending (e) of the verb, which applies only to the first-person singular in the present and active tense. These two cues are used to explicitly indicate that speakers are talking about themselves by using the first-person singular, whereas it is possible that one cue could be enough, and even none, as is often the case in high-context languages (just the infinitive verb). Thus, it is clearly important to understand whether the language being used is higher or lower in context when trying to communicate to a speaker of another language. For instance, Indo-European languages, on average, favour low- to medium-context communication, while many Far East languages, such as Chinese, Japanese, Thai, or Vietnamese, favour high-context communication.

Language differences worldwide

There is an incredible number of languages in the world (over 7,000), and much language diversity within nations. For instance, Switzerland has 4 official languages, Bhutan has 19, India has 22, as well as several hundred unofficial languages[8]. Perhaps surprising to English speakers, English is not the most prevalent language in terms of the number of native speakers, but it is the most commonly used language on the internet and in international business. However, it needs to be remembered that English is often an additional language. Of the approximately 1,350 million English speakers in the world, only around 370 million speak English as a 'primary' or native language (see **Figure 2.2**)[9]. Despite the sometimes-deceptive impression that English will increasingly be used everywhere for all occasions, people still commonly speak different languages in everyday interactions in most of the world. Further, people should not assume that everyone in international business is fully proficient in the language being spoken, as people differ greatly in their language proficiency. The notion that English is a universal language is not the case, especially from a historical and geographic perspective. There are many regional *lingua franca*, such as Greek in the Antiquities, Latin during a long historical period in Europe, and nowadays Russian, Turkish, Mandarin, Swahili and English in East and South Africa, French in West and North Africa, etc.

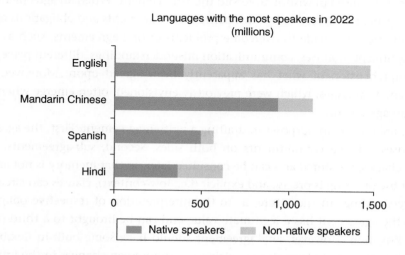

Figure 2.2 Most spoken languages in 2022

Source: Adapted from Ethnologue, 2022 (www.ethnologue.com/guides/most-spoken-languages)

Language is also strongly related to group identity and an object of pride for in-group members. There can be heated debate in multilingual countries around the respective status of local languages (e.g., the French versus the Flemish-speaking communities in Belgium) or conflicts and even wars involving language and cultural dominance, such as the conflict in Ukraine between Ukrainian and Russian languages in 2022. Showing respect for the communication partner's native language is important: disrespect, even understated, might offend.

Communicating through speech versus exchanging information through writing and reading (oral versus written language)

There is a major difference between oral and written communication: speech is often fuzzy and approximate and leaves no trace (unless it is recorded, which is rarely the case), whereas writing and reading are based on more explicit and accurate language and can be stored in a number of formats and later retrieved. However, the interface between oral and written communication is more complex. For instance, keeping silent, which is neither speech nor writing, is a means of communication, often intended to leave the other side with a disturbing sense of not knowing what is going on and feeling somewhat upset.

Generally, people combine speech and writing to achieve more efficient information exchanges. For instance, an agreement is often reached first by speaking, and then later formalised in writing to record the arrangement. When an agreement is put down on paper and agreed to by both parties, there are rights and obligations on both sides. Contracts are made to overcome problems of oral agreements, such as failing memory, unkept promises, communication misunderstandings, different perceptions, and comprehension of what has apparently been agreed upon. Moreover, tricky implementation issues, which were previously envisioned, often emerge when drawing up an agreement.

There are four main purposes in drafting a written agreement. First, the agreement summarises detailed commitments on both sides. Second, sub-agreements, in the form of clauses, are stored and can be consulted later, so that memory is not an issue. Third, if the phrasing is precise and explicit (i.e., low-context), clauses can circumvent misunderstandings in the future, as to the interpretation of respective obligations. Fourth, the agreement has a legitimate value and can be brought to a third-party in case of litigation. However, any agreement should have some built-in flexibility to deal with both expected events (e.g., delays) or unforeseen changes in the future.

Due to the difference in preciseness and explicitness between oral and written agreements, it is likely that parties will be obliged to go back to previous phases of the face-to-face compromise process, when in fact, they were convinced there was full agreement. Ambiguity in paragraphs may be intended or unintended; *bona fide* partners may have a hard time disentangling mere inadvertence from hidden intent.

A good verbal agreement does not necessarily lead to a well-written agreement and vice-versa. A good verbal agreement may generate perceived satisfaction on both sides and provide a relational and strategic framework for joint action. Conversely, an apparently well-written agreement may not lead to good outcomes at the implementation stage, especially when some joint resolutions cannot be put into practice and/or lead to unbalanced situations and contentious issues (e.g., unrealistic performance obligations). However, a well-drafted agreement contains detailed economic arrangements as to how the deal will be practically implemented.

The debate over verbal versus written agreements as a basis for trust between parties is often clipped into two stereotypical sayings: *Get it in Writing* versus *My Word is My Bond*. For cultures where *my word is my bond*, trust is a personal matter, and is people-based. In the *get-it-in-writing* mentality, trust is more impersonal, based on agreements, contracts, rules, commitment, and compliance. There is a potential dissymmetry in interpretations of clauses in any negotiated agreement, mainly due to misunderstandings, language problems, and divergent interpretation of obligations on both sides.

Use of local language in implementing marketing strategies cross-culturally

Language plays a central role in marketing communications when they take place in an international and multilingual context, since communication styles, as well as world views, are deeply influenced by the structure of languages. This is true for the major types of marketing communication tools, including advertising, personal selling, and public relations. These tools not only aim to communicate with customers, but also with all stakeholders in the market, including middlemen, business partners, public authorities, and even competitors.

Here, we provide the example of *brands* to show how much they are language-based, with more detail being provided in Chapter 5. Brands are signs based on sounds, written signs (letters or pictographs), and visual elements (logo-type, brand design). The linguistic content of a brand name has an influence on its verbal, auditory and cognitive meaning, and the way the brand is interpreted by consumers.

Several branches of linguistics (e.g., semantics, phonology, semiotics) enable us to assess how the sound, spelling, and design of a brand name is likely to transfer from a source to a target linguistic context. A brand name should generally be relatively easy to pronounce. A simple rule is that the brand name should not exceed three syllables, each composed of one consonant and one vowel.

Organisations looking to extend their brand into international markets have several options for the transposition of their existing brand name, including simple translation and transliteration. *Simple translation* is rarely used, as it may result in profound differences in meaning, scattered brand image, and inability to create international brand recognition. *Transliteration* is better, as it attempts to carry over the connotative meaning in the target language that exists in the source language. The best type of brand is the *transparent* brand, such as Sony, which is suitable everywhere. The corporate name Sony, formerly a brand name, arose from a replacement of the original company name (i.e., Tokyo Tsuhin Kogyo, Tokyo Industrial Telecommunication Company) by its product brand name, which proved to be successful.

A study of 100 multinational brands entering China found four common strategies[10]:

- **Adapt for sound,** ~43% sound similar to the original name, even if the meaning is completely changed (e.g., **AUDI**'s Chinese name is 奥迪, which sounds similar **ÀO DÍ** but means **profound enlightenment**).
- **Adapt for meaning,** ~24% have a similar meaning, even though they sound completely different (e.g., **GENERAL MOTORS**' Chinese name 通用汽亙 is pronounced **TŌNG YONG QI CHE**, which means **general motors**).
- **Adapt for sound and meaning,** ~22% try to find characters that produce the same sounds and the same meaning (e.g., **NIKE**'s Chinese name 耐克 sounds like **NAI KE,** which means **endurance conqueror**).
- **No resemblance**, ~11% chose a Chinese name with no resemblance to the original, either in sound or meaning (e.g., **HEINEKEN**'s Chinese name 喜力 sounds like **XǏ LI**, which means **happy power**).

Translation issues

In marketing communications, it is important to know that the message is understood as intended. Language translation is fraught with risk in this regard. Translation techniques, no matter how sophisticated, may prove incapable of achieving full message comparability.

There are four basic translation equivalence problems, as described below:

1. *Lexical equivalence*: Dictionaries and translation websites provide us with seemingly equivalent words. For instance, the English adjective *warm* translates into the French *chaud*. However, when back-translated *chaud* translates into *warm* <u>and</u> *hot*, showing that there is no precise lexical equivalence.

2. *Idiomatic equivalence*: This problem occurs when trying to translate a sentence such as *it's warm*. French has two expressions for this: either *il fait chaud* (literally, *it makes warm* meaning *it's warm [today]*) or *c'est chaud* (meaning *it [this object] is warm*). An idiom is a linguistic usage that is natural to native speakers. Idioms are most often non-equivalent: the present continuous (i.e., I am doing) has no equivalent in French, except *je suis en train de*, which is highly colloquial and not to be used in correct French written language. Idiomatic equivalence may also be problematic for regions within a country, as Roy et al. (p. 207)[11] state: 'The English phrase *"high risk"* can be translated as *"qiang feng xian"* in the middle and northern China but as *"gao feng xian"* in southern China. To Chinese from the south, the word *"qiang"* has two meanings, one is related to the "magnitude" and the other to "strength"; as such, it can be difficult to interpret the concept *"qiang feng xian"*.'

3. *Grammatical/syntactical equivalence*: This problem refers to the way words are ordered, sentences are constructed, and meaning is expressed in language. English generally proceeds in an active way, starting with the subject, followed by the verb, and then the complement, avoiding abstractions as well as convoluted sentences. Many languages, including German and French, start by explaining the circumstances in relative clauses, before they proceed to the action. This makes for complex sentences, starting with relative clauses that begin with *when, where, even though, although*, and so on. The Japanese language has a quite different ordering of words from Western languages: verbs are always at the end of the sentence.

4. *Experiential equivalence* is about what words and sentences mean for people in their everyday experience. Coming back to *chaud*, which translates into two English words *warm* and *hot*: the French think of warm and hot as one concept, whereas the English, the Germans and many others think of it as two. Similarly, the special experience of coldness in the word *chilly* cannot be adequately rendered in French. Translated terms must refer to real items and real experiences which are familiar in the source as well as the target cultures. An expression such as *dish-washing machine* may face experiential equivalence problems when people, even if they know what it is, have never actually seen this type of household appliance or experienced it.

―Activity 2.2―

Automatic translation

There are many automatic translation software applications available, and firms are tempted to use these to automate translations for business communication, business websites, etc.

Test some text from a website, or from a survey item, that you would like to translate. First, translate from English into several different languages, and then translate them back into English.

We did this with a well-established item from the 10-item CETSCALE[12] measuring consumer ethnocentrism, using the DeepL Translator, which claims to offer the 'world's most accurate and nuanced machine translation':

English item: Only those products that are unavailable in the U.S. should be imported

Translated into Japanese: 米国で入手不可能な製品のみを輸入すること

Then, translated back into English (US): Importing only products that are not available in the U.S.

Is this text equivalent?

In the case of preparing a local version of a market research questionnaire, a final local language questionnaire is first discussed and prepared by the researcher (who speaks the source language) and the two translators. It is advisable to have at least one translator who is a native speaker of the target language, and another who is a native speaker of the source language. This allows them to translate *into* their native language rather than *from* it, which is always more difficult and less reliable.

The back-translation technique is the most widely employed method of reaching translation equivalence (mainly lexical and idiomatic)[13]. Based on this technique, one translator translates from the source language into a target language (S1 => T1). Then another translator, ignorant of the source-language text, translates the first translation back into the source language (T1 =>S2). Then, the two source-language versions are compared (S1 = S2?). This procedure helps to identify probable translation errors. Discrepancies may arise from translation mistakes or derive from real translation equivalence problems. Any discrepancies are usually resolved jointly by those involved. However, back-translation can also instil a false sense of security in the investigator by inadvertently leading to spurious lexical equivalence. Simply knowing that words are equivalent is not enough. It is necessary to know the extent to which those literally equivalent words and phrases convey equivalent meanings in the two languages or cultures. Another technique, blind parallel translation, consists of having several translators translate, simultaneously and independently, from the source language into the target language. The different versions are then compared, and a final version is written.

Parallel and back-translation may, of course, be merged. When two languages and cultures present wide variations, such as Korean and French, combining parallel and back-translation provides a higher level of equivalence[14]. The European Social Survey, which is designed for cross-cultural comparisons, uses the TRAPD methodology, where an English source survey is translated by local national teams into all of the languages that at least 5% of the population speaks as a first language, after which it is reviewed for translation quality within each national team, adjudicated or verified for linguistic and semantic correctness and quality by an external provider, pretested and documented.

2.3 Language, worldviews, and mindsets

The Sapir-Whorf hypothesis: language influences worldviews

The first proponent of the idea that language has a decisive influence on culture was the linguist, Edward Sapir. Language creates categories in our minds, which in turn, directly influence the things we judge to be similar and those that *deserve* to be differentiated. It is proposed that language influences our *Weltanschauung* (i.e., our worldviews): our way of observing, of describing, of interacting, and finally the way in which we construct our reality. Sapir[15] (p. 214) writes:

> The fact of the matter is that the real world is to a large extent unconsciously built up on the language habits of the group. No two languages are ever sufficiently similar as to be considered as representing the same social reality. The worlds in which different societies live are distinct worlds, not merely the same world with different labels attached.

The linguist and anthropologist Benjamin Lee Whorf developed and extended Sapir's hypothesis. The Sapir–Whorf hypothesis contends that the structure of language has a significant influence on perception and categorisation. Whereas empirical testing of this hypothesis seems to have been fairly thorough[16], it is not considered valid by many linguists. For example, the gender given to nouns is not necessarily indicative of a particular cultural meaning (e.g., the gender of the earth, the sun and the moon, or of vices and virtues, may not convey any additional meaning); for most, it often seems to reflect an arbitrary choice. It may be the case, however, that this attribution of gender had a certain meaning at the genesis of the language, but that the meaning has since been lost.

Many languages, including Spanish, Portuguese, French, and Italian, use masculine and feminine noun classification. The gender, and often whether it is singular or plural, is usually coded in the ending of the word. **Table 2.2** provides some examples:

Table 2.2 Examples of nouns that have 'genders'

Italian		Spanish	
pizza	Feminine	perro	Male dog
risotto	Masculine	perra	Female dog
spaghetti	Masculine plural	señor	man, Mr.
lasagne	Feminine plural	señora	ma'am, Mrs.

Edward Hall was influenced by the view of linguistic relativity (i.e., the Sapir–Whorf hypothesis[17]); however, he did this without digging very deeply into linguistic issues[18] [19]. Accepting the Sapir–Whorf hypothesis (i.e., that language shapes world-views, perceptions, and communication), implies that business people from different cultures not only communicate in different ways, but also perceive, categorise and construct their realities differently[20]. This assumes a readiness to accept that words, even those that are translated with no apparent difficulty, offer only an illusion of sharing in the same vision of reality. It may be necessary to retain as many foreign words as possible in their original form, thereby keeping culturally unique concepts. We call this *untranslation,* which is widely practised for emic concepts. Asking questions of interpreters and/or team partners can help us to better understand the precise meaning of words or expressions and to identify shared meaning.

Language contains pre-shaped images of the real world that partly condition our experiences. A particular language can shape different assumptions (e.g., those associated with time, emotions, attitudes, and social hierarchy), and reflect how concepts are expressed (e.g., in the colloquial phrases used in marketing communications). The proposition that language actually shapes culture, and therefore cultural behaviour, is a major causal assumption that can be challenged, because often all that language does is simply reflect culture. That is why there are limits to this assumption.

Big Picture worldview versus down-to-earth, pragmatist mindset

On one hand, *ideologists* use a wide body of ideas, which provides them with a formal and coherent description of the world: Marxism or Liberalism, for instance. Every event carries meaning when it is seen through a broad intellectual framework. On the other hand, the *pragmatist* first considers the extreme diversity of real-world situations, and then derives principles inductively.

Ideologists tend to resent *pragmatists* as being too interested in trivial details, too practical, too down-to-earth, too data-oriented, and unable to look at issues from a higher standpoint. Conversely, *pragmatists* resent *ideologists* for being too theoretical, lacking practical sense, and too concerned with issues that are too broad to lead to implementable decisions. This can cause problems in communication, such as in the first stages of the negotiation process, where the differences between *ideologists* and *pragmatists* may create communication misunderstandings that will be difficult to overcome during subsequent phases. Indeed, developing common norms will be difficult in itself, although it is necessary if both partners want to be able to predict the other party's behaviour. A frequent comment in such situations will be: *One never knows what these people have in mind; they do not accept facts; their behaviour is largely unpredictable.*

Instrumental versus representative communication

It would be naïve to believe that languages only target fair and reciprocal exchange of true information. In terms of Shannon and Weaver's content-related communication model, the fair exchange of true information is called *representative communication*. The intention of the sender is to communicate a clear and unequivocal message, which may nevertheless be partly misunderstood due to noise and/or inadequate decoding. However, there may be many reasons why people send voluntarily distorted, sometimes unclear, and at times misleading, messages. For instance, an unwillingness to disclose one's position may explain why parties do not fully reveal their preferences, for fear that needs, priorities, and expectations can be rather accurately guessed by the other party. This *masked* communication involves hiding or disguising key information.

Instrumental communication is used as an attempt to persuade or manipulate the other party by delivering information, which is not false *per se,* but misrepresents the situation. Instrumental communication (e.g., *eat soup; it is good for you*) targets *persuasion* rather than mere information exchange. However, the expectations of the instrumental communicator, as to how the (possibly quite distorted) message will be decoded and understood by the other party, may not be met.

Beyond mere instrumental communication lies *strategic misrepresentation,* which involves knowingly delivering untruthful and manipulative information. A party may, for instance, convey false information on the value they assign to a particular issue or on key data (e.g., lying or equivocating on dates, commitments, etc.). Cultures do not put the same value on communication attitudes, such as frankness, speech openness, and instrumentality. Lying or misrepresenting information may be perfectly acceptable in some cultures and frowned upon in others, although some form of deception is practised everywhere. Lying can include mere omission (e.g., hiding key information), minor lies, or actively deceitful communication (e.g., forging accounts). The greatest prudence and caution are called for.

2.4 Recommendations for successful intercultural communication

Writing together… in English

Written communication is ubiquitous in international business and cross-cultural marketing, be it for exchanging information with foreign partners, negotiating globally, drafting international contracts, or when jointly preparing a project or a business plan. There are many collaborative tools available to teams in the digital space that go beyond email (e.g., Skype, Dropbox, and Google Docs) that can make collaborative work much richer and easier. There are also many digital tools that help non-native speakers to usefully participate in the joint drafting of a report, including actively using spell-check, grammar-check, dictionaries, Google Translate, and automatic translation instruments (e.g., DeepL). These tools can be combined with translation-back-translation to check meaning equivalence, as well as having a native speaker edit the draft text. The benefits of using a copyeditor are enormous, not only for the particular task at hand, but also for long-term learning about proper rules in English grammar.

Experience, unfortunately, shows that non-native English speakers generally make little use of these easily accessible language verification tools. Appendix 2.1 offers some advice from a non-native English speaker on how to write in English and gives an overview of how to improve, not only in style, but first and foremost in the readability and comprehensibility of a non-native English text. Below, we also provide a useful checklist of down-to-earth advice for both English and non-English speakers.

CHECKLIST: DOWN-TO-EARTH ADVICE FOR BOTH ENGLISH AND NON-ENGLISH SPEAKERS

The following precautions should be seriously considered when negotiating how the language gap may be bridged in terms of task distribution and balancing contributions, while taking into account different abilities and levels of proficiency in English:

1. Avoid slang and vernacular language, colloquial expressions, as well as purely idiomatic expressions that are known only by native speakers in a particular country (see NTC's Dictionary of American Slang and Colloquial Expressions).
2. Actively self-reflect on your accent, speech pace, tonic accentuation, pronunciation, etc., which are likely to affect the clarity of what you say.

3. Avoid pushing non-native English team members to pretend they are proficient English speakers (when, in fact, they are not) and to pretend that they understand (when they do not really catch what you say), so that they don't attract ridicule or lose face.

4. For non-native English speakers, do not hesitate to ask for clarification, re-phrasing, or further explanation of a word or an expression which you do not understand.

5. Regularly check with both sides that the meaning is really shared.

6. Avoid differences of opinion by using rational and documented arguments, rather than being excessively persuasive and trying to win the argument at any cost, as this can cause frustration and resentment that goes with the feeling of having lost a battle.

7. Be cautious about the way you expose lying, including strategic misrepresentation of verifiable information. If you feel that your partner or partners are insincere, and this is confirmed by supportive evidence, do not expose the alleged misconduct by direct communication, because it could make them lose face. Rather, choose indirect and understated statements that will save face; however, be clear with your arguments so that you convey the message that you are perfectly aware of the misconduct and want their behaviour to stop.

8. Avoid fake feedback. Pretending, whether consciously or unconsciously, is a form of self-lie that is intended to save face. However, pretending impairs communication. Fake feedback (e.g., mumbling lip-service) by the receiver, which induces speakers to believe that they have been understood, when in fact they have not, undermines the communication.

Managing language misunderstandings and negative emotions

During collaborative teamwork (e.g., between X-Culture team members), it is likely that some conflicts will arise from language mistakes, confusion in conveying information, and misinterpretation of what was written or said by participants, especially when they have lower proficiency in English than other team members.

Conflicts have two aspects: (1) an objective base in terms of actual contradiction and possibly incompatible, irreconcilable claims, and (2) a subjective base in terms of negative interpersonal feelings that come from conflicts that may quickly escalate. A simple misunderstanding can erupt into rivalry in an attempt to attain personal gain at the other side's expense. At the extreme, this may result in people parting ways, even if there was a win-win potential.

Negative emotions often arise from misinterpretations. These emotions (e.g., anger) result in individuals being less accurate in judging the interests at stake and more centred on their own interests; however, it also has a general effect of reducing joint outcomes. Thus, it is important to manage language misunderstandings and associated negative emotional states in joint cooperative tasks. Managing language misunderstandings can result in greater team cohesion and enjoyment of the task, as well as less motivation for opportunistic free-riding, as all members of the team feel valued and are less likely to exploit weaknesses (e.g., exploiting low language proficiency by feigning an even lower ability to comprehend the task).

Positive and negative emotions both have a role to play in intercultural interactions, as they are neither all good nor all bad. Emotions contain both an element of affect and an accompanying physiological arousal that can lead to different courses of action. On one hand, positive emotions can lead to being more flexible and encouraging of others to be persistent in their tasks, especially since positive affective states increase confidence levels. However, they may also heighten expectations, resulting in disappointment with the actual outcomes. On the other hand, negative emotions, when handled well, may have a positive influence on the collaboration process by drawing attention to an unfair situation or an opportunistic move that needs to be corrected. However, they more often result in conflict escalation, where people take matters personally, when they should see them in a more objective, distanced, and self-controlled manner.

While negative emotions may serve to inform the parties that an existing situation is untenable, they may also result in a negative conflict spiral. Negative spirals are partly based on selectively choosing information cues that confirm the negative feelings, leading to an escalation of negative feelings (no longer based on hard facts) toward the counterpart. Negative spirals also result from systematic reciprocation of contentious communication. They are particularly likely to occur in cross-cultural interactions, due to differences at three levels:

1. differences in internalised values and norms,
2. differences in emotional expression, and
3. differences in linguistic styles.

A conflict spiral appears as circular, as it is based on repeated contentious communication whereby each side *responds* to the other side's contentious communication with negative reciprocation.

Negative emotions may arise from cultural misunderstandings between individuals from low- and high-context cultures. Kumar[21] explains how Americans (from a low-context, task-oriented culture) and Japanese people (from a high-context, relationship-oriented culture) experience a goal conflict that generates negative emotions, which increase behavioural incompatibility and damage the relationship. Negative emotions not only affect the ability to process information and the quality of information exchange, but they also generate frustration on both sides. And when aroused, people generally revert to habitual behaviour. In this case, Americans react by being more aggressive and the Japanese by escaping. The conflict then escalates even further because aggression amplifies the Japanese desire to escape, while Japanese withdrawal increases American frustration.

A number of conflict resolution and communication strategies have been recommended for breaking negative spirals in cross-cultural encounters. First, *actively monitoring emotions* can help to avoid negative spirals without becoming overly conflict-avoidant. Second, focusing on *motivated information processing,* where information is selectively processed to support the desired outcomes, can guide interpretation, rather than emotions. Third, embracing *reciprocation, combined with non-contentious communication,* is likely to help break negative spirals in negotiations. Reciprocation implies being a good listener and being ready to respond to positive moves on the part of the communication partner by sending valuable information in a give-and-take manner. Non-contentious communication implies avoiding being dominant, argumentative, confrontational, and challenging others to the point that they feel the need to defend themselves. However, it is important to remember that emotions are informative and convey messages. They cannot be simply ignored.

2.5 Chapter summary

In this chapter, we describe cross-cultural communication as much more than phrases and words. Effective communication also considers both verbal and non-verbal elements, especially contextual factors, as well as feedback mechanisms to verify the accuracy of the message. Cultures differ in their preferences for high-context, indirect versus low-context, direct communication, which can confuse and frustrate intercultural communication and lead to serious misunderstandings and misplaced judgements. We explain how to avoid cultural misunderstandings and improve communication effectiveness in international business.

Appendix 2.1 Some advice from a non-native English speaker on how to write in English

- **Basic rules (syntax)**
  - Sentences should start with the main clause using SVO (Subject-Verb-Object), as much as possible. For example, *Brian purchased an i-Phone.*
  - Do not use OVS (Object-Verb-Subject which is possible in German; *i-Phone purchased by Brian*) or SVAO (Subject-Verb-Adverb-Object which is possible in French; *Brian purchased quickly an i-Phone*).

- Put adverbs before verbs (English = SAVO; *Brian quickly purchased an i-Phone*). Adverbs come before verbs except for the verb « to be ».
- You may occasionally place the adverb after the verb (SVOA; *Brian purchased an i-Phone quickly*), but this should remain the exception, not the rule.
- Avoid long relative clauses at the beginning of the sentence (*Quickly, so that he could get back to the meeting, Brian purchased an i-Phone*).
- In English, circumstances, situations, and conditions generally come **after** not **before** the basic action or state (*Brian purchased an i-Phone quickly, so that he could get back to the meeting.*).

- **Use of compound words**
  - The French language has few compound words. Therefore, the French use *de la* (of the) to tie up words which are simply put in reverse order in English. For instance, '*Le marché de la pâte dentifrice*' directly translates as '*market of the toothpaste*' meaning '*the toothpaste market*' and '*Les agents de la société étrangère*' directly translates into '*The agents of the foreign company*' meaning '*foreign agents*'.
  - Avoid long successions of words (e.g., *La gouvernance des entreprises du secteur public* meaning *public corporate governance*).
  - Omit definite (e.g., *the*) and indefinite articles (e.g., *a*), as much as possible.

- **Depersonalising your text**
  - Avoid overusing possessive pronouns. In English, possession is less often referred to than it is in French or German. To avoid using too many personal and possessive pronouns use passive voice (*We collected data = Data were collected*). This makes the text more scientific and more impersonal. You may, however, use the active voice with *I, we,* etc. from time to time, to show a proactive orientation.
  - Use plural forms rather than a singular noun to indicate a generic concept (e.g., *managers* rather than *the manager*; *executives* rather than *the executive*, and *consumers* rather than *the consumer*).
  - A significant advantage of the plural form for generic terms is that you do not need to restart with 'he' or 'she'; you use a neutral 'they'. **Texts should not be gender biased**. It is becoming common practice in English to avoid binary gender labels (e.g., male/female, his/her) unless it is necessary. This is even done when the subject is singular (e.g., The customer bought an i-Phone but they were unhappy with it.).
  - The word *person* is feminine in many languages (e.g., French and German). However, even the use of *She* rather than *He*, has largely been replaced by *They* in most English contexts.
  - American spelling is more common than British; however, it is important to consistently use one or the other.

- ○ The possessive apostrophe before or after the *s* conveys plural (*The shops' products*) or singular (*The shop's products*). However, this distinction can also be avoided (*Stanford's students – Stanford Students; Enron managers' conception – Enron managerial conception*).

● **Clarity and repetition**

- ○ *Repeat words* for the sake of *clarity* rather than avoid repetition for the sake of *élégance*. Do not use *apparent synonyms* to avoid repeating a particular word (i.e., employee, subordinate, staff member, worker). English readers will look for a reason why you use different words. Repeat the same word when you mean the same thing.

- ○ Do not overly replace meaningful words (employees, managers, top executive, etc.) with personal pronouns (they, he, she, etc.), which may not be clear references. Repeat the word for the purpose of clarity.

- ○ Be careful about *faux-amis* (false friends; words that look similar but have different meanings), e.g., *competition* in English is not *compétition* in French but *concurrence*; *regulation* in English is not *régulation* in French but *règlementation*; *based on* in English is not *basé sur* in French but *fondé sur* (i.e., caused by). Conversely, *located in* or *at* in English is basé *à* or basé *en*.

- ○ Avoid direct (but lazy) translation (e.g., a *criminal offense* is not *une offense criminelle*, but *une infraction pénale*).

● **Style and logic**

- ○ The run-on sentence, a long-winded sentence that tends to be complicated and that usually contains more than just one idea, can and should be separated into at least two shorter and clearer sentences.

- ○ Simplify by avoiding wordiness (i.e., *The last, but not least, point is that* Brian purchased an i-Phone = Brian (S) purchased (V) an i-Phone (O)). Delete what is unnecessary, including fake linking words that convey little or no meaning, such as *Moreover, Furthermore*, and *Indeed*.

- ○ Avoid mixing present with past tenses.

- ○ Find the right *Subject* and the right *Verb*.

- ○ Avoid spelling errors due to inattentiveness (e.g., *the invisible hand has often been cited in the past decades **h**as a 'magical instrument; Lake of Constancy* rather than *Lack of Consistency*, or ***k**now* instead of *now* because of the omission of letter ***k***).

- ○ Be careful of conjunctions and/or. In English *and* is clearly conjunctive (linking), whereas *or* is clearly disjunctive (separating). For instance, *ou/oder* should often be translated 'and/or' rather than simply 'or'.

● **Use the language tools in software and internet resources**

- ○ Always use spell-check, but do not exclusively rely on it (see examples above).

- Use the synonym dictionary, which is very useful for searching for the right word.
- Use online dictionaries (Collins, Reverso, Lexilogos, Larousse, Langenscheidt, Pons, etc.) to make sure you know the correct meaning.

- **Writing reports**
  - When writing a report, try to have the whole report edited by a native speaker, especially if different parts have been written by different team members.
  - Carefully read the memo describing assigned tasks and assess what you are expected to do and what you are *not* required to do.
  - Use important keywords in simple sentences.
  - Avoid long and convoluted explanations that are difficult to understand.
  - Be focused and avoid digression.
  - Try to be readable, including the use of visual grammar (e.g., bullet points, sub-headings, etc.).
  - Leave space if someone is to comment on your draft.

References

1. Hemingway, Ernest (1976). *The Snows of Kilimanjaro and Other Stories*. New York: Charles Scribner's Sons.
2. Hall, Edward T. (1981). *Beyond Culture*. New York: Doubleday.
3. Status is related to a set of behaviours that an individual legitimately expects from others. Status has therefore a strong impact on communication behaviour. Status is strongly dependent on each national culture, especially its level of Power Distance.
4. Gudykunst, W. B., Matsumoto, Y., Ting-Toomey, S., Nishida, T., Kim, K., & Heyman, S. (1996). The influence of cultural individualism-collectivism, self construals, and individual values on communication styles across cultures. *Human Communication Research*, *22* (4), 510–543.
5. Ueda, Keiko (1974). Sixteen ways to avoid saying 'No' in Japan. In J. C. Condon and M. Saito (Eds.), *Intercultural Encounters in Japan* (pp. 185–192). Tokyo: Simul Press.
6. Hans Boehm, managing director of the German HRM Association quoted by Woodward, (1999, p. 15). Woodward, N. H. (1999). Do You Speak Internet? *HR Magazine*, 44 (4), 12–16.

7. Vas, Taras, Caprar, Dan V., Rottig, Daniel et al. (2013). A global classroom? Evaluating the effectiveness of global virtual collaboration as a teaching tool in management education. *Academy of Management Learning & Education, 12* (3), 414–435.

8. Eberhard, David M., Simons, Gary F., & Fennig, Charles D. (Eds.) (2022). *Ethnologue: Languages of the World.* Twenty-fifth edition. Dallas, Texas: SIL International. Online version: www.ethnologue.com

9. Eberhard, David M., Simons, Gary F., & Fennig, Charles D. (Eds.) (2022). *Ethnologue: Languages of the World.* Online version: www.ethnologue.com. www.ethnologue.com/guides/most-spoken-languages

10. Fetscherin, M., Alon, I., Littrell, R., & Chan, K. K. A. (2012). In China? Pick your brand name carefully. *Harvard Business Review.*

11. Roy, Abhik., Walters, Peter G. P., & Luk, Sherriff T. K. (2001). Chinese puzzles and paradoxes: Conducting business research in China. *Journal of Business Research, 52* (2), 203–10.

12. Sharma, Piyush (2015). Consumer ethnocentrism: Reconceptualization and cross-cultural validation. *Journal of International Business Studies, 46* (3), 381–89.

13. Usunier, Jean-Claude, Van Herk, Hester, & Lee, Julie (2017). *International and Cross-Cultural Business Research.* London: Sage Publications.

14. As described in Usunier et al. (2017), two Koreans translate the same French questionnaire F into two Korean versions, K1 and K2. A third Korean translator, who is unfamiliar with the original French text F, translates K1 and K2 into F1 and F2. A final Korean questionnaire, K3, is then prepared by comparing the two back-translated French versions F1 and F2. English is used to help compare them as it is widely used and more precise than either French or Korean. This example could be refined: the number of parallel translations may be increased, or back-translation processes may be independently performed.

15. Sapir, Edward (1929). The status of linguistics as a science. *Language, 5,* 207–14.

16. Ferraro (2017). See also the Sapir–Whorf hypothesis as used in George Orwell's *1984*: www.angelfire.com/journal/worldtour99/sapirwhorf.html

17. Carroll, John B. (1956). Language, Thought and Reality: Selected Writings of Benjamin Lee Whorf. Cambridge, MA: MIT.

18. The reason may be that Hall was also deeply influenced by psychoanalysis and emphasised the non-verbal, unconscious side of communication, at the expense of the verbal side, which tends to be favoured by linguistics. See Rogers et al. (2002).

19. Rogers, E. M., Hart, W. B., and Miike, Y. (2002). Edward T. Hall and the history of intercultural communication: The United States and Japan. *Keio Communication Review*, *24*, 3–26.

20. Sapir, Edward (1929). The status of linguistics as a science. *Language*, *5*, 207–14 and Carroll (1956). Classical references on how language influences worldviews.

21. Kumar, R. (1999). Communicative conflict in intercultural negotiations: The case of American and Japanese business negotiations. *International Negotiation*, *4*(1), 63–78.

3
INTERCULTURAL INTERACTIONS IN BUSINESS AND MARKETING

Learning objectives

After reading this chapter and completing the activities, you should be able to:

- Understand how intercultural interactions widely vary in terms of people involved and location as well as by types of encounters.
- Learn how to deal with culture clash, ethnocentric attitudes (both one's own and the other side's ethnocentrism), and stereotypes.
- Develop skills for overcoming communication misunderstandings by astutely using courtesy and politeness and by rationally adjusting to your counterparts' own rationality.
- Understand the basics of intercultural business negotiations and become aware of how your own personality and interaction style may help improve your negotiation performance by cultivating both cultural and emotional intelligence.
- Use the set of recommendations at the end of this chapter for effective intercultural teamwork in your X-Culture project.

Introduction

In a globalised world, intercultural interactions in business and marketing (e.g., cross-cultural sales encounters, or designing cross-cultural messaging with a local advertising agency) are inevitable. However, no two intercultural interactions are the same; they involve different situations and diverse cultures, as well as unique people (and their personalities). Exposure to an unfamiliar culture or way of life can lead to culture shock, which is a feeling of disorientation that often affects expatriates in a foreign culture, businesspeople negotiating abroad even for a short period of time, and students in a foreign exchange programme.

Chapter Overview

Intercultural interactions may take place face-to-face or online, leading to quite different types of exposure to a different culture. In the following sections, we describe the unique issues in intercultural communication and explain how to deal with misunderstandings and conflict:

- **Section 1** presents the **intercultural interaction process** and explains how it differs according to the type and context of the interaction, with a special focus on whether the interaction is task-related or not (e.g., relationship building).
- **Section 2** explains and illustrates a number of **problematic issues** related to ethnocentrism, stereotypes, and cultural hostility that may lead to misunderstandings. Building on shared interests (e.g., sports, joint interests, hobbies, religious or non-religious convictions) and shared values (e.g., benevolence, universalism) facilitates interaction, as shared characteristics and beliefs can bridge the gap generated by perceived differences.
- **Section 3** explains how to deal with **communication misunderstandings and conflict escalation**. We argue that individual characteristics matter as much as cultural attitudes.
- **Section 4** focuses on **negotiations**, a frequent type of intercultural interaction. We explain how culture and personality, and emotional and cultural intelligence, contribute to a win-win approach to **intercultural negotiation**.
- **Section 5** discusses **key qualities that can enhance intercultural interactions**, including having awareness, alertness, open-mindedness, and reflexivity, as well as metacognitive thinking (i.e., the higher-order dimension of cultural intelligence). These are all key resources for intercultural interactions because they enable people to change their views according to new experiences and insights.

- **Section 6** deals with how **behaviour can be adjusted in intercultural interactions**, based on a model offering different possible sequences that link cross-cultural awareness, knowledge acquisition, and intercultural adjustment. This model proposes a set of 27 recommendations for effective intercultural teamwork.

3.1 The Intercultural Interaction Process
Types and context of intercultural interactions

Intercultural interactions vary considerably depending on the situation, location, duration, type of encounter, exposure to unfamiliar language and people, communication channel, etc. There is a huge difference in the depth and scope of the interaction between an expatriation experience of being fully immersed for several years in a foreign country, having daily contact with locals, possibly in their language, and a simple online interaction without video (e.g., voice, email). Given that culture shock is a common experience, we need to consider the factors that affect the nature of intercultural interaction, listed below:

- The length and frequency of the intercultural interaction.
- The degree of immersion in a different physical (geographical), national, or cultural context, from almost zero (e.g., virtual, online) to almost full (e.g., expatriation).
- Whether the interaction occurs while remaining in one's own location or occurs when abroad in a country that is unfamiliar (e.g., a culturally and linguistically distant place).
- The identity of and relationship with the participants (e.g., business partners, family, friends, colleagues, etc.).
- The channel through which communication takes place (see Chapter 2).
- The level of interaction, with most including both vertical (e.g., superior-subordinate) and horizontal (e.g., peers) interactions, to differing degrees.
- The type of interaction, with most involving both task- and non-task-based interactions, to differing degrees.

Two of the most important factors to consider in intercultural interactions are the **type** and **level** of interaction, as these are both strongly influenced by cultural norms. **Table 3.1** characterises the communication elements likely to be present under different combinations of task versus non-task and vertical versus horizontal levels of interaction.

Table 3.1   Characterising intercultural interactions by type and level of interactions

	Vertical interactions	Horizontal interactions	Mixed/undefined interactions
Task-related interactions	Tasks are allocated via instructions, orders, control, feedback	Tasks are allocated via cooperation, teamwork, mutual aid, skills, and abilities	Few cues for allocating tasks, which can lead to confusion
Non-task-related interactions	Interactions will be influenced by status, power differentials, formalism	Interactions will be influenced by informality, personal preferences	People may not feel at ease at first

The level of intercultural interaction and cultural norms: vertical, horizontal, or mixed/undefined

While different levels of intercultural interaction exist in all societies, the *nature* of the communication is likely to differ depending on the task (e.g., teamwork) and cultural background (e.g., the power distance level in a particular society). Power distance, where less powerful members of society expect power to be unequally distributed, is relevant to both level and type of interaction. Both horizontal interactions (i.e., between peers, especially in an egalitarian setting) and vertical interactions (between superiors-subordinates in a hierarchical setting, whether it is actual or perceived) exist at all levels of power distance. However, in a high power distance culture (e.g., Malaysia, Philippines, and Saudi Arabia), even horizontal interactions may be influenced by perceptions of hierarchy, related to age, seniority, status, etc. Conversely, in a low power distance culture (e.g., Austria, Israel, and New Zealand), vertical interactions are likely to be more easy-going and informal than in high power distance cultures.

Mixed-undefined situations are at the fringe between horizontal and vertical interactions. They often result from quite different role expectations and improper status perceptions which blur the intercultural interaction, especially at first contact. Cultural intelligence, however, which is introduced later in this chapter, helps in managing mixed-undefined situations, in both task and non-task contexts.

The type of intercultural interaction and cultural norms: task versus non-task

Different cultures have a preference for the degree of task and non-task interactions, especially in the initial stages of communication. In some cultures, task-related interactions are central from the beginning, especially those that deal with giving instructions to others, assigning, or distributing tasks in a team (even among peers, after informally taking the lead), jointly performing tasks (e.g., searching for data, interviewing), evaluating others, etc. In other cultures, prior to focusing on the task, it is important to understand who the other is, through non-task interactions.

Task-oriented cultures (e.g., Germany) tend to primarily focus on the task at hand. These task-oriented cultures foster a pragmatic orientation, focusing on results and consequences, especially when a joint project is developed based on egalitarian horizontal interactions. Task-oriented cultures tend to promote a non-territorial orientation, where concerns for joint outcomes dominate over the concerns of each player for their own outcomes, and everyone is considered to be on an equal footing. A task orientation can serve to curb or moderate conflicts, and induce parties to jointly address actual issues. In contrast, **non-task oriented cultures** tend to focus on relationship building that is often only indirectly related to the task. Getting to know one another is a typical and important non-task interaction. In cultures where there is an assumption that personal acquaintance is a necessary step for future task-related interactions, it needs to be prioritised. If *getting down to business* occurs too quickly, people from relationship-oriented cultures, such as Japan, will not feel at ease.

The process of intercultural interaction

Culture clashes, which arise from divergent cultural values, assumptions, and behaviours, are more likely at the initial stages of intercultural interactions, when people expect behaviour from the other side to correspond to what they are used to, as well as to what they consider to be the most appropriate for effective teamwork. The process of intercultural encounter can be described as an interaction in which each partner follows their own, *but different*, set of rules. In this situation, at least one partner needs to adapt their behaviour, or the intercultural interaction will not work properly. However, people tend to adjust to the other party's behaviour in ways that derive from their own culture's stereotypical norms, as it is naturally difficult to step out of one's own cultural assumptions. People, therefore, tend to adapt their behaviour to the other party, only to the extent they perceive as being useful for smoothing the process and improving the outcomes.

On average, cultural adaptation, provided that it is done properly – without naïve imitation – is positively experienced by the other side. For instance, Japanese buyers positively experience cultural adaptation by American sellers, despite the marked tendency in Japan to make a clear-cut distinction between in-group members (*nihonjin*) and out-group members (*gai-jin*). However, cultural adaptation is not necessarily symmetrical. For instance, Japanese negotiators have been found to adjust more than American negotiators in intercultural interactions: they tend to use more direct information sharing and less indirect communication with Americans than they do in interactions with other Japanese negotiators[1].

There are, of course, multiple levels of 'culture' in and across societies, as discussed in Chapter 1. Many people belong to different subcultures that have their own operational knowledge, beliefs, and standards, including international business professionals, immigrants, bilinguals and even teenagers, who may switch between their parents and peer culture. A common *professional culture* may help overcome the barriers related to cross-cultural understanding. That is why national culture often appears as a relatively poor predictor of the intercultural interaction process and outcomes, and why culture should not be used to directly predict behaviour[2].

Learning about partners

It is more difficult to learn about partners when both the situation and culture tend towards vertical (hierarchical) interactions. In this case, cultural codes are likely to be pronounced, and the people involved in the intercultural interaction must in some way decide who will be *superior* and who will be *subordinate*. If the power differential results in the subordinate shying away from delivering personal information and trying to protect themselves, then non-task interactions will become more difficult, especially if the superior is highly task-oriented and not concerned with relationship building. In this case, the risk of conflict (implicit or explicit, covert or overt) is significant and may result in a culture clash early in the intercultural interaction. A *culture clash* is a conflict arising from divergent cultural values, assumptions, and behaviour.

People tend to see similarities before they see differences, especially when interacting with similar-aged peers who share a common educational background. Often people will start from a *universalist assumption that we are all the same, open-minded individuals in a globalised world, sharing similar values and behaviour*. Naturally, they are wrong, but it pays to be aware that this universalist assumption is normal and based on benevolence towards others, as well as a somewhat self-serving self-image (i.e., as anti-racist, rejecting stereotypes of other nations and cultures, etc.).

Cultural dimensions, personality, and interactions

When people interacting do not share the same cultural assumptions, intercultural interactions are likely to be more problematic. Potential differences in important cultural assumptions can be identified by comparing country-level scores on various dimensions, such as individualism and collectivism and power distance.

Power distance and personality
in intercultural interactions

When investigating the **interaction between personality and culture** in predicting behaviour in intercultural interactions, it is useful to practise *thought experiments* (i.e., logically and prospectively thinking about an imaginary situation, in order to assess possible outcomes in the real world). At a minimum, these thought experiments should be supported with data on cultural dimension scores, and some literature search on Google or Google Scholar[3]. As a first step, team members can establish where the largest cultural differences are likely to be, by examining cultural dimension scores, as outlined in Chapter 1 (e.g., Hofstede or Schwartz dimensions). For instance, **Figure 1.2** in Chapter 1 shows a large difference in power distance between Venezuela and German-speaking Swiss. This difference will be exacerbated when relevant cultural norms combine with strong personality types in intercultural teams.

Let us imagine different combinations of personality traits (dominance versus subservience) in countries that differ in the degree of Power Distance (PD) (see **Table 3.2**). Countries with high PD (often combined with collectivism) will emphasise status and role, where less powerful members expect power to be distributed unequally. Individuals in high PD cultures may have personalities that are more dominant or more subservient, leading to an instinctive search for either a subordinate or a superior position. Similarly, individuals in low PD cultures may also be more dominant or subservient. The case of a *dominant person from a low PD society* facing a *subservient person from a high PD society*, may work because of their apparent complementarity, although there is a risk of too much submissiveness on the part of the high PD interactant. In contrast, a dominant person from a low PD society facing another dominant person from a high PD society may resent his counterpart as being overly dominant.

Table 3.2 The influence of culture and personality on intercultural interactions

		High power distance (PD) culture	
		Dominant personality	Subservient personality
Low power distant culture	**Dominant personality**	Low PD partner may resent his counterpart as being overly dominant. When these dominant personalities clash, the low PD partner may be at a disadvantage.	The interaction may work because of their apparent complementarity, but can be undermined by too much submissiveness from the low PD partner.
	Subservient personality	The differences may be too great, leading to frustration and misunderstanding in the interaction.	Frustration is likely to arise from this interaction, especially for the high PD partner who is expecting guidance but does not find it.

Beyond this, personality traits (individual dispositional variables) may either soften or, on the contrary, exacerbate PD orientation (cultural). For instance, in terms of the Schwartz value system[4], a person from a high PD culture who values self-transcendence (benevolence and universalism), may not display dominance, while another person from a low PD culture who values self-enhancement (power and achievement), may display more dominance than one could imagine based on the low PD country score.

Individualism/collectivism and teamwork

A similar *thought experiment* might consider differences between people from individualist and collectivist cultures. In individualist cultures, people are more likely to have an independent self-concept, where they view their personal attributes (e.g., abilities, values, and attitudes) as central, whereas in collectivist cultures, people are more likely to have an interdependent self-concept, where they view themselves in terms of their relationships and social roles[5].

- People from an individualist culture, who have an independent self-concept, are more likely to see performance as being driven mainly by individual achievements, fostered by interpersonal competition, with a focus on individual rewards and recognition[6].
- People from a collectivist culture, who have an interdependent self-concept, are more likely to value interpersonal relationships as a prerequisite for team performance, which is regarded as a consequence of joint effort.

Teamwork problems are likely to be exacerbated when the team includes different cultures and personality types, especially when a high level of cooperation is necessary to complete a task. When team identification is lacking, team members will continue to think, feel, and act as individuals, team identity will suffer, and consequently, team performance will be lower. Conversely, if team members identify with their team, team identity will be on the rise, leading to smoother and more spontaneous cooperation, resulting in increased team performance both objectively (i.e., joint output) and subjectively (i.e., team member satisfaction).

Cultural versus personal determinants of task-orientation

Thought experiments can also be based on an amalgamation of cultural and personal orientations to help understand how different types of people are likely to deal with the ordering of task and non-task interactions (e.g., relationship building).

We demonstrate this with an example of two polar ideal-types based on opposing cultural assumptions:

- **The Deal Making type corresponds to Western cultures, where people are more likely to focus on the task**. This type is more likely in cultures that are individualist with an out-group-universalistic orientation and low power distance, where individuals are more likely to have an independent self-concept, a *doing* mentality, and are principally utilitarian (mostly centred on interests, however not exclusively on self-interest). In this case, they will have a preference for an objective/hard-facts assessment of reality, a discrete and economic view of time, direct and explicit/context-free communication, proactive behaviours reflecting deliberate decision making, and a preference for written contractual arrangements and litigation if need be.
- **The Relationship Building type corresponds, by and large, to non-Western cultures**, where people are more likely to focus on non-task elements, especially in the early stages of interactions. This type is more likely in collectivist cultures with an in-group orientation and high power distance, where individuals are more likely to have an interdependent self-concept, a *being* mentality, and see relationships rather than tasks being at the centre of the team interaction. In this case, they will have a preference for a subjective assessment of reality (even though facts also matter, but may be (mis)interpreted), a holistic, non-economic, and relaxed view of time, indirect and implicit/context-bound communication, where decision making and implementation are difficult to disentangle, and there is a strong concern to develop relationships mainly based on personal and oral arrangements, rather than detailed written agreements.

The Western Deal Making type may actively discourage relationship building (except for mere lip-service and initial icebreaking), given the emphasis on low-context and *doing (i.e., skills and abilities)*, especially when the task-orientation is relatively depersonalised and highly time-conscious. In contrast, the Non-Western Relationship Building type may lead to the task being subordinated to relationship building (i.e., non-task), given the emphasis on high-context and personalisation, where shared identity is paramount.

As can be seen above, culture is complex. Although this type of thought experiment is useful for describing individuals as members of a particular cultural group, the combination of cultural categories may inflate preconceived views that do not correspond to real-world individuals, with unique personality traits and experiences. Such simplification may contribute to stereotyping, partly reinforcing ethnocentrism and prejudices. The next section examines these topics.

3.2 Ethnocentrism, stereotypes, and misunderstandings in intercultural interactions
Ethnocentrism and Self-Reference Criterion

The concept of ethnocentrism was first introduced by G. A. Sumner[7] more than 100 years ago, to distinguish between *in-groups* (those groups with which an individual identifies) and *out-groups* (those regarded as antithetical to the *in-group*). Ethnocentrism has been extended by psychologists to the individual level, where it relates to the natural tendency of people to refer spontaneously to the symbols, values, and ways of thinking of their own ethnic or national group (i.e., their ingroup). Ethnocentrism may lead to disinterest in, and even contempt for, the culture of other groups. Ethnocentrism should not be regarded too negatively as a major cognitive and/or affective fault, but rather as a fact of life. It is, however, a potential limitation in establishing a rapport with others who have a different ethnocentric background. We are all partly shaped by our native culture and language and the worldviews and attitudes they convey. As it is quite problematic to put oneself in someone else's shoes, most people do not even try. The Self-Reference Criterion refers to our spontaneous and unconscious tendency to refer to our own thought framework (mainly tied to our culture, which, in general, we did not choose), to interpret situations, evaluate people, communicate, negotiate, or decide which attitude to adopt. The interpretation of situations, choice assessment, and decision making are all influenced by ethnocentrism.

The following steps may be taken in order to try to eliminate the decisional bias related to the Self-Reference Criterion in intercultural interactions[8]:

1. Define the problem according to *your* behavioural standards and ways of thinking.
2. Define the problem according to (what you know and/or can guess from) *your foreign partner's* behavioural standards and ways of thinking.
3. Isolate the influence of the Self-Reference Criterion on the problem as you perceive it, and identify how differently your foreign partner perceives it.
4. Redefine the problem (and often the objectives), removing the bias related to the Self-Reference Criterion, and then try to find joint solutions and make decisions which fit with both cultural contexts.

However, this process is challenging. For instance, when people wait in line at Disneyland in the USA, discipline with respect to queues is strong. Waiting in lines is well organised, with defined corridors and information on the waiting time. In other countries, where there is a sense of *free-for-all* and waiting lines are *not* orderly or organised, the free-riding problem will be more serious and more difficult to tackle. Despite sincere efforts to remove biases from these two different standards and ways of thinking about the problem of queuing, redefining the problem may still prove insufficient, as it assumes it is possible to understand the intricacies of a particular culture without being a native of that culture.

Stereotypes

Stereotyping, based on widely held, over-simplified beliefs about a group, may be quite strong at first contact. Stereotypes often influence behaviour at a subconscious level, as they require little cognitive effort and operate as a cognitive summary and an affective self-defensive mechanism, in the absence of more detailed information. It takes much higher cognitive effort to put aside stereotypes, in order to identify and understand an unfamiliar culture. This is demonstrated by the difficulties encountered by immigrants when integrating into a host society, even those who have voluntarily migrated.

As a cognitive summary, ethnic or national stereotypes are based on beliefs about distinctive cultural or behavioural features of members of a definite ethnic or national group. If people from other cultures perceive Americans as being tough and forthright in business, or the British as insincere, it is for the most part due to stereotypes, which give a distorted view. American lack of modesty is, in fact, related to a different hierarchy of values that promotes a strong task orientation and sense of self-interest. Stereotypes represent an over-simplification which, though perhaps intellectually useful in reducing information and conserving our differences, can become dangerous. Stereotypes are often used to capture the salient traits of a *foreign* national culture, which means they focus on what is different or unique and often poorly understood. It is easier to lazily stick to one's own values and behaviour and consequently transfer onto the foreign partner the burden of adjustment than to decentre oneself and try to put oneself in the other's shoes. This is especially true when considering oneself a *civilised* observer and the partner as a less *civilised* person with behaviours that can be seen as primitive, ritualised, irrational, and/or possibly superstitious. The partner's behaviours and values, construed through an outsider's lens, are incorrectly interpreted.

An old stereotypical joke about Europeans goes something like this: '**Heaven** is where the cooks are French, the mechanics are German, the policemen are English, the lovers are Italian, and it is all organised by the Swiss. **Hell** is where the policemen are German, the mechanics are French, the cooks are British, the lovers are Swiss, and it is all organised by the Italians.' While this joke captures some information about long-established cultural capabilities, it is useful to remind us that cultures are complex, and that we cannot simply combine the best aspects across cultures, while rejecting the worst.

Self-shock

Cultural awareness is more complex than simply *getting to know the other*. Problematic representations of the *other* may evolve into a confrontation with oneself, in a process called *self-shock*[9]. Experiencing how others actually *are* may be somewhat destabilising, with identity confusion being a typical feature of self-shock. Self-shock is probably one of the principal causes of stereotyping. Stereotypes often protect *the self* much more than they really provide information on *the other*.

When people from different cultures meet, such as when expatriate managers meet local executives or international sellers meet local buyers, the intercultural encounter often takes place in the absence of previous knowledge and experience of the other culture. At first, one might think that the *basic problem is getting to know the other*. But in the intercultural encounter, there is in fact, a *progressive unfolding of the self* which can be attributed to 'a set of intensive and evocative situations in which the individual perceives and experiences other people in a distinctly new manner and, as a consequence, experiences new facets and dimensions of existence'[10].

In intercultural encounters, one's personal identity is questioned by a mirror effect. Within our own cultural context, we have unconsciously built our *self-image*. That is, we necessarily construct an image of ourselves from observations based on the responses of others to our behaviour. This is emphasised by Erikson (1950, p. 13)[11]: 'Identity is the confidence gathered from the fact that our own ability to maintain interior resemblance and continuity equals the resemblance and continuity of the image and the sense that others have of us.' However, the process of maintaining personal identity can be problematic in intercultural encounters, because (1) this process mostly happens unconsciously, and (2) it requires skills in interpersonal communication.

Self-shock, unlike culture-shock, is seen as a reaction to differences between oneself and the other, and is a concept that extends to differences *within the self*. The root of *self-shock* lies in the intimate workings of the relationship between the *ego* (that is, personal identity), our behaviour, and *the other*, not only as they *actually* are, but also as *perceived* by us.

Self-shock emerges as a deep imbalance between our need to confirm our identity and our ability to do so. In one way, this situation places the individual in a position of a double-bind. The self-shock situation increases our need for the reinforcement of our personal identity, while at the same time resulting in a loss of ability to satisfy this need. Thus, one can understand more easily that certain stereotypes or abrupt judgements about foreigners may directly result from our attempts to defend ourselves against the painful double constraint of self-shock.

International empathy: a naïve concept

In the concept of *international empathy*, we can catch a glimpse of the immense naïvety of those who, with good intentions, argue in favour of being open-minded, sincerely interested in the other, ready to listen, watchful and alert, etc. This communication tactic, although well meant, may only last for an instant – the time during which the personal identity of the *empathiser* has not yet come into play. The idea that an *empathiser* can understand what other people from other cultures feel, to actually see things from the other's viewpoint, and imagine themselves in their position, is optimistic.

However, there are some concrete issues that can make being involved in intercultural interactions a little easier. It may be worth thinking about:

- Which personality types and/or personal backgrounds are best suited for specific intercultural interactions and/or for intercultural interactions in general?
- Are we able to communicate better with particular countries and cultures?
- How can we increase our intercultural interaction skills?
- If an adjustment must be made during the intercultural encounter, who should be the one to adapt?
- Whether or not learning can be bilateral, especially where long-term relationships are likely?

Cultural hostility and racism

Limits to *cultural borrowing* clearly appear when the borrowing is resented as a threat to one's own cultural coherence. This is especially true of religious practices, social morals, and even daily customs. It is impossible to import polygamy or clitoral excision for babies into cultures where monogamy and child protection are established practices. There must be a minimum level of coherence and homogeneity in cultural assumptions and behaviour within the cultural community if people are to synchronise themselves and live peacefully together.

Racism is often confused with cultural hostility, whereas in fact it precedes cultural hostility. *But cultural hostility does not necessarily imply racism*: one may be hostile to people of (some) other cultures, without being racist. Behind racism there is a theory that, because of their race (i.e., physiology), some human beings are inferior at various levels (intelligence, creative abilities, moral sense, etc.). However, racist theses and opinions have been progressively abandoned over the last two centuries. The idea that there are differing intellectual abilities among people of different races or ethnic groups has been shown to be unreliable due to the type and contents of IQ tests. Moreover, studies show that the *inter-individual* variability of genetic characteristics is much larger than the *inter-racial* groups variability[12]. In other words, there are more genetic differences among Europeans, or among South African Zulus, than genetic differences between the average European and the average Zulu[13].

In contrast to racism, *cultural hostility or animosity does not imply prior prejudices* as to who is inferior or superior according to race or culture. There is a strong affective involvement when a person feels that their own cultural values are under threat. This feeling may result from either or both of the following situations:

1. Simple interactions with people whose cultural values are quite different, and in which we do not feel at ease. Communication is experienced as burdensome and there is little empathy. A defensive response may then develop, based on unconscious, minor cultural hostility.
2. Collective reactions to perceived identity threats. Cases are so numerous worldwide that it would need many pages to quote them exhaustively; however, many are based on conflict and competition[14]. *Identity is a matter of culture rather than race.*

Both territorial conflicts and economic competition may cause cultural hostility. The Chinese are sometimes considered negatively in the USA. China has a large trade imbalance with the USA and also is culturally and politically distant. Cultural hostility, when directed at successful nations, is often a fairly ambiguous feeling, in that admiration and envy for the other's achievements go along with contempt for many traits of the envied people and obvious unwillingness to understand the root causes of the other's success.

3.3 Dealing with communication misunderstandings and conflict escalation

Conflicts have positive sides. They intensify awareness of problems, often allow change and adaptation, sometimes strengthen intra-group relationships, and may increase awareness of self and others. Beyond this, conflicts encourage psychological development, such as a more realistic self-appraisal, and they can stimulate the exploration of more creative joint solutions. However, conflicts are more known for their negative aspects; thus, the underlying view is that conflicts are a bad thing, especially when they escalate. Conflicts may foster misperception and bias, provoke inflated emotional involvement, and therefore decrease communication efficiency. In intercultural interactions, they magnify perceived differences, possibly leading to conflict escalation by boosting competitive processes.

The seeds for non-rational conflict escalation

Non-rational conflict escalation in intercultural interactions is based on a snowballing combination of personality clashes, communication misunderstandings, disagreements about the ways to proceed (mindset issues), and, last but not least, uncompromising players on both sides. Other team members may try to act as mediators, withdrawing or aligning with one or the other contestant.

Conflict de-escalation is stalled by subjective investment in keeping to one's own position and not losing face. To resolve these kinds of conflicts, it is useful to employ several strategies:

1. debrief the communication misunderstandings;
2. talk rather frankly (if culturally possible) about the personality clash to show that it is detrimental to the task at hand;
3. focus on a joint *doing orientation* favouring task completion; and
4. reach an agreement upon the ways to proceed (mindset issues).

Surface-level repair of the relationship between the parties in conflict is generally enough to restore a joint task orientation. It is better to focus on saving face for everyone involved in the conflict, rather than striving unnecessarily for deep reconciliation. Subjective conflicts in interdependent teams with people siding in two opposite camps are fortunately rare.

Courtesy and apology in intercultural interactions

Courtesy, politeness, civility, and respect are found across all societies; however, they are coded differently. The common aim is to acknowledge status and position, as well as send preliminary positive signals of considerate behaviour to the other side. However, readiness to behave appropriately (i.e., being open-minded, sincerely interested in the other, ready to listen), and to accept local customs, at times lead people to involuntarily offend their counterpart(s). In these circumstances, an apology may be required.

The objective of apologetic statements and behaviour is to quash possible conflict early, so as to avoid conflict escalation. Courtesy and apology in intercultural interactions stand at the interface between high- and low-context communication norms. The degree of formality must be considered. For instance, a common practice in the USA is to automatically address others by their first name. The same is true in many countries, including Iceland, Canada, and Australia. However, in more formal countries, such as Germany, Austria, Switzerland, and Sweden, as well as many Asian countries, it is better not to address new contacts by their first names unless invited to do so.

The meaning and function of apologies also vary cross-culturally. The Japanese, for instance, apologise more frequently than Americans, especially when what they are apologising for is not even their responsibility. Americans apologise because they feel guilty for some action and want to acknowledge their own responsibility. In both cases, the function of apologies is to repair possible damage to the trusting relationship caused by someone's misbehaviour. However, apologies for competence violation are more effective for Americans, who are often *task-related, doing oriented, individualists*, while apologies for integrity violation lead to greater trust repair for Japanese negotiators, who are often *people-related, being oriented, collectivists*[15].

A core set of courtesy rules exists worldwide. To be polite and courteous, we often need to avoid being overly direct[16]. Thus, politeness is always high-context communication in any culture. The set of universal rules is mostly in the form of *don'ts*, such as not coughing on someone, not spitting at a person, or slapping another's face. However, the degree of contextuality varies according to language and culture. The word *courtesy* is derived from the word 'court', meaning the residence of a king or emperor. It emphasises the kind of noble behaviour that enhances self-respect through the respect granted to others. Most languages have such a word. German, for instance, has the word *höflich* (polite), based on the German word for court, *Hof*. Foreigners are forgiven much, provided they are not arrogant and show consideration for their hosts, even if they may be ignorant of the host's customs. Modest behaviour by the foreigner facilitates the acceptance of cultural mistakes by the host. If you upset the host, it is advisable to ask for clarification, where needed.

Apologies may take many forms and can be offered without taking things so far that your position would be undermined. It is important to understand that communication rules can be especially sensitive when problems occur. For instance, there are two forms of apology in Japan[17], the *sunao* apology, which is a sort of gently submissive apology given with good grace, and a *sincere* form of apology, which is more from the heart. These apologies are codified in Japanese conduct manuals, which provide many readily usable apologetic expressions. Conversely, most Westerners tend to favour direct, spontaneous, and non-formulaic apologies, in which sincerity is conveyed through original expressions. It is easy to find *savoir faire* manuals which describe local norms of courtesy and apology, as well as to ask for insider information. However, apologies should be kept within the limits of what is strictly necessary for avoiding misunderstandings and conflict. Beyond a certain threshold, overly apologetic statements may harm both the credibility and the position of the apologiser.

Adjusting rationally to different types of rationalities

The difficulty in *rationally adjusting* in intercultural interactions is that there are different *types of rationality*; the first being based on a *positivist, calculative, and utilitarian logic* and the second on a *normative, subjective, and relational reasoning*. There is a clear difference between *positivist* judgements (i.e., based on verified facts, evidence, proof, and shared experience) and *normative* statements (i.e., based on a standard or norm that may or may not be relevant to the interaction).

1. Advice based on a *positivist judgement* might be something like: *look at people and relationships as they are, that is, search for empirical cues, facts, and evidence.*
2. In contrast, advice based on *normative* statements might be something like: *Be nice, understand your partner, put yourself in their shoes, and separate interests from people. Be relationship-oriented but do not lower your aspirations, don't be soft, yielding, and weak.*

The key issue is then interpretation, as interpretation is language- and culture-based and misunderstandings are likely to arise.

The first concept of rationality (positivist) bases decision making on an individual's calculative, precise, and explicit logic; therefore, on economic, deal-making, and value orientations in the utilitarian paradigm. This is more likely in individualist societies, where people value independence and are seen as more mature if they act in a manner that is consistent with their internal attitudes[18]. In contrast, the second concept of rationality (normative or relational) is more likely in a collectivist society, where people value interdependence and are seen as more mature if they can put aside their own personal feelings and act in a socially appropriate manner[19]. This means that in collectivist societies, norms are likely to be more important than in individualist societies.

Another consideration is whether it is possible to be both rational and emotional simultaneously. Models linking emotions to rationality question whether emotions are a *threat to being rational* in intercultural interactions or whether they can be *an element of being rational,* assuming that emotions can be controlled, consciously created, and directed to influence the other side.

Pure positivist rationality can be, at times, opposed to a 'relational rationality', which is seen by outsiders as a more fuzzy, indirect, and imprecise calculation. However, in most cases both rationalities can be astutely combined in intercultural interactions, following the *'or/and' conjunctive* approach in which both detached and relational rationalities can be usefully combined, rather than the *'either/or' disjunctive* approach in which they are dichotomously opposed, that is, radically incompatible.

3.4 Negotiating across cultures

A frequent type of intercultural interaction is negotiation across cultures. Negotiations can involve a range of different business issues, including the development of joint business projects with foreign partners, the joint design of a local advertising campaign, or any kind of intercultural teamwork. It can also include resource allocation activity (i.e., *bargaining*), the joint search for solutions (i.e., *problem-solving*), and a collective decision method when there are no rules and/or no hierarchy.

Intercultural business negotiation: the basics

Negotiation may be defined as an activity (therefore *task* and *doing* oriented), with two or more players who are aware of their divergent interests, know that they are independent, but choose to actually seek an arrangement that ends this divergence and thus creates, maintains, or develops a relationship between them. The functions of a negotiation are first trade and economic exchange (trading/dealing), but can also include interactive decision making (e.g., defining and implementing a joint project), conflict resolution (i.e., a peaceful alternative), and drafting joint rules (institutionalisation).

The scope of negotiation is very large, ranging from sales contracts to business deals (e.g., company takeovers, joint ventures, mergers, and acquisitions), and marketing activities (e.g., negotiation with distribution channels, advertising agencies, middlemen, and so on). Industrial relations are a great area for negotiation, mostly between employers and employees around compensation issues, work contracts, working conditions, etc. Companies are also obliged to negotiate key issues with public authorities, such as business regulation and taxation, and to use lobbying to influence rule design by legislative bodies and implementation by public authorities. The scope of negotiation increases as and when rules and hierarchy play a diminishing role.

Negotiation, which is usually multi-issue and open to a *win-win* situation, is often confused with *bargaining*, which is usually single-item, centred on price, and generally a *win-lose* situation (discussed further in Chapter 5 under Pricing). The decline of traditional bargaining activities, especially in Western countries, is due to the compulsory display of price tags imposed by regulation. This diminishes the role of bargaining, but it still exists on a much more limited scale (e.g., bulk purchases and some large-ticket items in consumer durables). As a consequence, many buyers and sellers have lost the traditional skills related to bargaining rituals for the exploration of exchange prices. Pure bargaining is good hands-on training for business negotiations. Individuals from countries where bargaining is legally forbidden may be at a disadvantage, because of their lack of hands-on experience, as against people coming from cultures where bargaining is a common daily experience.

Negotiations are built on deals (task-oriented outcomes) and relationships (non-task-oriented development of human/economic bonding). A ***deal*** is based on the concrete, sometimes physical, often measurable, objective attributes of a discrete transaction (e.g., type of good or service, order size, delivery date and conditions, payment terms, and so on). A ***relationship*** is based on human connections and feelings/emotional bonds, and it generates a sense of being in some way attached to the other party. It progresses on a foundation of joint experiences, sympathy, or antipathy. Deals and relationships may be divided or combined.

At the extremes, there are two distinct negotiation types that correspond to these two components of negotiations[20]. A *Deal-Making Type* starts from a 'deal first' focus, emphasising calculative rationality, in which relationships are not necessary. In contrast, a *Relationship-Building Type* begins by establishing a connection, with the deal being a consequence of good relationships, where rationality is based on self-interest aligned with other-interest.

The division between the deal and relationship results from the predominantly Western assumption, in its extreme form, that people (e.g., their identity-related bonds and commonality: age, gender, shared in-group, common educational background, shared language, etc.) can be separated from transactional interests. For other cultures, relationship-building (considered by Westerners as 'non-task') is a pre-condition for entering into deal (task-related) negotiation.

Classical approaches to negotiation are either:

1. *integrative or cooperative* (often called *win-win*), which first aims to increase the joint outcome and later to distribute it among the parties; or
2. *distributive* (often called *win-lose*), where a party is first and foremost concerned with defending and possibly increasing their own outcome, and defending their own territory and position, at the risk of possible confrontation.

An integrative orientation relies on a *problem-solving approach,* which is based on culturally relative assumptions. This approach assumes:

- a *doing* orientation (to solve a problem is to *do* something) that focuses quite often on the *task-related* part of negotiation
- that both partners are *fair* (an English word that is untranslatable in many languages). *Fair* means being open and honest in communication and interaction. This value is not prioritised in all cultures
- reciprocal behaviour, based on a quick response to the other party's openings on a give-and-take basis, where concessions on each side are precisely measured and balanced.

In intercultural negotiation, taking a *problem-solving approach* has been shown to have a contagious effect: when a negotiator uses this approach, the partner's satisfaction may increase, especially if they reciprocate, leading to an increase in individual and joint outcomes.

Negotiation is always rather horizontal. However, perceived elements of status and role can change the process to slightly more vertical kinds of interaction (buyer/seller, large/small company, etc.). Power differentials, dependence asymmetries, and perceived subjective-versus-objective dependence are factors that increase the verticalisation of a negotiation setting that is naturally horizontal.

BATNA: THE BEST ALTERNATIVE TO A NEGOTIATED AGREEMENT

Intercultural teams, such as those involved in the X-Culture project, are *negotiating with peers,* who are close in age and education. They are involved in a task-oriented joint project. Consequently, they may have a much stronger sense of equality than in most traditional negotiation settings. Although a number of features in global virtual teamwork play in favour of a cooperative-integrative-problem-solving approach to negotiation, there are walk-away possibilities that may activate their BATNA by leaving the team.

Before starting a negotiation, the potential consequences of not reaching an agreement should always be considered. The BATNA sets the lowest acceptable value for a negotiated agreement. One's own BATNA corresponds to the best alternative among out-of-negotiation alternatives; not to the best alternative among those being negotiated. A reserve price (conceptually near to the BATNA) is the price level at which it is of no consequence to reach a negotiated agreement or to finish in an impasse.

Emotional/cultural intelligence

The key skills required from people engaged in intercultural negotiations are patience and flexibility. Patience helps individuals to both create and obtain value in negotiations, because they are willing to spend time on exploring alternative solutions and later claim their fair share of the joint outcome. Ideally, intercultural interactors must be calm and active listeners, and able to master their emotions. Courtesy and respect for the other party's cultural codes (e.g., *Ningensei,* described below), in addition to intercultural communication skills, are required. Authority should be shown without being commanding or pushy; role authority, as well as personal empowerment, can be displayed, as long as it is without unnecessary display of status, which is at odds with the horizontal, egalitarian setting of the negotiation.

Opportunistic behaviour can be both a cultural norm and a personality trait. Some people feel unashamed about failing to respect their commitment and fulfil their agreed-upon obligations. Resistance to provocations, such as the other party lying or not respecting their commitment, is another key skill for intercultural negotiators, who should avoid reading too much into this situation, especially when the other party's behaviour is ambiguous and equivocal. An apparent lack of commitment may be due to unforeseen events and circumstances that the other party hides for fear of being ashamed and losing face. Similarly, it is advisable not to presume the opposing party's personality is naïve and lacking in conviction, when in fact their cultural norms may value a modest and unassertive self-profile. Empathy, language proficiency (or at least sensitivity to language issues), and the ability to disentangle the deal from the relationship are other key intercultural negotiation skills.

Cultural intelligence[21] and emotional intelligence can be developed either though training or by recruiting adequate intercultural negotiators[22]. *Emotional intelligence,* according to psychologist Daniel Goleman[23], involves not only the awareness of one's own and the other party's emotions, but also the ability to empathetically understand how emotions on both sides interact and combine. Emotional intelligence relies on active self-control (i.e., not only pure emotional restraint) and the capacity to regulate one's own mood and behaviour in a way that will positively transfer to the other side's capability to regulate their own emotions. However, as emphasised by Earley and Mosakowski, *cultural intelligence* differs from emotional intelligence (p. 139)[24]:

> A person with high emotional intelligence grasps what makes us human and at the same time what makes each of us different from one another. A person with high cultural intelligence can somehow tease out of a person's or group's behavior those features that would be true of all people and all groups, those peculiar to this person or this group, and those that are neither universal nor idiosyncratic.

Cultural intelligence helps people to interact with diverse groups of people in unfamiliar and ambiguous environments. It is related, for instance, to the ability to delay judgement, possibly suspending it for some days, and actively retrieve new cues for understanding, and persistence when facing hostility or incomprehension, and thinking before acting. The Cultural Intelligence Quotient (CQ) is defined as an interactive system of knowledge and skills linked by cultural metacognition. It includes four dimensions[25]:

1. Metacognitive QC focusing on higher order thinking and mental processes that help make sense of cultural knowledge;
2. Cognitive QC focusing on knowledge of norms, practices, and conventions, as well as frameworks for cultural values;
3. Motivational CQ focusing on expending energy toward learning and functioning in different cultural situations; and
4. Behavioural CQ focusing on appropriate verbal and non-verbal actions with interacting in different cultural situations.

Personality and interaction style

An introductory caveat is in order: *Do not try to be someone else*. It is tempting to *change* some aspects of oneself in the hope of being more effective in intercultural interactions. Therefore, it makes sense to try and understand one's own personality traits based, for instance, on the Meyer/Briggs personality type inventory (MBTI). The MBTI proposes personalities on four polar dimensions:

- Extroversion versus Introversion
- Sensing versus Intuitive
- Thinking versus Feeling
- Perceiving versus Judging

It is not clear-cut that any one type of personality is universally superior to others. *Extrovert*s seem more adapted as intercultural interactors because of their sociability and orientation to the outer world. However, *introverts* may be good listeners and keep a strong focus on their interests. *Sensing individuals* are facts-oriented, practical, and precise, while intuitive people privilege the big picture, metaphors, and innovation. *Thinkers* are logical and objective (much like in the *logos* orientation described in the next section), while *feelers* are more subjective in their approach to interaction. *Perceiving individuals* place the emphasis on information-seeking, data-gathering, and understanding situations, while remaining highly flexible. Finally, *judgers* are concerned with controlling events and planning action[26].

An initial strategy for improving one's performance is to adopt an *interaction style* which fits with one's personality. It is beyond the scope of this book, dealing with culture and business, rather than personality and behaviour, to comment at length on the issue of choosing an interaction style. However, a number of books which are cited in the end of chapter note[27] offer detailed insights.

A second strategy is to choose, if possible, *interaction situations* that correspond to one's own personality traits. Some competitive personalities may be more adapted to one-shot deals, short-term and bargaining-oriented interactions, in which their hardsell talents will triumph. In contrast, more long-term and collaborative-oriented personalities may feel more at ease with the relationship-building type of interaction.

3.5 Three culturally based frameworks that inform negotiation styles

We present three frameworks below, which may help individuals to assess their own style, building on their own strengths and trying as much as possible to offset their weaker points. The first guiding framework is of ancient Greek origin, Aristotle's Rhetoric building on *ethos* (morality), *pathos* (empathy), and *logos* (rationality). The second framework is based on four Confucian behavioural principles, originally Chinese, but shared by the Japanese under the name of *Ningensei*. The third framework is based on the symbols expressed in the Chinese five-element system of Water, Wood, Earth, Fire, and Metal (*Wu Xing*). The combination of strengths and weaknesses expressed in each element and in their interactions (each element generating and moderating other elements) is a useful symbolic resource for the self-assessment of one's own skills in intercultural interaction.

Framework 1: Argumentation and persuasion, Greek style

The Rhetoric of Aristotle, with its three components of *ethos, pathos, logos* is a nice guiding framework for developing persuasive skills, because they are essential aspects of cooperation[28]. It is a symbolic system because it roughly corresponds to an effective Deal-Making Type, and Western categories of *morality, sympathy,* and *rationality*. These aspects are helpful for assessing one's strengths and weaknesses in the negotiation process.

- ***Ethos***, which is the Greek word for 'character'. Not only is the word 'ethic' derived from ethos, but many other words use this root. Ethos corresponds to the moral sense in a personality (i.e., the capacity to address moral issues as questions rather than ready-made normative answers as to what is good or bad). Personal goodness and benevolence are part of ethos (similar to the Confucian *Rén* as well as the Japanese *Amae* as explained in the next section). ***Ethos conveys a message of individual credibility and character which contributes to persuasive power***. By *ethos*, Aristotle meant credibility, authority, and legitimacy:

   'We believe good men more fully and more readily than others: this is generally true whatever the question is, and absolutely true where exact certainty is impossible and opinions are divided . . . his character may almost be called the most effective means of persuasion he possesses.' – Aristotle (McKeon, 2001, p. 1329)

- ***Pathos,*** which is a broad concept relating to 'suffering' and 'experience', and also, more generally, to feelings and emotions. The words *pathology*, *empathy*, *sympathy*, and *pathetic* are derived from the Greek ***Pathos, which refers to emotions in general, and in the present context to the emotional connection between the negotiator and their counterpart***. Other-regarding orientation, in the form of positive pathos, is a key component of persuasion skills. Pathos is defined by Aristotle in the following way, insisting that a negotiator's own emotions, both positive and negative, can be used to persuade partners by appealing to their emotions:

   'Secondly, persuasion may come through the power of the hearers, when the speech stirs their emotions. Our judgments when we are pleased and friendly are not the same as when we are pained and hostile.' – Aristotle (McKeon, 2001, p. 1330)

- ***Logos***, the Greek root of many words in English relating to facts, science, logic, and rationality (e.g., logical, therefore convincing). Speech, reasoning, and discourse, whether oral or written (presentations, as well as books and articles), are central in *Logos*. Facts and statistics, scientific proof, data, evidence, as well as historical and literary sources, are the typical means used by Logos to generate a sense of truthfulness and inevitability in the arguments made by a negotiator. ***Persuasion is achieved by a logically articulated, rational*** *speech which proves the truth of arguments used in intercultural interactions*. Aristotle defines the appeal to logic and reasoning to convince in the following terms:

'Thirdly, persuasion is effected by the speech itself when we have proved a truth or an apparent truth by means of the persuasive arguments suitable to the case in question.' – Aristotle (McKeon, 2001, p. 1330)

Aristotle's framework of rhetoric has limits; however, it draws our attention to the need to use all three pillars of persuasive skills, as well as the necessary balance between them. Individuals may assess their natural tendencies and abilities in mobilising *ethos, pathos,* and *logos*. For instance, rights-oriented negotiators who combine *logos* and *ethos* should be careful to also develop *pathos*, the second pillar of persuasive skills, if they do not want to appear as insensitive and dry.

Framework 2: Other-regarding orientation, East-Asian style

Confucian thought focuses on the cultivation of virtue and the maintenance of ethics. Some of the basic Confucian ethical concepts and practices include *rén, yì, lǐ,* and *zhì*[29]. This framework roughly corresponds to an effective Relationship-Building Type, with an emphasis on the perspective of moral and social behaviour rather than on logic and rationality, as in the Western Aristotelian framework described above. This set of moral guidelines for human interaction is found in most East Asian countries. The Japanese concept of *Ningensei* exemplifies the same four interrelated principles of Confucian philosophy: *jen, i (amae), li,* and *shu*[30].

- **Rén (仁),** meaning 'benevolence' or 'humaneness' is at the heart of human behaviour when people manifest compassion toward other human beings. Benevolence and empathetic behaviour related to **Rén entails active listening, caring for the views of partners, and looking out for their feelings and true intentions**. However, there are pitfalls to possibly *excessive* other-regarding orientation. In terms of the Dual Concern Model, which balances concern for one's own goals and the goals of others through assertiveness and cooperativeness, Rén may translate into disproportionate concern for the other party's outcomes. This concept may remind a Deal-Making Type to balance consideration for the needs of both sides.

- ***Yì (義/ㄫ)*** comprises remaining righteous and cultivating a moral disposition to do good. Confucian *Yì*, called *i* by the Japanese, also termed *amae*, is **concerned with group welfare as it directs human relationships towards the common good**. According to Goldman (p. 33)[31],

  'The *i* component of *ningensei* surfaces in Japanese negotiators' commitment to the organization, group agendas, and a reciprocity (*shu*) and humanism (*jen*) that is long-term, consistent, and looks beyond personal motivation.'

- ***Lǐ (禮/礼)*** is a system of ritualised behaviours and propriety norms that govern individuals in everyday life. **Li codes behaviour in a precise and formal manner, and is supposed to smooth the interpersonal and social expression** of *jen*, *shu,* and *i*. The Japanese *meishi* ritual of exchanging business cards can be considered as typical of *li*-coded etiquette[32]. However, codes corresponding to formal manners differ across cultures. They need not necessarily be imitated by cultural outsiders unless they have a practical purpose (such as the *meishi* ritual) in the non-task interaction phase. The comprehension of alien or foreign social interaction codes in intercultural interaction commands respect, however, not imitation.

- ***Zhì (智)***, or *Shu* in Japanese, is based on a norm of generalised reciprocal behaviour essential in relationship building. It obliges the individual to refrain from actions and behaviour toward others that would be unpleasant if directed at oneself. This mirror game **enables us to understand what is right and fair, or wrong and unfair in both one's own and others' behaviours**.

  Zhì / Shu is a practical protective device in Confucian philosophy which negatively considers individual failure to sustain the moral values of *rén* and *yì*. Similarly, the Japanese equivalent of *Zhì*, *Shu* emphasises the importance of reciprocity for the cultivation of human relationships. *Shu* is an affective and intuitive means of coding messages and involves 'belly communication' when negotiating[33].

Framework 3: Five Chinese elements in intercultural negotiation: generating integrative collaboration[34]

In the Chinese philosophical tradition, five basic elements (*Wing-Xu*) compose our world: *Wood* (*mu*), *Fire* (*huo*), *Earth* (*tu*), *Metal* (*jin*), and *Water* (*shui*)[35]. Each element has a symbolic meaning, and their balance is important for individuals. The five elements are traditionally regarded as the foundation of everything in daily life, including personalities and natural phenomena. They have their own character and can generate or destroy one other. Each of these five elements gives a symbolic force to persons, who should use them shrewdly, since each element (1) generates another symbolic element and (2) is moderated and counterbalanced by still another symbolic element (see **Figure 3.1**)[36].

- **Wood** relates to vegetation and flowers and expresses beauty and benevolence. *Wood* articulates destiny, representing lavish, brilliant, blooming, flourishing aspects. In intercultural negotiation, ***Wood stands for the richness and quality of arguments.***
- **Fire** represents features related to strength or softness, to power and influence, as well as to bravery and forcefulness. *Fire* is related to the sense of commitment and to the sense of propriety. In intercultural negotiation, ***Fire provides individuals with stamina, respectability, and good manners.***
- **Earth** fundamentally represents a link to material life and to the real world. *Earth* is related to depth, fidelity, and honesty. *Earth* provides the status, rich or poor, and represents the birth and growth of everything. ***In intercultural negotiation, the Earth element corresponds to both a deep sense of the real issues at stake, and a rather pragmatic, or realistic attitude***.
- **Metal** is associated with both righteousness and practical decision making. *Metal* determines the life span, longevity, and foretelling (i.e., predicting, forecasting) dangers and difficulties, penalties, and dead ends. *Metal* is also associated with prudence. In intercultural interaction, ***Metal governs the ability to predict possible negative events, to be precise in drafting contracts, and to value justice, righteousness, and honesty (e.g., ethical standards).*** It also provides the individual with strength and the ability to reach a decision that is applicable in practice and mutually profitable for both sides.
- **Water** relates to imagination and wisdom. Because of its liquid, fluid, and agile nature, *Water* promotes talents and represents aptitude, brightness, as well as an agile and accurate mind. In intercultural negotiation, it can lead to ***strong ability to invent creative solutions, to be flexible (e.g., not be stuck in the middle or adopt a positional stance).*** *Water* also relates to the ability to clarify complex situations and intricate issues at stake.

The five elements provide intercultural interactors with symbolic resources that guide their involvement in the interaction process. However, going too far in pursuing the path indicated by a first element results in generating the next element on the Wu Xing circle, possibly fostering its negative side, which then requires a third element to intervene as a moderator, and re-balance the 'triangle'. That is why the *Wu Xing* is based on a circle and five arrows inside, between a first element, a second element generated by the first, and a third element which generates the first element and acts as a moderator of excesses in the second element (see **Figure 3.1** and **Table 3.3**).

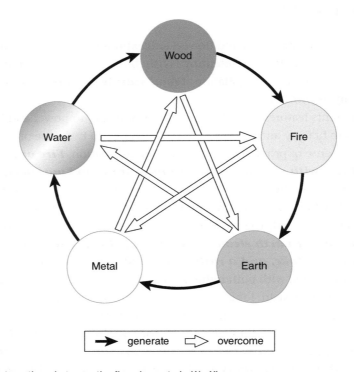

Figure 3.1   Interactions between the five elements in Wu Xing

Source: Adapted from 'The Five Elements (Wu Xing)' [37]

Table 3.3   The five Chinese elements and intercultural interaction behavior

Element 1 generates......	...... Element 2, which is......	...... moderated by Element 3.
Water (imagination and creativity)	*Wood* (brilliant, blooming ideas)	*Metal* (practical decision-making)
Wood (brilliant, blooming ideas)	*Fire* (commitment/propriety/ power)	*Water* (imagination and creativity)
Fire (commitment/propriety/ power)	*Earth* (material life-deal-fidelity)	*Wood* (brilliant, blooming ideas)
Earth (material life-deal-fidelity)	*Metal* (practical decision-making)	*Fire* (commitment/propriety/power)
Metal (practical decision-making)	*Water* (imagination and creativity)	*Earth* (material life-deal-fidelity)

COUNTERBALANCING ELEMENTS TO BALANCE NEGOTIATIONS

Water supplies the power of imagination and agility of mind. In turn, *Water* generates (i.e., nourishes) *Wood*, which stands for the richness and quality of arguments, problem-solving abilities, and the creative exploration of joint solutions. However, making arguments (excessive *Logos*) should not be to the detriment of decision-making. *Wood* needs a counterbalancing element which it finds in *Metal*. *Metal* penetrates *Wood* by cutting, sawing, drilling, nailing, screwing, etc. Excesses in the *Wood* element are moderated by the practical decision making orientation in *Metal*.

Wood-based argumentation generates (i.e., feeds) *Fire*, possibly too strong a commitment at the risk of a lack of self-control. Trying hard to convince the opponent and being passionately committed to one's goals should not translate into a lack of self-control. However, *Fire* is moderated by *Water*, which quenches *Fire*. Excessive commitment can be moderated by the *Water* element bringing brightness, wisdom, and a flexible mind.

Fire, related to the sense of commitment, generates *Earth* (i.e., *Earth* is a crusty surface produced by the cooling of magmatic *Fire*). The risk with *Earth* is that negotiators become so solidly fastened, that they turn out to be too single-minded and possibly stubborn. Therefore, *Earth* is moderated by *Wood*, the underlying symbolic image being that *Wood* parts *Earth* (e.g., tree roots breaking up soil, and even rock). *Wood* in the form of roots or trees can prevent *Earth* erosion. Single-mindedness and excessive resolve related to the deep-seated *Earth* element should be curtailed by coming back to more sophisticated, diverse, and creative arguments, that is, by breaking up a too solid and steadfast position. This is especially true for positional confrontation.

Earth, which represents the link to material life and to the real world, generates *Metal*, since its soil contains ore and minerals. *Metal* commands practical decision making, deal-orientation, and awareness of risk and danger. However, too much *Metal* may result for a negotiator in excessive deal-orientation, narrow focus, and mean practicality, as well as a counterproductive obsession to make things work. Being overly concerned with possible negative events and their unpleasant consequences are the possible undesirable aspects of the *Metal* element for a negotiator. *Metal* needs a balancing element, which it finds in *Fire*. *Fire* melts *Metal*. The strength and robustness of *Metal* should be used by the negotiator, but moderated by *Fire*, which prevents cold-hearted decision making, with no *Pathos* or empathy.

(Continued)

Metal, associated with practical decision making, generates *Water* (i.e., *Water* runs off *Metal*). *Water* (imagination and creativity) is moderated by *Earth* (linked to material life and pragmatism) because creative ideas should, as much as possible, remain realistic. *Earth* absorbs, dams, or muddies *Water*. Creativity should find down-to-*Earth* limits.

A balanced self-orientation in intercultural interaction requires reflexivity, moderation, patience, and prudence. Be yourself, try to remain sincere and genuine, while being prudent and impartial. Do not try to be someone else. This may lead to difficult trade-offs between being yourself and wearing a mask, which may be to some extent necessary in some social situations. The paradoxical recommendation of *negotiating rationally in an irrational world*[38] acquires new meaning in the world of intercultural negotiation, where rationality is crucial. In fact, where different cultures are involved in negotiation, complex calculative, economic, and utilitarian rationality has to interact with a relational, group and identity-based rationality.

3.6 Adjusting in intercultural interactions

Metacognitive cultural intelligence[39] relates to reflexivity and consciousness (self-awareness) in intercultural interactions. The three items in this subscale relate to being conscious, adjusting, and checking for accuracy when using cultural knowledge in interactions with people from different and/or unfamiliar cultures.

The AKA (awareness-knowledge-adjustment) model of intercultural interaction

The AKA (awareness-knowledge-adjustment) model of intercultural interaction starts from a *linear* sequence beginning with becoming aware, followed by an information search and a thoughtful elaboration, and later serving as a base for further practical adjustment. However, in daily intercultural interaction, the sequence is far from always linear, starting for instance with adjustment and coming only later to knowledge and awareness (or vice-versa).

Awareness

When interacting with partners from different cultures, awareness involves not only awareness of one's *own*, but also awareness of the *others'* culturally based values, assumptions, and behaviour, as well as progressively becoming aware of how culture-based attitudes and behaviour may sometimes fit well, but in other cases be discrepant. Unique experiences during intercultural interactions, which may be recorded in a diary, provide the opportunity to cultivate awareness by debriefing specific critical incidents with partners from different cultures[40]. Discussing the critical incidents can build awareness by integrating a reciprocal understanding of one's own cultural background with those of acquaintances and partners from different cultures. Self-shock (previously described as a mirror effect) results in becoming aware of the relativity of cultural assumptions and beliefs in the world of diverse cultures. Ethnocentrism is then partly discovered and understood by being reflexive and self-critical.

Cultural knowledge types

There are many ways to learn about other cultures. *Surface knowledge* can be gained from descriptions of local customs, etc., *intermediate knowledge* can be gained from engaging with cultural productions, whereas *deep knowledge* usually needs to be acquired through personal experience.

Deep Knowledge consists of learning about a country/culture's history, geography, language(s), literature (especially well-known novels and short stories from local authors with global recognition), *etic* scores on cultural dimensions (e.g., Hofstede, Schwartz values), as well as *emic* accounts of particular norms and experiences, which may entail living in a country for some months or more as an expatriate or exchange student. This deep knowledge refers to the cognitive dimension of the CQ (cultural intelligence) scale[41], based on six questions asking whether respondents know: (1) legal and economic systems of other cultures; (2) rules (e.g., vocabulary, grammar) of other languages; (3) cultural values and religious beliefs; (4) marriage systems; (5) arts and crafts of other cultures; as well as (6) the rules for expressing non-verbal behaviour in other cultures.

Intermediate Knowledge derives, for instance, from watching foreign movies that can be very good cultural informants because they sketch daily life in a culture, including living environments, foods, travel, friends, and family interactions, especially those in which the members come from other cultures. Another way is to explore Dollar Street[42] which was created by Anna Rosling Rönnlund, who collected and organised photos that show how people really live.

Surface Knowledge is based on country-culture description, such as those found in culturegrams[43], in *how to* travel guides describing local customs, dos and don'ts, tips for appropriate behaviour, etc. These are useful in combination with the more profound sources.

Adjustment

Adjustment deals with motivation for change and behavioural fine-tuning in intercultural interactions. It implies changing communicative behaviour (verbal and non-verbal) to improve intercultural interactions and getting things done, despite a somewhat complicated process due to cultural and language differences. The capacity for adjustment in the cultural intelligence (CQ) scale is measured by two dimensions: Motivational CQ, which is related to enjoyment, self-confidence and coping with adjustment to a different culture, and Behavioural CQ, which is related to change in verbal behaviour (e.g., accent and tone; use of pause and silence; rate of speaking) and non-verbal behaviour (e.g., bodily and facial expressions), when a cross-cultural situation requires it.

Activity 3.1

Dollar Street

Search up Dollar Street on the internet and explore the lives of more than 450 families, their homes and their possessions in over 65 countries. You can visit their homes around the world without travelling there, to get a deeper insight into how people live, from looking at more than 40,000 photographs and 7000 videos. Across countries, families are lined up from the poorest to richest by their total consumption value per adult (in dollars adjusted for purchasing power parity).

Pick a region or consumption level and explore the differences in how people live, their homes, what they eat, and even the next big thing they plan to buy.

Sequences and styles in intercultural adjustment

There are several ways of adjusting behaviour in intercultural interactions, each of which has merit. They depend on which step is prioritised in successive steps in the intercultural interaction. In the AKA model, ***awareness, knowledge, and adjustment*** may follow different sequences:

- **Awareness-Knowledge-Adjustment** is the first sequence in the AKA model. This starts with awareness, followed by the acquisition of knowledge, leading to adjustment. This corresponds to a sensitive (subtle, perceptive, reactive) adjustment pattern in intercultural interactions. It involves listening, open-minded attention, non-judgemental attitudes, but also asking for information and feedback from the person you are paying deep and thoughtful attention to. Knowledge will be accessed in part by asking for insider sources easily accessible to outsiders. However, there is a risk of over-adjustment, by appearing as excessively concerned with cultural empathy. When showing empathy, an AKA-sensitive person should not try to *mimic* the status of an insider. Conversely, they should not over-emphasise differences as being radical, which risks propagating and reinforcing the stereotypes of one's own people.

- **Knowledge-Awareness-Adjustment** is another possible sequence, where formal acquisition of knowledge and learning is first, followed by awareness of problematic issues in the intercultural encounter, and finally adjustment based on the assumed ability to apply knowledge as solutions to perceived problems. This corresponds to an intellectual model, in which people think before acting. Many texts recommend this sequence; however, there is a risk of being *too* rational, logical, and cerebral. This can limit understanding to a stereotypical summary that later blocks awareness and adjustment. Acquiring formal cultural knowledge has value only in combination with other learning/coping strategies before or after experiencing intercultural interaction.

- **Adjustment-Awareness-Knowledge** corresponds to an experiential model (do first, learn after). AAK actors experience intercultural interaction with little or no advance preparation. The joint task and virtual collaboration raise their awareness, and then if they feel a need to go deeper and understand more, they may attempt to retrieve cultural knowledge and try to debrief their intercultural experience. A risk for AAK experientials with strong egos is to impose their own cultural style on the intercultural interaction, regardless of the risks that it might lead to a possible culture clash. Another risk is being seen as a meddler due to snooping, or improvising with no definite approach to intercultural interactions, even though they may want to make it work.

- **Adjustment-Knowledge-Awareness** is an alternative sequence, where people adapt and adjust first, without being really aware of the intercultural interaction process, and later search for cultural knowledge which will help them debrief the experience.

A choice is often necessary: intercultural interactions involve dilemmas and conflicts which should be solved by making clear, negotiated choices based on *either* your cultural framework, the partner's cultural framework, or a mix of both. Mere empathy is an inadequate solution. Beyond the fact that it is quite difficult, and sometimes misleading, to *put yourself in another's shoes*, the other party rarely demands that you do this.

3.7 A set of recommendations for effective intercultural teamwork

Recommendations for effective intercultural teamwork can be divided into several stages.

1. **Preparing**

   Rule 1: Be prepared for the other side's unpreparedness

   Rule 2: Map the human landscape and prepare for respectful behaviour

   Rule 3: Assess intercultural obstacles (and opportunities) as early as possible

   Rule 4: Examine key elements in both people and tasks and prepare for understanding their interface during the teamwork process. Empathy is not enough

2. **Communicating and dealing with people**

   Rule 5: Make time for adequate preliminaries (especially if it is a first-time encounter)

   Rule 6: Give *face* to the other side and to your team partners; also protect your own *face*

   Rule 7: Be ready for different communication styles

   Rule 8: Constantly check the accuracy of communication

   Rule 9: Do not over-interpret, especially when faced with ambiguous moves from partners

   Rule 10: Let your intuition guide you in the interpretation of non-verbal communication

   Rule 11: When interacting in English, use simple and clear words as well as short sentences

3. **Developing strategic behaviour in intercultural teamwork**

   Rule 12: Define what your basic interests are

   Rule 13: Identify the expectations of the other party and the common ground for collaboration

   Rule 14: Be ready to breach cooperation, while avoiding mentioning walk-away options

Rule 15: Be equipped for tough strategies from the other side

Rule 16: Do not over-invest in benevolent, integrative moves if the other party is not likely to reciprocate

4. **Managing issues, power, and time in the collaborative process**

Rule 17: Adjust communication style when needed

Rule 18: Be prepared to resist some rough and manipulative tactics; bring them to light

Rule 19: Control your concessions

Rule 20: Never tell the other side when you are early in finishing a task

Rule 21: Plan modestly, but firmly monitor tasks and deadlines

Rule 22: Be ready for a temporal clash

5. **Fostering trust and developing relationships**

Rule 23: Build a trusting relationship by being reliable and asking the other side to reciprocate

Rule 24: Check that your partners are neutral and do not play against you

Rule 25: Avoid conflict escalation because it harms the relationship and, therefore, the collaborative process

Rule 26: Introduce 'arbitrating' outsiders (e.g., mediators, conciliators) as late as possible in the teamwork process, and only if conflict resolution has failed after several attempts

Rule 27: Try to develop what could be a long-term relationship, even if the task timeframe seems short

3.8 Chapter summary

This chapter deals with ways and means to adjust in intercultural interactions and reviews a number of key concepts in the field (ethnocentrism, stereotypes, empathy, cultural hostility, and misunderstandings). It highlights the role of culture, personality, as well as emotional and cultural intelligence in adjusting rationally, especially when performing a joint task within a culturally diverse team and/or when negotiating across cultures.

References

1. Adair, W. L., Okumura, T., & Brett, J. M. (2001). Negotiation behavior when cultures collide: The United States and Japan. *Journal of Applied Psychology, 86*(3), 371–385.

2. Tinsley, C. H. & Brett, J. M. (1997). Managing workplace conflict: A comparison of conflict frames and outcomes in the U.S. and Hong Kong, Paper presented at the Annual Meeting of the Academy of Management, Boston.

3. See for instance Gundlach, M., Zivnuska, S., & Stoner, J. (2006). Understanding the relationship between individualism–collectivism and team performance through an integration of social identity theory and the social relations model. *Human Relations, 59*(12), 1603–1632.

4. Schwartz, S. H. (2009). Culture matters: National value, cultures, sources and consequences. In C.-Y. Chiu, Y. Y. Hong, S. Shavitt, & R. S. Wyer Jr (Eds.), *Problems and Solutions in Cross-cultural Theory, Research and Application* (pp. 127–150). New York: Psychology Press.

5. Markus, H. R. & Kitayama, S. (1991). Culture and the self: Implications for cognition, emotion and motivation. *Psychological Review, 98*(2), 224–253.

6. Hofstede, G. (2001). *Culture's Consequences,* 2nd edn. Thousand Oaks, CA: Sage Publications.

7. Sumner, G. A. (1906). *Folk Ways.* New York: Ginn Custom Publishing.

8. Lee, J. A. (1966). Cultural analysis in overseas operations. *Harvard Business Review,* March-April, 106–111.

9. Zaharna, R. S. (1989) Self shock: the double-binding challenge of identity. *International Journal of Intercultural Relations, 13*(4), 501–526.

10. Adler, 1975, p. 18. Adler, Peter S. (1975). The transitional experience: An alternative view of culture shock. *Journal of Humanistic Psychology, 15*, 13–23.

11. Erikson, Erik (1950). *Childhood and Society.* New York: Norton.

12. Segall, Marshall H., Dasen, Pierre R., Berry, John W., & Poortinga, Ype H. (1990). *Human Behavior in Global Perspective.* New York: Pergamon Press.

13. See Chapter 5 of Segall et al. (1990, pp. 93–112), which asks whether there are racial differences in cognition? and offers an in-depth review of the empirical studies of the difference in intellectual performance across ethnic groups.

14. For instance, Transylvanian Hungarians and Romanians, people in ex-Yugoslavia, Armenians of High Karabakh and Azeris of the Azerbaijan enclave in Armenia; Walloons and Flemings in Belgium; Protestant and Catholic communities in Ulster; etc.

15. Maddux et al. (2011); see also their literature review on cultural differences in the meaning and functions of apologies. Maddux, W. W., Kim, P. H., Okumura, T. and Brett, J. M. (2011). Cultural differences in the function and meaning of apologies. *International Negotiation, 16*(3), 405–425.

16. Morand, D. A. (1996). Politeness as a universal variable in cross-cultural managerial communication. *International Journal of Organizational Analysis, 4*(1), 52–74.

17. Sugimoto, N. (1998). Norms of apology depicted in U.S. American and Japanese literature on manners and etiquette. *International Journal of Intercultural Relations, 22*(3), 251–276.

18. Triandis, H. C. (1995). *Individualism and Collectivism*. Boulder, CO: Westview.

19. Triandis, H. C. (1995). *Individualism and Collectivism*. Boulder, CO: Westview.

20. See Jean-Claude Usunier (2019). Intercultural Business Negotiations: Deal-Making or Relationship Building, Abingdon: Routledge.

21. See Earley, P. C., & Mosakowski, E. (2004). Cultural intelligence. *Harvard Business Review, 82*(10), 139–146.

22. Key bargainer characteristics are examined in Hernández Requejo and Graham (2008, pp. 130–137). The issues around negotiator selection and training are treated in Maude (2020) *International Business Negotiation: principles and practice*. Bloomsbury Publishing, Chapter 13, and in Foster (1995, pp. 275–277). Hernández Requejo, W. & Graham, J. L. (2008). *Global Negotiation: The new rules*. London: Macmillan. Foster, D. A. (1995). *Bargaining Across Borders*, New York: McGraw-Hill.

23. See Goleman, D. (2006). *Emotional Intelligence*. New York: Bantam Books.

24. Earley, P. C., & Mosakowski, E. (2004). Cultural intelligence. *Harvard Business Review, 82*(10), 139–146.

25. Ang, S. & Van Dyne, L. (2008). Conceptualization of cultural intelligence: Definition, distinctiveness, and nomological network. In S. Ang & L. Van Dyne (Eds.), *Handbook of Cultural Intelligence: Theory, Measurement, and Applications* (pp. 3–15). Armonk, NY: M. E. Sharpe.

26. Kalé, Sudhir H. (2003). How national culture, organizational culture and personality impact buyer-seller interactions. In P. N. Ghauri & J.-C. Usunier (Eds.), *International Business Negotiations* (pp. 75–93). Oxford: Pergamon/Elsevier.

27. Cellich and Jain (2004) in Chapter 3 (pp. 43–52) describe typical negotiation styles and offer advice as to how to select one's own negotiation style based on a 35-statement Personal Assessment Inventory (pp. 50–51). G. Richard Shell (2006) in his landmark book, *Bargaining for Advantage*, provides advice both for collaborative people (who need to become more assertive, confident, and prudent) and competitive negotiators (who need to become more aware of other people and of their legitimate needs) in two different sets of seven 'tools' adapted to each negotiation and personality style. Maude (2014) mentions extroversion, and risk-seeking versus risk avoiding as personality characteristics that may have an influence on performance. He also usefully highlights the role of interpersonal attractiveness, that is, the degree of fit between individual personalities, as having a positive impact on cooperation in negotiation.

See also Wheeler (2013) *The art of negotiation: How to improvise agreement in a chaotic world*. Simon and Schuster.

28. See Weiss, Joshua N. (2015). From Aristotle to Sadat: A short strategic persuasion framework for negotiators. *Negotiation Journal,* July, 211–222.

29. https://en.wikipedia.org/wiki/Confucianism

30. Goldman, A. (1994). The centrality of 'Ningensei' to Japanese negotiating and interpersonal relationships: Implications for U.S.-Japanese communication. *International Journal of Intercultural Relations*, *18*(1), 29–54.

31. Goldman, A. (1994). The centrality of 'Ningensei' to Japanese negotiating and interpersonal relationships: Implications for U.S.-Japanese communication. *International Journal of Intercultural Relations*, *18*(1), 29–54.

32. Goldman, A. (1994). The centrality of 'Ningensei' to Japanese negotiating and interpersonal relationships: Implications for U.S.-Japanese communication. *International Journal of Intercultural Relations*, *18*(1), 29–54.

33. In Mastumoto's (1988) words. Matsumoto, M. (1988). *The Unspoken Way: Haragei – silence in Japanese business and society*. New York: Kodansha International.

34. My thanks to Pr. T. K. Peng from I-Shou University, Kaohsiung, Taiwan for cultural insider validation.

35. Compared to the Western four-element system, *Earth, Air, Fire,* and *Water*, two man-transformed elements (*Wood* and *Metal*) exist in Chinese elements which do not occur in the Western – purely natural – framework. One element (*Air*) exists in the Western framework, but it does not exist in Chinese elements.

36. For a complete presentation of the linkage between Wu Xing and personality traits see https://fr.slideshare.net/DieselDave8/wu-xing-wu-shen-personality-traitsarchetypes-who-do-you-think-you-are

37. Figure 3.1 is adapted from: 'The Five Elements (Wu Xing)' available at www.travelchinaguide.com/intro/astrology/five-elements.htm, Accessed September 26, 2022.

38. See Bazerman and Neale's (1992), Chapter 18. Bazerman, Max H. & Margaret A. Neale (1992). *Negotiating Rationally*. New York: The Free Press.

39. See Earley, P. C., & Mosakowski, E. (2004). Cultural intelligence. *Harvard Business Review*, *82*(10), 139–146, and Ang, S., Van Dyne, L., & Rockstuhl, T. (2015). Cultural intelligence: Origins, conceptualization, evolution, and methodological diversity. In Michele L. Gelfand, Chi-yue Chi, & Ying-Yi Hong (Eds.), *Advances in Culture and Psychology* (pp. 273–323 (cit. 311–12)). Oxford: Oxford University Press.

40. It may be useful to be aware of the examples of critical incidences, along with different cultural assumptions, provided in Chapter 1.

41. Ang, S. & Van Dyne, L. (2008). Conceptualization of cultural intelligence: Definition, distinctiveness, and nomological network. in S. Ang & L. Van Dyne (Eds.), *Handbook of Cultural Intelligence: Theory, Measurement, and Applications* (pp. 3–15). Armonk, NY: M. E. Sharpe.
42. Dollar Street www.gapminder.org/dollar-street
43. www.proquest.com/products-services/culturegrams.html CultureGrams™ offers concise, reliable, and up-to-date country reports on 182 cultures of the world.

PART 2
CROSS-CULTURAL
MARKETING
DECISION MAKING

Globalisation has occured at a rapid pace over the last century. The continuous expansion of cross-border marketing has been backed by the progressive elimination of barriers to trade, and the emergence of a global consumer culture. However, in the early 2020s, the onset of the COVID-19 pandemic and increasing geopolitical tensions, including the war in Ukraine, created a perfect storm for the global supply chain. These events led to product shortages, healthcare crises, severe travel restrictions, global price spikes in fuel and food, the creation of millions of refugees, and a dramatic increase in poverty.

Countries, firms, and consumers were largely blindsided by these events. In 2019, who would have predicted that people would be refused admission to hospitals and to morgues, due to overcrowding, even in wealthy countries? In 2021, who would have predicted that Russia would invade Ukraine? Who would have predicted the impact this war would have on the Ukrainian people and infrastructure, on changes in cooperation between countries, and on changes in access to food and fuel worldwide? In 2022, who would have predicted that over 1000 major companies, including McDonald's, Coca-Cola, and Starbucks, would withdraw totally from Russia amidst threats of expropriation or nationalisation of foreign-owned assets for those who leave? With other developing geopolitical tensions, civil wars (e.g., Ethiopia, Myanmar, Syria, and Yemen), and major climate events (e.g., bushfires, floods, and droughts), it is clear that firms cannot afford to make major decisions in isolation.

Firms need to consider how major global drivers (i.e., socio-economic trends, geopolitical shifts, environmental challenges, and technological advances) may impact important stakeholders (i.e., consumers, suppliers, and legislators) in ways that can lead to dramatic changes in the balance between the need for more (a) local adaptation or global uniformity, (b) automation or humanisation, (c) simplicity or complexity, and (d) protectionism or collaboration[1]. We consider the international environment and how cross-cultural differences may impact the success of a firm's decisions throughout Part 2 of the book.

- In Chapter 4, we focus on market entry and expansion decisions across cultures. We explore the evolution of international business strategy, the selection of new target markets, modes of entry and selection of channels, and dealing with foreign partners.
- In Chapter 5, we examine cross-cultural marketing strategy and implementation, including international product and branding decisions, international distribution, pricing under different market conditions, and the influence of culture on communication strategies.

In Chapter 6, we focus on how to develop a culturally sensitive business plan, including the conceptualisation of clear aims and questions, finding tools, concepts and theories that help to define the type of information needed, and how to develop and communicate recommendations.

4
MARKET ENTRY AND EXPANSION DECISIONS ACROSS CULTURES

Learning objectives

After reading this chapter and completing the activities, you should be able to:

- Analyse the types of international markets your company aims to serve and learn how to define an internationalisation strategy.
- Understand how the World Trade Organisation (WTO) legal environment impacts businesses worldwide.
- Develop skills in the selection of target markets, based on analytical tools and published data, while taking into account the various risks associated with international operations.
- Review the main modes of entry of foreign markets and make adequate choices in terms of operations, distribution, and intermediation.
- Learn how to deal with local partners in foreign countries and adjust to their culture and ways of doing business.

Introduction

The challenges to globalisation (e.g., geopolitical clashes, the COVID-19 pandemic, and major climate events), discussed in the introduction to Part 2, have impacted markets worldwide. This has, at least temporarily, reset the balance between global and local products and services, as governments encourage consumers to purchase local (or regional) over global, with the aim of reviving the local economy and shoring up the supply chain. Whether these changes are short or long-term is yet to be seen, but it does illustrate how global events can have a strong and often unexpected impact on international markets and the process of internationalisation. Firms need to understand the risks inherent in international markets, especially when selecting and entering new target markets.

Chapter Overview

In this chapter, we discuss market entry and expansion decisions across cultures. We describe frameworks that illustrate the advantages and disadvantages of each choice, in the following sections:

- **Section 1** examines key concepts in **International Business Strategy**, such as the underlying logic of scale economies and experience effects in the globalisation of markets, as well as theories of internationalisation. The distinction between Global and Multi-domestic industries and markets is especially relevant for designing business strategies. The opening of markets globally has happened because of the long-term evolution of the regulatory framework of international trade. We briefly describe how Multilateral Trade Negotiations and the WTO's 18 trade treaties have organised the opening of international trade over the last 70 years. These factors also influence the internal push for firms to internationalise to save transaction costs and better control their international operations.
- **Section 2** deals with the **selection of target markets.** A number of analytic tools are presented, and meaningful cultural and contextual factors are taken into account for the choice of markets (e.g., cultural distance, psychic distance, the liability of foreignness). The assessment of foreign environments and evaluation of risks in local markets (e.g., commercial risk, political risk, credit risk, etc.) is examined in a way that balances opportunities and risks.
- **Section 3** describes the different **modes of entry** into foreign markets (i.e., exporting, foreign direct investment, licensing agreements). Modes of entry are clarified across the stages of international development and as a function of the firm's resources and learning process.
- **Section 4** deals with **exporting** in more detail, including intermediation choices (e.g., in the country of origin or in the country of destination) and channel management. We highlight the basic features of export operations and distribution in foreign markets through home-country or host-country

intermediation (agents, dealers, franchisees). Major choices in foreign distribution are clarified, and key differences in distribution channels worldwide are summarised. We propose some criteria for choosing foreign distribution channels.

● **Section 5** deals with **foreign partners**, especially contracting with middlemen while adjusting to local environments and facing competition as a new entrant. We successively review a number of contracts (international sales contracts, export contracts, agent/distributor contracts, licensing/franchising contracts, and international joint ventures), and explain how typical clauses in these contracts should be negotiated, what precautions should be taken, and how relationships with local partners should be managed.

● **Section 6** explains different ways of **controlling foreign operations**, either control through proprietary know-how and marketing/management knowledge and/or control through the property (equity stake, cash investment, etc.).

4.1 International Business Strategy
Scale economies, experience effects, and the internalisation process

Internationalisation has been described as a process of learning and progressive commitment vis-à-vis international markets[2]. There is often a need to search for market opportunities beyond the domestic market. Global markets offer opportunities for building large-scale and experience effects.

The logic of economies of scale (the cost advantage experienced when a firm increases output) and experience effects (efficiencies gained by learning or experience) is central in the internalisation process (i.e., producing items internally rather than supplying from the external market), because it helps define (a) the optimal size of a firm in terms of its global activities, (b) to what extent it should be more or less specialised, and (c) whether it should integrate its global operations within the organisation structure (internalise) or use intermediaries, agents, and middlemen (externalise).

Experience effects are related to the cumulated volume of production (i.e., manufacturing scale):

$$C_n = C_1 \, n^{-\lambda}$$

where C_n is the cost of the *nth* unit; C_1 is the cost of the first unit ever manufactured, *n* is the cumulative number of units produced, and λ is an elasticity parameter that links unitary cost (i.e., production of a unit) to cumulative volume of production. λ is strongly dependent on industry and technology, as described below. However, experience effects and economies of scale are not automatically related. While experience effects increase cost-competitiveness through economies of scale (the cost advantage gained by higher production of one product), they also increase cost-competitiveness through economies of scope (the cost advantage gained by producing a variety of products), learning (the cost advantage gained by improving performance via the *learning curve*), and technological improvements (e.g., cost-reducing materials and product design, elimination of unnecessary features, etc.). In fact, learning and technological improvements may be less related to the scale of production than to the ability to incorporate feedback from the market and invest in strong research and development (R&D).

Despite the attractiveness of growth and potential economies described above, there are limitations to the positive effects. **First**, different products and industries do not offer the same potential for scale and experience effects. For instance, artisan cheese has a lower potential than potato crisps or electronic products, based on Moore's Law, which posits significant gains from experience in production, based on historical observations that the number of transistors in a dense integrated circuit doubles about every two years. **Second**, new manufacturing techniques (e.g., robotic technology and flexible production lines) have reduced the cost of smaller production runs. **Third**, lower cost is not the only competitive advantage. **Fourth**, size does not *per se* command learning and experience, and size without learning does not lead to experience.

There are also limitations to expanding operations abroad due to various kinds of distances. Here we discuss physical distance, with other types of distances – linguistic, cultural, psychic, legal, and political – being discussed in the next sections of this chapter. *Physical distance* is an obvious obstacle, not only in terms of kilometres or miles, but also in terms of the costs involved in loading/unloading goods. The long-term trend of decreasing shipping costs per kilometre is now offset by the hazards related to large ships, especially sea and coastal pollution, as well as logistical issues related to crises (e.g., COVID-19 and geopolitical tensions). Transportation costs differ by destination and product. For instance, costs related to loading/unloading goods (containerisation/roll-on/roll-off ships, multimodal transportation) have been greatly reduced in major hubs, but these costs may be far greater where there is less automation and higher labour costs. Transportation costs also differ according to product attributes (e.g., weight, volume, perishability, value, etc.), which influence the costs of international shipping tariffs. While physical distance is symmetrical, transportation costs are not (e.g., transportation costs from New York to Tokyo may not be the same as from Tokyo to New York, even for the same load).

The capacity of a particular good to be transported internationally is related to its unit cost per kilogram. It is largely uneconomical to transport cement more than 100 km, except in very sparsely populated countries like Australia and Canada. This is similar for larger products with small margins. A small, cheap car needs to be produced near the final consumer, while a higher-priced luxury car can be transported overseas. Due to the unit cost per kilogram, electronic products, portable computers, and computer chips are barely impacted by shipping costs. During the golden period of Japanese exports (the 1970s to 1990s), Japanese firms specialised in products that had the potential for high levels of experience effects and low transportation costs (e.g., electronic goods, music instruments).

Long-term evolution of the regulatory framework of international trade and the opening of international markets

Understanding trade agreements is important when planning for international expansion, as these agreements not only offer stability but can also provide significant cost savings in trade between specified countries. Trade agreements may lower customs duties, dismantle non-tariff barriers, and remove domestic protectionist measures as much as possible, increasing the size of accessible international markets for the most competitive companies worldwide.

Multilateral trade negotiations (e.g., treaties and agreements between nations) have organised the regulatory framework of international trade for more than 70 years. The basic principles in the General Agreement on Tariffs and Trade (GATT) treaty (1947) were taken over by the World Trade Organization (WTO, based in Geneva) in 1995. These principles govern regional trade agreements, including customs unions and free trade zones (according to the GATT 1947, Article 24 on Customs Unions and Free-trade Areas). The European Union is not only a single market, but also a customs union, with duties set at zero between member-states and a common external tariff vis-à-vis external countries. The North American Free Trade Agreement or NAFTA (involving Canada, Mexico, USA) is a free trade zone; however, it has no common external tariff, as is the case for most regional trade agreements that are weakly structured in institutional terms.

Examples of the many important basic principles adopted by the WTO from the GATT treaty 1947 (see full list of Articles[3]), include the General Most-Favoured-Nation

Treatment clause (Article I), the National Treatment for Internal Taxation and Regulation (Article III) and Subsidies (Article XVI). The General Most-Favoured-Nation Treatment clause provides for multilateral rather than bilateral trade and is non-discriminatory; however, regional trade agreements are provided for in Article 24 on Customs Unions and Free-trade Areas. Basically, the principle of National Treatment for Internal Taxation and Regulation holds that a member-state must treat foreign exporters in their domestic markets no less favourably than it does domestic firms. The principle of reciprocity (not formally applied in international trade treaties) holds that trade regulations should be compared across member states. If a more advantageous regulation exists in state A than in state B, exporters of state A would be entitled to take advantage of this more favourable regulation in state B. However, this is very difficult to implement in practice. Finally, Article 16 restricts the use of subsidies, akin to raising a tariff barrier, which are a key target of the Agreement and the 18 international trade treaties managed by the WTO.

In addition to the more obvious tariff barriers, non-tariff barriers also apply protectionist measures, through industrial norms, safety standards, and technical regulation. Firms often wonder whether non-tariff barriers are aimed primarily at the safeguarding of local ways of doing (e.g., electric plugs still massively differ worldwide) or actually amount to deliberate protectionism. That is, non-tariff barriers may be legitimate *culture-bound* local techniques, or ways of keeping foreign competition at a distance. The process of harmonisation of technical, hygiene, and safety standards through international organisations, such as ISO, CEN, CENELEC, ETSI, Codex Alimentarius, among others, has been intensive over the last 40 years. However, protectionism appears to be on the rise again since the COVID-19 pandemic, and with rising geopolitical tensions.

Non-tariff barriers, 855 of which were identified in the Tokyo Round study (multilateral Trade Negotiations taking place from 1973 to 1979), cover a range of barriers to international trade. These include:

* quantitative restrictions, such as quotas, contingents (quantitative limits on imports, e.g., only 10,000 cars), or contingents with limited or zero duties, beyond which full customs duty applies;
* technical barriers to trade, such as technical and industrial norms or standards;
* hygiene and safety norms and regulations; and
* other restrictions to trade, such as customs formalities, valuation for customs purposes, favouring local suppliers in public procurement, delaying of spare parts imports, requiring a pile of customs documents with translations, jumbo customs fees, delays when going through customs, etc.

Market barriers, contrary to non-tariff barriers, are natural obstacles to international exchange that should not be confused with legal and procedural obstacles, such as tariffs (e.g., customs duties) and non-tariff barriers. Among the main market barriers are linguistic barriers (e.g., the Japanese writing systems with *Hiragana, Katakana, and Kanji*), barriers due to local preference for domestic products (e.g., Germany), and informal barriers related to protectionist attitudes in retail distribution systems (e.g., Finland, Japan, Switzerland, and many other countries, especially industrialised countries).

Will we witness the end of the multilateral era for international trade, which has driven international marketing and merchant globalisation over the last 70 years? The rise of nationalistic and populist parties in a number of countries may give the impression that we are at a turning point, with increasing protectionist attitudes, trade conflicts, and consumer patriotism. However, most countries have lost a large part of their national sovereignty and control over these issues because their markets are too small, and they are bound by international trade treaties and/or integrated into regional alliances (such as the EU). There is a great deal of built-in interdependence after 70 years of GATT, 25 years of GATS (General Agreement on Trade in Services, 1995), and the 18 WTO treaties, which set the background rules of international trade and, therefore, international marketing at a macro level. In addition, consumption has been largely globalised, even if it remains partly creolised, due to the inventive capacity of local cultures to merge indigenous and foreign/global items.

There will certainly be more bilateral trade talks (and treaties) between major countries and significant regional zones, including both customs unions, such as the EU, and free-trade zones, such as NAFTA. However, it is unlikely that there will be a rise of strong and generalised protectionist tendencies, as was the case after the 1929 economic crisis.

Despite its impressive performance in increasing global welfare, multilateral trade has unfortunately given rise to major imbalances in trade flows, where some countries have huge surpluses and others abysmal trade deficits. The need to rebalance bilateral trade flows will have a deep, but slow, influence on concrete international trade policies for firms who are engaged globally. Some exports and specific trade flows will be impacted, although more as symbolic threats during trade negotiations than as concerns of significant magnitude. Exports are therefore more at threat than other internationalisation patterns, including subsidiaries and joint ventures (FDI), local partners (agents, dealers), licensing, and local distribution networks, which provide much better support for continued international operations, especially in times of sporadic trade conflict. Competitive patterns will become more multi-domestic (i.e., competition in each particular national or regional market area) and less global, except in industries that have already achieved worldwide oligopolistic rivalries, such as mobile phones, computers, and the like.

TRADE WARS

Geopolitical tensions can impact exporters, sometimes with little or no warning. For instance, China imposed duties of around 120% to 220% on most Australian wines in March 2021 until 2026, following 'anti-dumping' allegations that were believed in Australia to be in retaliation for a call for an investigation into the origins of COVID-19. Regardless of the cause, the market value for Australian wine in 2022 was reported to have fallen by 98% from its peak of A$1.2 billion in 2020[4]. The Australian government appealed to the WTO, and an independent panel was appointed to try to resolve the issue. Since then, other commodities, including beef, timber, cotton, barley, lobsters, and coal, were also hit with high tariffs and trade restrictions. However, like most trade wars, both sides have been affected, with small to medium business owners and consumers paying the price.

Michael Porter's thesis about world markets[5]

A key issue is whether companies should (and can) remain *local players*, or whether the need for survival obliges them to become *global players* (multidomestic versus global industries) (Porter, 1986). **Table 4.1** shows which factors influence globalization or localization of business activities on demand and/or supply side.

In Michael Porter's view of preventive and reactive strategy, based on competitive forces, the bargaining power vis-à-vis both customers and suppliers, and the pressure of substitute products and technological alternatives, he makes a quite relevant distinction between global and multidomestic industries:

- In **global industries**, competition is open on a worldwide basis because of the absence of regulatory barriers, high opportunities of experience effects, homogeneous consumer behaviour across countries, the quasi-absence of market barriers, and the relative weakness of transportation costs, customs duties, and non-tariff barriers. Typical examples of global industries are laptop computers and mobile phones.
- In **multidomestic industries,** national markets are fragmented per country for a particular region of the world. However, international competition still exists and takes place separately in each domestic market (e.g., pharmaceuticals, motor insurance). If products, consumer behaviour, or elements of the marketing mix depend on culture (*culture-bound*), multi-domesticity is stronger. Thus, industries fall along a dynamic continuum from purely global to fully multidomestic. For example, some service industries (e.g., the finance industry) have progressively changed from multidomestic to global over the last 30 years under the auspices of GATS (General Agreement on Trade in Services, 1995).

Table 4.1 Globalization and localization factors

Globalization factors ►	Globalization Factors - HIGH	Globalization Factors - LOW
(Mostly supply-related)	Interconnected markets worldwide	Disconnected markets worldwide
Localization factors	No custom duties	High custom duties
(Mostly demand-related) ▼	No non-tariff barriers	Significant non-tariff barriers
	High level of global product acceptance	No global product acceptance
	High potential for economies of scale	Low potential for economies of scale
	Limited impact of transportation costs	High impact of transportation costs
Localization factors -LOW	***Global industries***	Multidomestic industries as
Global product acceptance	Purely global industries with few players world-wide, no local players	***Multilocal industries***
World standards prevail		Mostly local players, a few owned by global players
Local consumers willing to buy foreign products and services	e.g., computers, portable phones, consumer electronics, ...	e.g., cement, beer, restaurants, banking, ...
No or little language barrier		
Localization factors - HIGH	***Multidomestic industries***	***Local industries***
Geographically limited market areas	Few players world-wide with local players competing on the domestic market scene	Only local players, no global player
Local consumer culture (ethnic)		e.g., local services and manu-facturing industries, often SMEs, producing local items for local consumers
Local consumer behaviour	e.g., pharmaceuticals, food, hygiene, detergents, cement, publishing	
Idiosyncratic distribution systems		
Language is important		
Local regulations favouring national players		

Companies usually need to reconfigure their activities, including the location of these activities internationally, in order to maximise efficiency at each stage of the value chain, including production, distribution, and service, and gain a competitive advantage over their competitors by delivering a valuable product to end customers. A systematic approach to value chain analysis may lead to cost competitiveness, increased customer satisfaction, and therefore improved market share and profit.

Theories of internationalisation and business strategies in the global environment

Theories of the internationalisation of the firm attempt to explain:

1. The emergence of multinational companies;
2. Why firms enter certain national markets rather than other markets where they choose not to go;

3. Why they choose particular entry modes, such as foreign direct investment, exporting, licensing agreements, franchising, etc.; and

4. How they can coordinate and control different dimensions of their international operations, such as manufacturing, marketing, logistics, R&D, etc.

Figure 4.1 shows how foreign operations choices relate to products/services, foreign entry modes, target market characteristics, organisational structure, and finance and personnel.

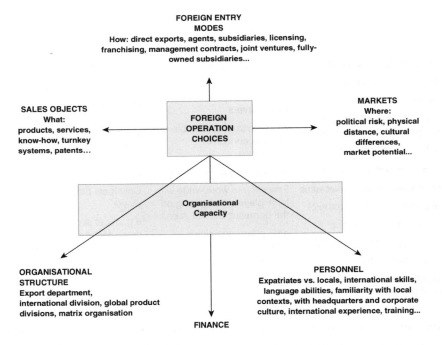

Figure 4.1 Dimensions of internationalisation and foreign operations choices

Source: Adapted from Lawrence S. Welsh and Reijo Luostarinen, Internationalisation: evolution of a concept. In *The internationalisation of the firm: A reader*: Edited by Peter J. Buckley and Pervez N. Ghauri, Academic Press, London, 1993, page 158.

The International Product Life

Companies are pushed towards internationalisation by a number of convergent factors. **First**, the search for experience effects and economies of scale drives firms to hunt for larger markets. **Second**, the International Product Life Cycle (IPLC)⁶ implies moving operations according to phases in the product life in the country of origin. This concept, which originates from the notion of product life cycle developed in marketing, was first proposed by Raymond Vernon to explain international corporate development. There is a correspondence between the stage in a product life cycle and the mode of entry in foreign markets, as well as the nature of the marketing policy followed by the firm.

In **Figure 4.2**, the two initial stages (product launch and growth) of the marketing cycle are combined into a single stage. During the first stage, at least one major firm has made significant research and development (R & D) investments, enabling them to offer new products, often high-tech, worldwide.

- In **Stage 1,** the product is expensive to recover the R & D, its novelty attracts early adopters, and the high price permits high costs associated with limited manufacturing capacity. A small number of factories located in the countries that initiated the R & D supply foreign markets by exporting.
- In **Stage 2,** markets rapidly grow, the product becomes commonplace, and the number of manufacturers increases. In this stage, each firm invests in advertising and promotion to try to create a monopolistic market by creating a unique position in consumers' minds. Market sizes in many countries have become large enough for manufacturing subsidiaries.
- In **Stage 3,** the product has become common. Marketing policies emphasise the price component, and therefore components are sourced at the lowest possible cost, factories are relocated in low-wage countries, and products are re-exported to the main markets, including the parent company's market.

This model applies well to many industrial goods, especially high-tech products, such as consumer electronics. However, there are limitations to the IPLC model of international operations. For many products, there are no significant product-related R & D investments, as research and development targets manufacturing processes and production systems, rather than new product development. This is the case for the food industry, where country heterogeneity in consumer preferences plays a key role, whereas the IPLC model assumes their complete homogeneity. Finally, transportation costs may surpass the cost advantage obtained in Stage 3 by producing in low-cost countries.

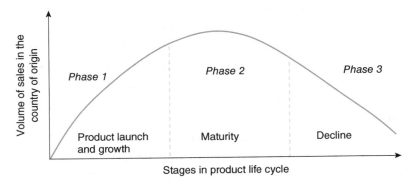

Point of strength in the marketing mix	Novelty of the product	Distribution promotion advertising	Price
Factors explaining the internationalisation stage	Technological advance due to previous R & D	Emergence of competitors in foreign countries	Search for low-cost sources for purchasing and/or manufacturing
Stage of internationalisation	Exports from the home country	Foreign subsidiaries with production and sales operations	Production in low-cost countries and e-export to home country

Figure 4.2 International Product Life Cycle

Source: Adapted from Vernon, R.P. (1966). International investment and international trade in the product life cycle. *Quarterly Journal of Economics*, vol. LXXX, no. 2, 191–207.

Internal causes pushing firms to internationalise

Market-related factors are not the only things that drive a firm toward internationalisation. The capacity to save transaction costs (e.g., costs of contracting with foreign intermediaries, commissions and fees, and costs related to monitoring their behaviour and performance) has pushed multinational companies (MNCs) away from pure market-based solutions (i.e., exporting to, or finding intermediaries to sell their products in the market) toward building a vast network of integrated subsidiaries. Many international firms do this by integrating former intermediaries (i.e., taking over formerly independent agents and transforming them into a fully owned sales subsidiary or taking over a foreign manufacturing or subcontracting firm). MNCs also strive to internalise their competitive or firm-specific advantages in order to protect themselves from competitors and possible imitation.

Eclectic theory of international production

John Dunning's eclectic theory of international production[7], also known as the ownership, location, internalisation (OLI) framework, is an evaluation framework that international companies should follow in order to decide if it is beneficial to pursue foreign direct investment (FDI). Eclectic theory explains FDI from the perspective of internalising competitive advantages, as well as other *firm-specific advantages*, such as assets that are proprietary to a firm, whether tangible or intangible (e.g., technologies, patents, trademarks, know-how in manufacturing, organisation, and marketing). One of the main advantages of internalising firm-specific advantages is protecting proprietary knowledge from being imitated and copied by competitors. Firm-specific advantages are better protected, developed, and capitalised on in a fully owned subsidiary, with a clear hierarchical attachment to headquarters, than they are with independent partners who might opportunistically exploit and disseminate those advantages.

Location-specific or *country-specific advantages* are external (i.e., non-firm) advantages related to local markets and countries, in terms of human resources, raw materials, cost of manpower, etc. Country-specific advantages are key determinants of target location choices, especially from a comparative perspective, in which a number of *candidate countries* are compared for FDI. The multinational firm decides about its internationalisation strategy by maximising the transfer and protection of its firm-specific advantages, and by using relevant country-specific advantages.

Globalisation of competition is a dynamic process. If an international company wants to remain globally competitive, it must constantly outpace its most significant competitors, and therefore be ahead of them in its internationalisation process. The time lag between external factors of internationalisation (often quick and unforeseen) and internal factors (often a lengthy learning process) implies that internationalisation evolves over time (see **Figure 4.3**). Therefore, it is necessary to have some lead time over competitors in terms of organisational learning regarding international operations. The example of the many multinational companies from smaller countries, such as Sweden and Switzerland, shows that going international is essential for growth when the home market is small. The Swedish School on the internationalisation of the firm (Uppsala, Stockholm School of Economics), as well as the academic contributions made by other Nordic countries (Finland, Denmark) in the field of corporate internationalisation, show that they recognised the problem and potential early on. However, the model, which emphasises learning (both organisation and human resources) and progressive and increasing commitment vis-à-vis international markets (Vahlne and Johanson, 2017)[8], is now questioned with the advent of *born global* companies (Oviatt and McDougall, 2005)[9]. Born global companies (e.g., Cochlear, an Australian company producing implants for the profoundly deaf) pursue globalisation from the beginning without having to go through a lengthy learning process.

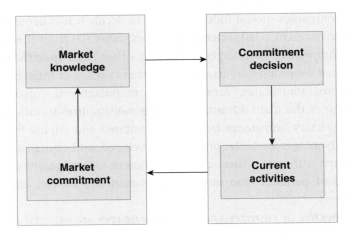

Figure 4.3　The progressive process of learning about and commitment to foreign markets

Source: Adapted from Vahlne, J. E., & Johanson, J. (2017). From internationalization to evolution: The Uppsala model at 40 years. *Journal of International Business Studies, 48*(9), 1087–1102. Printed with permission of Springer Nature.

4.2 Selection of target markets

Analytical tools are available to help identify and organise the information that is crucial to consider in the selection of target markets. For instance, the **SWOT** approach identifies internal factors (strengths and weaknesses), as well as external factors (opportunities and threats) that can help the potential investor to understand which markets have more potential, and fewer associated risks[10]. These types of analytical tools offer guidance and flexibility in the factors that should be considered, including cultural and contextual insights (e.g., cultural distance and political risk). Small to medium enterprises that use a systematic approach in selecting target foreign target markets perform better than their rivals[11].

The choice of target country has to consider political risk, as well as the business climate (i.e., the ease of doing business in a country independently of its political risk), and the perspectives of the local market (i.e., primary demand, growth, competition), the local taxation system, the existing tax treaties (bilateral fiscal conventions), and the local foreign exchange and the degree of freedom in transferring funds abroad. **Appendix 4.1 offers a detailed Checklist of criteria for deciding about target (country) markets.**

Assessing foreign environments and appraising risks in local markets

In general, risks related to international operations are largely balanced and often compensated for by opportunities, even in the riskiest markets and countries. A major external opportunity lies in the identification of emerging and developing markets in countries where primary demand is still growing (non-saturated markets). Other opportunities include lower taxation rates (tax avoidance, not fraud), much lower labour costs (to be gauged, however, against local manpower productivity, which may also be quite low), and more economic freedom in general.

Business risks in the international environment

Commercial risk includes issues around trust, concerning distant and often unknown business partners. The worst course of action is blind trust, which may lead to a negative and traumatic experience. For example, companies that are new to exporting often fail to be paid because they exported to a foreign market without checking for the risks of opportunistic behaviour from their foreign client. There are formal/legal solutions that are widely practised, especially for the first contract, which is based on the International Chamber of Commerce (ICC) standard terms for international trade (e.g., Incoterms, Letter of Credit, etc.). However, drafting and signing international contracts has its limitations, as avenues to enforce international contracts can be costly and time-consuming. One way to get around this is to take out international trade operations insurance. This is a solution frequently used for large deals (e.g., turnkey plants, large international projects). For these reasons, developing relationships in the long term with just a few partners is probably the best course of action.

Other major risks that cannot be ignored in international operations include political risk, credit risk (i.e., not being paid for a buyer's credit), legal risks related to the differences in legal systems worldwide, and financial risks related to foreign exchange and the potential losses due to exchange rate fluctuations. Here we address political risk, which may be related to other types of risk, and can change quite suddenly to dramatically affect a firm's performance.

Political risk in the international environment

Political risk is not solely about serious political events, such as riots, revolution, coups, terrorist attacks, hostages, etc. Political risk can also translate into negative consequences for foreign firms, including the following:

- nationalising firm assets (i.e., expropriation/confiscation);
- inserting a local partner into the foreign firm;
- prohibition of repatriation of funds (e.g., dividends, royalties);
- threats to expatriate personnel or mistreatment of local staff;
- unilateral breach of contract;
- payment failures;
- export restrictions to manufacturing (i.e., incurring expenses for manufacturing parts and/or equipment that cannot be any longer exported because of political risk); and
- loss of assembly equipment (i.e., having assembly equipment in a country where negative political events make it impossible to repatriate equipment, which must be left on site and possibly damaged).

A number of consulting companies, as well as large international banks, identify criteria and weightings to calculate and publish a *Composite Index of Political Risk* (Country Ratings), which is based on the following formula:

$$I_p = \sum_{i=1}^{i=n} P_i . N_{ip}$$

Where I_p is the Index of political risk for country p (country risk); N_{ip} is the rating of country p on criterion i (n criteria), and P_i = Weighting of criterion i in the overall rating.

The most often-used criteria in political risk indices relate to different types of heterogeneities (e.g., linguistic, ethnic, and religious heterogeneity and conflicts), which, if not properly managed by the groups and the local authorities, may result in bloody conflicts or even long-lasting civil wars or military incursions (e.g., Russia's invasion of Ukraine). Some current examples of ethnic and religious division can be found in the Middle East (e.g., in Afghanistan and Israel). However, political stability and the degree of democracy should also be considered key factors in considering political risk. In situations where voting is based on ethnic/religious belonging, and more powerful groups can prevail over rival groups (e.g., minority ethnic groups), as is the case in many African countries, the risk is increased. In addition, the latent, or sometimes explicit, influence of neighbouring political powers (e.g., Pakistan and Afghanistan) is often cited as a factor increasing political risk.

Income disparities, as well as inequality in wealth across different strata of the population (measured by GINI, the General Inequality Index), also contribute to social instability, lack of consensus, and finally to political risk. Non-realistic foreign exchange control systems (e.g., Iran or Venezuela) and the non-convertibility of the local currency (Argentinian Peso is virtually impossible to convert; its value was 1:1 with USD in 1992, but in September 2022 it was worth less than 1c), are a ferment of corruption and a disincentive for local entrepreneurs. This often translates into rather negative attitudes towards foreign firms and foreign direct investment, etc.

Rating Agencies, such as BERI (Business Environment Risk Index) and ICRG (International Country Risk Guide), issue country ratings and full analyses of countries. Country risk ratings are also prepared by major international banks and financial rating agencies, such as Moody's, Standard & Poor's, etc. The *World Competitiveness Report* issued by the World Economic Forum, which organises the annual Davos global conference, and the *CIA World Factbook,* are also first-rate sources for finding comparative country information. Both are easily accessible on the internet.

Political risk: Coverage/Insurance

The impact of political risk differs according to the mode of a foreign operation (local subsidiary, exporting, joint venture, etc.). Various strategies can be used to avoid or cover political risk:

1. The simplest and most effective is a *Go/No Go Strategy*, whereby a multinational company systematically avoids high-risk countries, because there is enough potential in low-risk countries.
2. The second strategy reduces risk by investing little cash in foreign contexts (e.g., Coca Cola, which initially exported through local bottlers but has now moved to fully owned subsidiaries).
3. The third strategy is preventive, where the network of subsidiaries is organised so that none of them can effectively work without supplying to, and purchasing from, other subsidiaries (i.e., the 'empty shell' strategy). If local company assets are nationalised by a foreign government, the subsidiary is unable to survive without other subsidiaries in the network.
4. The fourth strategy is to cover political risk through an insurance policy for international operations. This is more frequently used for large project sales than for foreign direct investment.
5. A fifth strategy is to confront local authorities; however, this rarely occurs because firms, even large multinational companies, are weaker than sovereign states.

Insurance contracts can be used to cover non-payment in case of political risk or commercial risk. These contracts may protect exporters against manufacturing risk, as well as credit risk, but not against risks related to the nationalisation of local subsidiaries. Credit insurance is often available from semi-public bodies (Hermès and Kfw in Germany, Coface in France, US Eximbank in the USA, ECGD in Great Britain, etc.), and increasingly from private insurance companies. Large international operations (e.g., turnkey plants) are often financed by a loan to the foreign buyer, where the loan repayment must be insured at 90–95% for risky foreign buyers to be financed (financing schemes are coordinated within the OECD Consensus).

IDENTIFYING MARKET OPPORTUNITIES

Appendix 4.1 lists criteria that should be considered in the process of selecting new target markets. The most important criteria for the industry and the firm's priorities can be selected and ranked for the selection of (1) regions of the world, then (2) countries within selected regions, and then (3) consumer segments within and across selected countries. At each step, the analysis becomes more detailed, as shown here:

1. Regions can be compared using relevant, easily accessible, secondary data at the macro level (e.g., cultural similarity, geographic proximity, political stability, labour costs, and potential for economic growth).
2. Countries within selected regions can then be compared on more detailed secondary data at the meso level, which should include industry and consumer information (e.g., market size, product ownership, and the level of competition).
3. Consumer segments within and across countries can then be compared using secondary and often primary data at the micro level to help identify and better understand segments with the most potential (e.g., buyer behaviour and lifestyle factors).

After the new international market(s) have been chosen, an in-depth comparison with the home country should be undertaken to identify relevant differences at the macro (e.g., demographic, economic, political, legal/regulatory, business, and cultural environments), meso (e.g., competitive product positioning, and wholesale, distributor, retail, and online landscape for getting products to consumers), and micro (e.g., customer tastes, preferences and buying criteria) levels. The more distinct the differences are, the more attention needs to be paid to potential customisation of the marketing strategy.

ACCESSING SECONDARY INFORMATION

One of the major issues in cross-cultural and international market research has to do with limited availability of data and limited resources to collect it. Fortunately, it is relatively easy to locate preliminary information about a region or country of interest online, including macro-environmental factors (e.g., political, legal, geographical, economic, and cultural information) and even meso- and micro-environmental factors (e.g., market size, distribution systems, presence of local and global competition, and consumer information). This information can be compiled into an initial industry or buyer behaviour analysis that can inform the initial stages of marketing decisions. Access to secondary information over the internet is fast, easy, and cheap, but it is also somewhat difficult to validate. As such, the source of the information, and any potential biases, should be considered.

The internet can also provide a wealth of other relevant information. Consumer ratings, comments, blogs, and other posts can be researched to examine product and competitor reputation in order to identify new opportunities. For established businesses, it can be useful to track exposure to websites, products, advertising, company information and patterns of use (e.g., search patterns). It is also easy to communicate directly with customers and potential customers through bulletin boards and by interacting with comments. Further, online surveys and focus groups can be used to collect primary data. The main caveat is that much of this information is limited to the more active users, who may, or may not, represent the target audience.

4.3 Modes of entry into foreign markets

Entry modes differ on the basis of whether cash investment and/or local partners are involved.

1. Modes of entry with foreign direct investment (FDI) include sales and/or manufacturing subsidiaries and joint ventures (with a local partner).
2. Modes of entry with local partners without cash investment (i.e., know-how rather than equity-based) include licensing, franchising, and management contracts.

3. Modes of entry without local partners or cash investment include exporting
    (direct, intermediated from the home country or in the country of destination).

The *choice of foreign entry modes* for international marketing operations should take
into account the triplet (1) target country, (2) product(s) or service(s) proposed and
(3) mode of entry. Different modes of market entry are discussed below.

Foreign Direct Investment (types of subsidiaries and main choices)

Foreign direct investment either creates a local subsidiary from scratch (i.e., a greenfield investment) or takes over a local company. There are several key reasons for
foreign direct investment:

-   The **first** key reason is to be present in a target market, because tariff barriers
    (high duties), non-tariff barriers, high transportation costs, and/or market
    barriers all preclude exporting into the market.
-   The **second** key reason is the search for cost reduction, especially for
    manufacturing operations. Cost reductions can be found in lower labour costs,
    closeness to sources of raw materials and other key inputs, and closeness to
    markets and consumer demand. For manufacturers involved in foreign direct
    investment, a convenient cost-cutting solution is to locate in a Free-Trade Zone
    (FTZ, also called Export-Processing Zone; a limited area generally in a seaport,
    with no customs duties, limited taxation, and manpower available from the
    nearby surroundings).
-   A **third** key reason is for an international company to learn new
    competencies and increase its knowledge base, including country/linguistic
    competencies, negotiation skills, and intercultural management abilities and
    management knowledge.

Some subsidiaries only deal with manufacturing to cut costs, based on country-
specific advantages, whereas others (i.e., integrated and mixed subsidiaries) include
the creation of a sales subsidiary that takes care of local marketing, managing distribution, and providing direct contact with final consumers. *Integrated subsidiaries* locally
manufacture and market products and/or services from the parent company, without
being dependent on supplies from other subsidiaries. In contrast, in *mixed subsidiaries*,
manufacturing and marketing are relatively independent. In this case, there can be a
different product range for production and sales, with exports to and supplies from

other subsidiaries. This leads to the integration of manufacturing and sales subsidiaries within a global organisation, with different manufacturing and/or sales specialisation for each subsidiary and a global sourcing organisation.

The systematic search for the best possible location for each element of the value chain is a key determinant of a multinational company's organisational decisions. Two decisions are key for the control of international operations: (1) whether the subsidiary is a fully new operation (*a greenfield investment*) or an acquisition (a takeover), and (2) whether it is a partnership (possibly with a minority interest) or fully owned. **Figure 4.4** highlights key aspects of an FDI decision, as a decision tree.

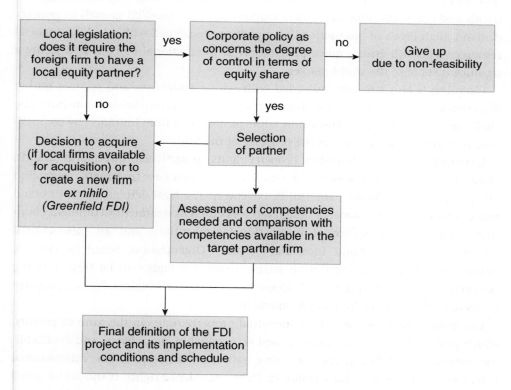

Figure 4.4 Important aspects of an FDI decision (decision tree)

Licensing agreements

A license is a right to manufacture and/or commercialise products or processes corresponding to a particular technology. It is often associated with patents and trademarks, but not always; technology is also embedded in non-patented know-how (e.g., industrial designs, technical manuals, procedures, or pure know-how). However, there are two main strategic risks associated with licensing agreements: (1) the licensee may become a competitor, and/or (2) the licensee may be incompetent, in that they do not perform adequately, leading to market failure and the closure of a market for which it has been granted exclusive rights.

When is licensing a proper international marketing strategy? **First**, licensing may be imposed by the host country because of restrictions on imports (prohibitions, limitations), import-substitution policies (targeting the replacement of imports by local manufacturing), and transfer of technology policies (import know-how and technology, rather than products). **Second**, licensing may fit with market trends and corporate resources, where markets have double-digit growth in primary demand, high levels of international competition, combined with a lack of financial resources. This will ensure quick penetration in international markets and secure a significant share of the world market.

Licensing is also strongly associated with selling know-how and services (rather than products), either technology-based expertise or marketing-based know-how. The challenge then is spreading know-how while protecting it from imitation by competitors, thus keeping know-how as the property of the firm.

Licensing is related to industrial property rights, in particular, trademarks (brands, brand names). The acceptability of a particular brand name for trademark registration must be proven (originality, anteriority, coverage). The legal determination of brand name versus shop sign, model or design receives different treatment in different countries. Despite the existence of international conventions and an international organisation (WIPO, World Industrial Property Organization, based in Geneva, Switzerland), trademark registration largely remains a matter to be treated at the national level, except in the EU. Trademarks are different from intellectual property rights (copyright for books, records, movie films, etc.).

Licensing is also associated with industrial property rights in the form of patents, which protect the inventor's rights (based on originality, precedence, and applicability). Patents are still largely registered on a national basis, despite some international patent conventions (e.g., Paris Union of 1899, precedence right). It should be noted that patent registration has the drawback of 'informing' competitors. Furthermore, what is technically original is not necessarily patentable, since industrial applicability must be demonstrated in a number of countries. Finally, there is much diversity in registration and patent prolongation procedures across countries. The international protection of industrial property rights has been the subject of negotiation in the WTO, with the TRIPS agreement (Trade-Related Industrial Property Rights), which continues to be an issue (see WTO website).

Type and purpose of contract, interdependence, and market relationship

Licensing/franchising contracts are deals that revolve around patented technology and know-how (i.e., non-patented technology), as described above. Industrial property rights are a central issue in such negotiations, with the caveat that industrial property rights must be understood in the same way by both partners (for cultural differences on industrial property rights, see Li[12]). Respecting industrial property rights and complying with industrial property rules may be a problematic issue, based on whether the industrial property rights constitute a private or a public good[13]. Asian countries, especially China, do not attach the same formal and legal importance to industrial property rights as Western, especially American, negotiators do.

The *licensing deal* and *licensing relationship* are deeply intermingled in licensing agreements: the relationship is as important as the deal itself because such agreements involve long-term cooperation, with a win-win perspective and much integrative potential. However, there are significant potential benefits for the party adopting an opportunistic stance. There is often a large gap in terms of knowledge and information between the potential partners that encourages opportunistic behaviour on both sides. Control is key, especially for franchising, as well as being ready to litigate if needed in the case of trademark and patent infringement by the licensee or franchisee, or non-respect for the contractual rules. The major cultural-institutional-legal differences lie in the acceptance or not of the private appropriation of 'proprietary' knowledge versus inventions and knowledge, in general, being viewed as a public good.

Licensing involves different forms of industrial property rights related to trademarks, such as brands, brand names[14], and patents[15]. Licensing may also cover intellectual property rights related to copyright. A license is a right granted by the industrial property right owner (licensor) to manufacture and/or commercialise products or processes corresponding to a particular technology to a licensee. Licensing is most often associated with patents and trademarks, but not always; technology is also embedded in non-patented know-how: industrial designs, technical manuals, procedures, and/or pure know-how (i.e., individuals who know how to do it).

Clauses in licensing agreements

As in the case of agency-dealership contracts (explained in the next section), territorial clauses combined with exclusivity are the central parts of the license agreement. Rights to manufacture and/or commercialise combine with exclusivity/non-exclusivity. An exclusive license precludes the patent owner from manufacturing and/or selling in the granted territories, and no other licensee can be appointed. In a non-exclusive license, the licensee is generally not allowed to further license other companies. Manufacturing is generally limited to the territory of the licensor (i.e., the licensor gives up the right to manufacture in the licensee's country), while commercialisation may be allowed for both exclusive territories (i.e., the licensor gives up the right to sell in these territories) and non-exclusive territories. In this case, licensor and licensee may be in competition to win customers, which may pose problems. Parties may foresee joint manufacturing operations, which have the advantage of increasing the licensor's control over the quality, delivery dates, and reliability in delivering a product or service meeting the requirements of the licensed technology. However, the licensor must then significantly increase their financial and managerial involvement to the extent that both companies would create a joint venture, which would then be the licensee.

An additional issue is to decide which brand will be used for the products and/or services under the license. Licensors often prefer that their brand is not used by the licensee because there is uncertainty about their manufacturing and marketing abilities. The licensor's reputation could suffer from a licensee's poor image. The solution is generally to keep the licensee brand or corporate name and add in fine print 'Manufactured under license from [the licensor's corporate name]'.

The license contract often also includes a clause about reciprocal information, as concerns new developments, and a confidentiality clause by which the licensor is forbidden from sharing information on the licensed technology with third parties (e.g., customers, competitors).

As to compensation, licensors generally prefer a flat fee, because it protects them against the licensee failing to manufacture and/or market according to the license agreement. Conversely, licensees generally prefer a variable fee, because it protects them against an outdated product which may be unsellable in their market area. License negotiation will often lead to balanced solutions, where a flat fee is granted against know-how documents (plans, designs, technical manuals, procedures) and a variable fee is based on sales as an incentive for the licensee to succeed in creating value from the industrial property rights they have acquired for a specific time period, as well as the probation period and tacit renewal, all to be negotiated.

Franchising agreements

The respective obligations of the franchiser and the franchisee reflect a strong asymmetry between them. The franchiser, generally a large company, supplies brands and associated trade-related industrial property rights, such as shop signs, designs, and models. They also often provide a number of services, such as store/outlet location studies,[16] training for the franchisee's personnel, technical assistance, and often, supplies from a central procurement facility. They also grant access to technical know-how and commercial know-how for flat fees and/or yearly royalties.

The franchisee, generally a much smaller, local firm, brings capital equity for the franchised outlets, as well as daily management. Franchisees pay an entry fee and annual royalties and sign a contractual commitment not to compete with the franchiser in case of franchising contract termination. Popular domains for international franchises are services, hotels, fast-food restaurants, and fashion stores. Industrial franchises are rare; a case in point is Yoplait, a major cooperative for milk-based products that grants franchises to other cooperative organisations worldwide. Strict control must be exercised by the franchiser over its franchisees, without lenience, especially if franchisees behave opportunistically.

A ***management contract***, generally a long-term agreement, provides that a company, often due to a lack of local skills, subcontracts its daily operations (e.g., manufacturing, management of personnel, accounting, marketing services and training) to a separate firm that manages in return for a fee, based on a mix of percentages of revenues and gross operating profits. Many hotels operate under management contracts, using the brand name of a major hotel chain, which brings economies of scale, access to global reservation systems, and world-class hotel management competencies. Management contracts can be used as an alternative to foreign direct investment when local regulations restrict this type of investment; furthermore, they reduce the exposure to political risk.

4.4 Exporting strategies

Major choices in foreign channel selection

It is difficult to disentangle key distribution channel decisions (discussed in Chapter 5 as part of the marketing mix) from decisions about the mode of entry. As can be seen in **Figure 4.5**, different modes of entry have more or less direct access to the final consumer and markets. It is far easier to develop a strong competitive position if a firm deals directly with the final consumer and understands the local competitive scene.

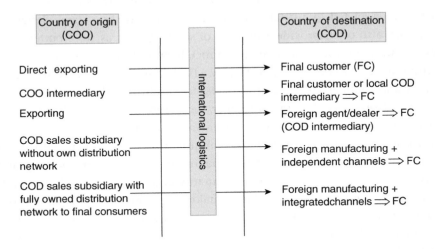

Figure 4.5 Major choices in foreign channel selection

Foreign markets can be accessed directly, or through intermediaries based in the home country (COO) or host country (COD), as well as through sales subsidiaries. Direct and indirect forms of exporting can be combined. When facing choices about foreign distribution policy in relation to entry modes, a company should consider the following questions:

- Should distribution be direct from the manufacturer to the final consumer?
- Should distribution start from the home country or in the country of destination?
- Which, if any, middlemen should be chosen, and how can relationships with key actors in local distribution channels be developed?
- Should distribution channels be independent or integrated?
- Should we prefer short or long channels?
- To what extent should a distribution system which has proven successful at home be extended to foreign markets?
- What is the best way to deal with locally embedded and cultural aspects of distribution channels?
- Which product range and services should be offered? Who stocks what, and who owns the stocked items?

● Should traditional or new international channels be chosen (e.g., brick-and-mortar retail versus direct marketing or E-commerce), or a combination of them?

Key differences in distribution channels worldwide

Major differences in the type and style of local retail outlets are related to population density, local retail regulations and traditions, the degree of concentration of major retail companies, opening hours, and the degree of automatisation (e.g., scanners, self-check-out). These differences also influence the product range carried in particular types of stores, even if the stores seem equivalent (e.g., a drugstore differs from a *droguerie*), as well as the services offered and interaction with shoppers in the store environment.

Culture is an important factor in distribution channels, especially whether people tend to view shopping as an opportunity to socialise, both with customers and merchants. Particular distribution systems, such as door-to-door selling (i.e., direct selling at home) may be popular in one country's culture and be almost non-existent in other places. The development of online versus brick-and-mortar depends on local conditions, especially the development of broadband internet, and the quality and reliability of the local postal service (true for any form of distance selling).

Short versus long distribution channels depend on the degree to which a complex, vertical chain of wholesalers and semi-wholesalers is necessary to reach retail outlets (as is the case with the Japanese distribution *keiretsu* system[17]), or whether major distributors are dominant and bypass intermediaries in the retail chain (as is the case in most countries of the European Union). The degree of conflict within the local distribution system, as well as the degree of openness to foreign suppliers, are other crucial factors. Smaller countries (e.g., Finland, Switzerland) have only a few players who tend to adopt a somewhat protectionist stance, defending the local brands whenever possible.

The criteria for choosing foreign distribution channels include:

1. **Consumers** and their characteristics;
2. **Culture** (distribution is tightly linked to local styles of interaction);
3. **Character** (image projected by the channel);
4. **Capital** (financial resources necessary to start and maintain the channel including fixed and working capital);
5. **Cost** (trade margins rather than to overhead costs);
6. **Competition** (in local channels, including local cartels);

7. **Coverage** (geographic coverage);
8. **Continuity** (the channel should continue to be usable, avoiding bankruptcy or other financial difficulties); and
9. **Control** (where the ideal situation is when the company creates its own distribution network).

Direct exports

Direct export, also called *open distribution* (i.e., without any intermediary, whether at home or in the country of destination), is often used by newcomers to exporting activities. A company receives orders from abroad and responds on the basis of taking the full risk in contracts, delivery, and payment. In international sales, export contracts are often short-term, one-shot deals with little or no interdependence, especially in a globalised market for standardised items, in highly competitive markets, where price is the main negotiation issue. There are three main types of direct exports:

1. new-to-export companies, which often passively provide their products for open distribution;
2. international sales contracts, usually for globally traded standardised business-to-business (B2B) items (e.g., commodities); and
3. direct export sales of customised industrial equipment, often hi-tech products and/or services, in B2B bilateral oligopolies.

The problem of new-to-export companies (generally small-to-medium enterprises (SMEs)) is the lack of experience with international shipments, payment problems, and an underestimation of opportunistic behaviours in distant markets. The second type, sales contracts for globally traded standardised items, is facilitated by online B2B purchase platforms (e.g., Alibaba, Europages) or online B2B marketplaces. Negotiation, which is often electronic, centres on price, quantity, shipping and insurance, and delivery date. This often comes with a strong power imbalance in favour of the single buyer facing a rather large number of competing sellers found on online B2B purchase platforms (i.e., a sort of monopsony or a market heavily influenced by a single buyer). Business originating from internet platforms, especially in a B2B setting, is a pure deal. The third case is based on direct exports; that is, the buyer and seller are acquainted and have a relationship based on product and/or service customisation, which requires face-to-face negotiation. This is a worthy solution for niche industrial companies with very few clients worldwide (e.g., from 5 to 50), selling specialised products, often high-tech, to foreign corporate customers in a B2B relationship.

Export sales contracts may be largely deal-oriented, especially in the case of a new, unknown partner, and/or in a politically unstable context, with high legal and cultural distance[18]. A strong deal orientation and an *a priori* one-shot deal generally mean little interest and no willingness to bridge the cultural and/or linguistic gap. This could also be the case in repeat business that is embedded within successive one-shot deals with no particular relationship being developed.

Direct exports are a good solution for niche companies with very few clients worldwide (e.g., from 5 to 50). They suit the case of industrial companies selling specialised products in a B2B relationship with foreign corporate customers. There are strong limitations for firms relying on export sales and open international distribution in terms of their development and entry into foreign markets. In most cases, after some preliminary business deals, it may be necessary to have a middleman in the home country or a local partner in the country of destination. This enables knowledge of and contact with the foreign market. Direct exports are not a real presence, unless in the case of niche industrial companies having very few clients (e.g., 10 to 20) worldwide, with whom they can be in direct contact in a full-fledged business relationship.

Exports intermediated from the country of origin

Apart from direct export sales, there is a variety of solutions for exporting without leaving one's home country. An *export commissioner* is an intermediary, paid on a percentage fee of the goods exported; this is generally done by a small-sized company or even an individual freelance businessperson with a particular product/country(ies) specialisation. For example, a ski equipment exporter may go through an export commissioner who has military forces as their main clients to sell their equipment to countries with few ski resorts (e.g., India, Nepal, China).

A second solution is *export piggyback*, a term in which the metaphor is quite clear. In an export piggyback contract, the partners are (1) a company (*the carrier*) that has established distribution networks in the target market and (2) another company (*the rider*), often a SME, which sells its products through the *carrier's* network in exchange for a commission. Piggyback exporting is typically used for products for which the *carrier* and *rider* are not competitors, but are complementary (e.g., the rider SME is a supplier of the carrier in the domestic market).

International trading companies are the third solution. There are several hundred international trading companies with worldwide operations (50 to 200 sales offices all over the world in major cities). Some Japanese general trading companies (*Sogo-Shosha*) are large and well known, such as *Mitsui Bussan, Mitsubishi Shōji, Sumitomo Shoji, Marubeni, C. Itoh, Nissho Iwai*, etc. They export for SMEs from all over the world which do not have easy access to foreign markets. It should be stressed that exporters sometimes do not even know who the final customer is and have, therefore, no consumer knowledge concerning their exports.

A fourth solution for 'easy exports' is to sell to *buying offices*, which the to-be-exporter can find in its home country. Buying offices are specialised procurement departments within large distributors searching for foreign suppliers, including department stores, brick-and-mortar traditional retailers, mail-order companies (catalogue sales), and pure online platforms. *Professional buyers* travel around the world to search for potential suppliers for items sold in department stores and catalogues, and often have permanent offices in key supplying countries. For instance, a Romanian or Bulgarian SME may export furniture through an IKEA buying office: the pieces of furniture are based on IKEA design, and IKEA exerts strict control over manufacturing quality in local plants. However, the exporting SME has no control over brands, final consumer prices, etc. Buying offices and trading companies do not necessarily offer much continuity in the export business, nor do they provide the opportunity to learn about foreign markets, local consumers, or local competitive scenes, and so the exporters do not gain international experience.

Exports intermediated by a middleman in the destination country

There is slightly more opportunity to learn about foreign markets when exports are intermediated by a middleman in the destination country, including agents, dealers, distributors, or importers-distributors. Another possibility is to have a *local branch* (popular for banking and insurance) or a local representative, which is not a subsidiary (i.e., not a local company, registered according to local corporate law with the parent company having most or all of its equity capital; that is, full control). A local branch depends for its accounting and financial reporting directly from its parent company abroad.

Agents

Agent/distributor and dealer contracts correspond to exports intermediated by a middleman in the destination country, generally a foreign agent acting as an intermediary with local customers. Such agents most often represent multiple exporting companies (possibly competitors, beware!). Foreign agents are generally paid through commissions on sales. The degree of marketing delegation from the exporter to the agent (on brand, promotion, advertising, sales documents, etc.) varies; it is often low. The exporting firm contracts with and invoices the final customer; the foreign agent is commissioned on the sale.

The foreign agent, being a small local partner, apparently has a weaker position compared to an international/global company in terms of size, professionalism, financial capacities, etc. However, the local partner brings key assets: a deep understanding of the local market, insider knowledge of the local culture, proficiency in the local language(s), familiarity with the institutional system, and a network of relationships with local companies. Who should adapt to whom in terms of language, culture, and negotiation style? Usually, the local partner will adjust, speaking English and pretending to be the typical international businessperson. However, this adaptation could be partly misleading for those who are adapted to.

Agency contracts may cover an exclusive, a non-exclusive, or a mix of exclusive and non-exclusive sales territories. If exclusive, the foreign agent will always receive fees for any sale on its contractual territory, even if the deal has been closed by the exporter without any agent's involvement. Conversely, in the case of a non-exclusive contract, the exporter may hire other non-exclusive agents for the same territory and/or directly sell to final customers, bypassing the agent(s). The main aspects of the agency contract abroad are:

1. the area(s) covered, depending on whether they are exclusive or non-exclusive sales territories, or a mix of both, according to particular sub-regions explicitly mentioned in the agency contract;
2. the product(s) and services covered;
3. the forms of commissioning (e.g., flat percentage fee, increasing or decreasing percentage according to sales figure, etc.);
4. the degree of marketing delegation (degree of leeway in terms of brands, trade documents, sales promotion efforts, if any);
5. maintenance of a spare parts inventory (it is possible, however not always the case), as well as after-sales service (rare for agents);
6. contract duration: probation period, tacit or explicit renewal;
7. clauses about possible cases of contract resolution and termination of the contract;
8. legal precautions: clauses designating the law governing the contract, arbitration clause, clauses about provisions for possible litigation; and
9. a possible clause concerning minimal sales to be reached by the agent for the contract to be maintained in force.

The first risk associated with agents is that of a hidden market closure, because the agent also represents a competitor of the exporting firm which is unaware of this bond. The closure may be either a total market closure or a partial market closure (for a particular product and/or part of the sales territory). The second risk is that local courts grant financial damages to former agents when agency contracts are terminated. Therefore, it is advisable to look at local practices and rules before choosing an agent.

Dealers in foreign markets: Main aspects

Dealerships are a stronger business relationship than agency contracts; a dealer represents a brand for a particular territory (generally on an exclusive basis) and offers after-sales service and spare parts. The dealer generally buys from its principal and resells to end customers. For example, Caterpillar, the world leader in earthmoving equipment, has a worldwide network of dealers; the Coca-Cola Company also uses local bottlers and beverage distributors as Coca-Cola dealers. However, Coca-Cola has increasingly created fully owned local subsidiaries over the last 30 years.

4.5 Dealing with foreign partners
Adjusting to local environments

Foreign companies in a local context initially lack hands-on experience and knowledge of the cultural and institutional environment. As foreign players, they lack the relational network, social skills, and know-how for dealing with local people that insiders have. They do not have local language proficiency, a key factor in facilitating communication and doing business. Firms operating abroad also face additional costs compared to local firms, a phenomenon called a *liability of foreignness* (LOF)[19]. LOF is dynamic and generally diminishes over time, after experience with, and adjustment to the local context. In this respect, good relationships with an agent, a dealer, or a partner in a local joint venture are likely to decrease LOF.

LOF is a concept different from that of *cultural distance*, but the two notions are related. Cultural distance is the degree to which cultural assumptions, norms and values, and legal and institutional systems differ between two countries, which has an impact on both companies and consumer preferences. Cultural distance has been operationalised, with the USA as a baseline country, often using the deviation between the two countries along Hofstede's four cultural dimensions (i.e., power distance, uncertainty avoidance, masculinity/femininity, and individualism) in a composite index[20].

LOF can be assumed to be higher in a very distant country/culture. However, as the preceding chapter on intercultural interactions explained, there are many ways to facilitate adjustment to the local context, partners, and consumers, in culturally distant contexts, and reduce LOF.

Additional ways to reduce LOF include the following:

- Having a local partner (agent, partner in a joint venture) present, especially if the relationship is long-term oriented and strong enough to overcome conflicts that will inevitably occur when implementing joint decisions. Learning from the local partner is likely to reduce the psychic distance[21] between associates, a concept at the border between individual values and the societal values reflected in the cultural distance.
- Using local brand names, utilising local personnel rather than expatriates, and nurturing a positive attitude to the local cultural and social environment (i.e., avoiding critical attitudes and demeaning judgements vis-à-vis the local culture and institutions). Facing competition as a new entrant is a particular facet of LOF. If local players are, in one form or another, members of an unofficial cartel and decide to bar, or at least hinder, the entrance of a foreign competitor into their *chasse gardée* (i.e., their private hunting ground), the potential entrant should be aware of this and try to get acquainted with one or two local players, and possibly enter into a partnership with one of them.

Negotiating and contracting with foreign partners

Typical intercultural business negotiation contracts between partners from different countries and cultures vary in terms of the (1) time span, (2) partner compatibility, and (3) understanding of what a signed contract involves. **First**, time span primarily refers to the contract period in effect; however, it may also apply to whether or not a duration is set, whether short-term contracts repeat over time, and how to deal with planning trouble, delay, postponement, and rescheduling. Special attention and care will be needed to avoid time-related conflicts and misunderstandings. This is illustrated by the termination of agency-dealership contracts, as well as with the complex and uncertain completion of turnkey projects. **Second**, partners, may share a common culture and a similar mindset, as might be expected between Western multinational companies, or they may each have a different culture, language, or mindset that affexts their interaction and their assumptions about the deal. **Third**, understanding what a signed contract involves in terms of rights and obligations is more difficult between high- and low-context cultures, as the terms of the agreement in high-context cultures is likely to be more implicit, and rely more on people and the relationship than is the case in low-context cultures, which rely on precise, explicit contractual clauses and frown upon the perspective of renegotiation. Even if there are joint legal frameworks for contracts (e.g., sales contracts), interpretation of agreements is subject to differences in language and legal traditions. The proportion of deal and the proportion of relationship, as well as their respective natures, differ in each type of contractual arrangement.

The following types of intercultural business negotiation (ICBN) contracts are examined:

- *International export sales contracts* range from deal-oriented to relationship-oriented negotiations according to the market background, standard versus customised item being traded, etc. International sales contracts and export contracts are predominantly deal-oriented, with one-shot discrete transactions, and limited relationship development, unless deals are repeated over time, and both partners are willing to enter into a relationship.
- In *agent-dealer-distributor contracts*, the relationship is important, and termination after successful collaboration needs to be managed with great care; sales deals with local customers are embedded within the contractual relationship with the local intermediary.
- In *license agreements*, the deal is reflective of the extent of the licensor's trust in the capacities of the to be licensee. In the post-agreement phase, the relationship is important.
- *International joint venture* negotiations are more relationship-oriented than deal-oriented; they are, at first, quite cooperative and future-oriented. Building a good working relationship to manage the international joint venture seems logical; however, relationships may not survive the acid test of actual international joint venture implementation and development.

International export sales contracts

Generally, export sales follow a deal-oriented pattern, legally and globally, with possibly a no-trust, no-relationship solution. This entails standard international sales contracts, which are key instruments to secure deal-related aspects. Such standard contracts are either imposed by the more powerful party (i.e., their own standardised contract) and/or derived from an international standard contract. Potential recourse to litigation is based either on arbitration (the International Chamber of Commerce [ICC] represents millions of companies in over 100 countries) or on the law and the courts of the powerful party. The deal conditions in terms of shipment, freight insurance, property, and risk transfer, are based on ICC Incoterms standards. The payment is secured by a Letter of Credit through the intermediation of banks as third parties.

For this type of export contract, especially in the case of globally traded standard-ised items, much of the negotiation takes place online, through dedicated websites, email, or videoconferencing, with little or no face-to-face negotiation. Relational expectations from the less powerful party may emerge over time after successful deals, especially if there are few alternative partners for the powerful party (e.g., a bilateral oligopoly market background). Repeat business and non-standardised (i.e., custom-ised) items may require some face-to-face negotiation, travelling to meet the sales partner, investing in significant transaction costs, on technology, specifications, deliv-ery schedule, shipping, etc. If, in addition, the representatives of both buyer and seller firms are the same over the years, asymmetrical loyalty expectations may arise from a non-Western partner (being relational, HC, etc.). Loyalty expectations must, however, be kept under strict control, because they are not in the very nature of this type of business agreement.

Agent-dealer-distributor contracts

As noted earlier, dealerships are a stronger business relationship than agency con-tracts. A dealer represents a brand for a particular territory (generally on an exclusive basis); it most often offers after-sales service and spare parts to local customers and buys from its principal and reselling to end-customers.

Contract negotiation processes. There are two levels of contract negotiation: the first level is based on repeated deals (sales contracts with customers in the foreign market), while the second level is non-repetitive (i.e., the intermediation contract with the foreign agent, which may cover several years before being terminated or renegotiated).

Interdependence issues have to be considered, taking into account that agents often represent many foreign exporters. The foreign exporter is bound to the local agent for several years. Relationship development is needed and should often be pro-active on the part of the foreign exporter.

Global companies, however, sometimes change their internationalisation strat-egies because they want to increase control over their foreign operations and consequently decide to replace foreign agents by sales subsidiaries. This strategic move may lead to contract termination with the local agent, despite the agent having done a good job over years, and regardless of the quality of the foreign-exporter/local-agent relationship.

Agency or dealership agreements are indeed embedded in the relationship, espe-cially if it is an exclusive contract. Implementation problems may arise on both sides. There may be very few deals, and the market is virtually closed to the foreign exporter if the agreement is exclusive. Alternatively, deals are closed with local customers without the agent being aware of it because they were negotiated in the foreign exporter's home country. For instance, when the exporter, a multinational firm, deals directly with the headquarters of another MNC because of centralised purchasing systems, its local subsidiaries are subordinated to the headquarters' decision and have no reason to contact the local agent, if even the subsidiary is aware of the local agent's existence.

Three-party sales negotiations follow the two-party negotiation of the agency-dealership contract. As in any intermediation, sales deals always involve foreign exporter, local agent, and local customers (see **Figure 4.6**). Choosing between a local agent and a sales subsidiary is a make-or-buy issue. A sales subsidiary will replace the local agent if direct contacts with the local market and with local customers, as well as integrated distribution, are required.

Opportunism on the part of local agents is rather frequent. First, the agent may, willingly or unwillingly, close the market, either by negligence and lack of involvement, or for the benefit of a foreign exporter's competitor, the foreign exporter being unaware of the local agent's covert and opportunistic behaviour. The risk of a hidden market closure can be divided into two threats: total market closure, and partial market closure (for a particular product or for a particular sales territory). Second, the local agent may unduly favour local customers, quietly forming a semi-coalition with some local customers against the foreign exporter (e.g., by reducing prices, granting special conditions, etc.), this being especially likely to arise in B2B markets. Third, the local agent may discreetly represent the foreign exporter's competitors, despite this being explicitly forbidden by the agency contract, assuming that exclusivity is bilateral.

Hence the key importance for the foreign exporter is a relationship with the local agent, which paradoxically consists of both *trust*, and a capacity to *control* the local agent's actions. This may give rise to expectations on the part of local agents that the foreign exporter will help even on personal, non-business-related matters (e.g., taking care of a son or daughter sent abroad for a study period). These highly personal demands may appear to be curious to some foreign exporters who may not be accustomed to rendering services as if they were almost a member of the extended family. Foreign export negotiators may even find such requests for friendly assistance in non-business-related matters somewhat shocking because this violates the Western norm of relatively strict separation between the personal sphere and business-related matters.

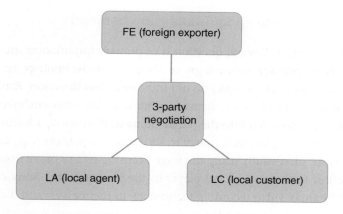

Figure 4.6   Three-party negotiations for agency/dealership agreements

As noted above, agency agreements may no longer support the objectives of one party, or context and circumstances may have evolved. In these cases, the agreement should be brought to an end. In case of termination, local courts often grant damages to former agents when agency contracts are terminated at the foreign exporter's initiative. Before starting the termination process, it is, therefore, advisable to look at local practices and rules and seek expert advice. Problems in dissolving an agency agreement have to be resolved by negotiation, especially when the agent has no responsibility in the circumstances leading to contract termination. Creative and positive solutions have to be envisaged for the termination issue. The first piece of advice is to avoid litigation, especially in a local court, which will certainly side with and support the agent; this is all the more likely when the local laws provide measures to financially repair agents, and the local jurisprudence has traditionally been generous in awarding damages to evicted agents. Consequently, it is advisable to agree on an out-of-court settlement with the terminated agent or dealer. If the foreign exporter's market presence is an objective for the future, any conflict that would result in a poor reputation for the foreign exporter in the local business environment is best avoided. A positive solution is to involve the local agent in the creation of the sales subsidiary, which will take the form of a joint venture in exchange for their acceptance of the agency contract termination. Finally, it is generally better to negotiate a termination indemnity with the local agent, rather than going to local courts and receiving a higher penalty.

Licensing/Franchising contracts

In technology sales, the following question is of primary importance: should the company license its proprietary technology, or should such technology be retained for internal growth? Historical examples do not indicate a clear direction. Rank Xerox kept their photocopying technology for themselves but were later overwhelmed by competition when the technology fell into the public domain. Pilkington, a British glassmaker, chose to license its float glass technology to its direct competitors (e.g., Corning Glass and Saint-Gobain), successfully using the huge licensing fees to move from its status as a local competitor to that of a global player in the glass industry. Sony chose to keep their superior Betamax video recording technology to themselves, and it never became the dominant standard in the market, except in the professional segment. Conversely, JVC chose to abundantly license its VHS technology, which became the arch-dominant standard in the market, especially in the consumer electronics segment.

Negotiation preparation should take into account the place of licenses and licensing, as a foreign market entry mode in the international business strategy of the licensor. Licensing abroad may be either a full mode of entry into foreign markets, or mere technology sales (versus selling products). The search for and selection of potential licensees requires being more careful in the case of foreign market entry mode licenses.

The strategic risk is that the licensee may become a competitor; an opposite risk is that the licensee may be incompetent, may not attain the desired objectives, and may close the market for which it has been granted exclusive rights. Either way, the licensor will suffer. A prospective licensee may later become a competitor or may try to opportunistically evade their duties for diverse alleged reasons (e.g., claiming to have developed a completely new technology, or exploiting local legislation that allow licensees to repudiate license agreements). Conversely, the success of the prospective licensee may be rather poor, causing the licensor to lose market potential granted to the licensee, without gaining much in licensing fees. In both cases (too good, too bad), the information asymmetry should be bridged before and/or during the negotiation process by requiring detailed and complete information from the prospective licensee and/or by performing audits, either financed by the licensee or by the licensor, or any negotiated scheme for sharing audit expenses. In any case, the licensor should try to hire their preferred auditing firm. If the prospective licensee refuses an audit, it is an indication that they are not confident about their own capacities to secure the optimum benefit of the license.

Sometimes licensing can lead to fake negotiations. For instance, when negotiating a know-how license a prospective licensee may deceptively negotiate in the hope of gathering technical information to copy, and then withdraw before closure for some sham reason. In such cases, the licensor may demand that the prospective licensee sign a non-disclosure agreement[22] before entering the licensing negotiation. A non-disclosure agreement strictly forbids the licensee to disclose information related to the to-be-licensed technology to third parties. It is often signed by the parties before entering into a negotiation.

International joint ventures (IJV)

In its most general definition, a joint venture is a cooperative agreement in which two or more businesses decide to pool resources in order to achieve a specific project or business activity (e.g., joint manufacturing, sales, R&D, etc.). A joint venture is often a separate company with assets and equity contributed by its owners and founders. In an international joint venture, two or more companies, or a MNC and a local partner, create a joint business entity for specific business activities. An international joint venture (IJV) has a strong cooperative stance from the outset, since it is an out-of-market, entrepreneurial alliance in which resources are shared, and partners have to agree on how the venture company will be managed. It is a long-term oriented joint project and is very open in the early phase of negotiation. Since it is based on combined resources, an IJV seems at first more integrative than distributive: value creation appears to dominate over value claims in the early stages of negotiation. Often partners already know each other (e.g., the local partner is the former agent, a subcontractor, or a distributor). There may be complementarities in the contributions brought by each IJV partner (e.g., manufacturing versus sales; local knowledge versus global experience; skills in technology and R&D versus operations/management; different types of assets being brought to the joint venture by each partner). However, despite a pleasant atmosphere in the early phase of negotiating the joint project, relationships may progressively deteriorate due to contextual differences, asymmetric contributions, power asymmetries, and the burgeoning discovery that interdependence is high after the venture has been formed and starts its operations. IJVs require a preparedness for continuous negotiation in the relational style.

Being a separate company, the objectives of the IJV cannot be reduced to those of the parent companies. The atmosphere of the negotiation may suffer from the dependence and autonomy of the joint venture negotiators (oriented towards *integrative value creation*) vis-à-vis their parent companies (more oriented toward *claiming value*). Also, problematic points at implementation must be carefully reviewed and discussed.

The main issues that need to be considered include:

1. the goals for the joint venture versus the goals of both partners;
2. the compatibility of objectives and the relational background between potential parent companies;
3. the joint assessment of critical (relevant) resources for the international joint venture;

4. the equity and asset contributions (e.g., cash, technology, facilities), as well as joint agreement on a balanced financial evaluation of partners' contributions;

5. integration in the local context and relationships with public authorities and future local employees, and management;

6. key management positions in the international joint venture (e.g., how are positions assigned and venture key staff recruited?);

7. clear assignment of responsibilities, management procedures, reporting;

8. the scope and nature of the relationship, especially in the case of significant cultural differences between partners;

9. the macro-environment, where the venture is going to operate, needs to be taken into account, particularly the local rules concerning international joint ventures and possible differences in legal traditions, especially if the country presents a rather hostile environment for both local employees and expatriate managers; and

10. communication and reporting rules and procedures that enable both partners to have similar information on how the international joint venture works.

There is no timeline for the international joint venture negotiation process. Negotiation is continuous until termination, although less intense during the periods when the international joint venture is established in routine manufacturing and/or sales.

There are two stages in negotiating international joint ventures: (1) a long negotiation at the start, followed by (2) continuous negotiation when running the venture together. The **first stage** is to negotiate the agreement, which can take several months and frequently more than one year, with regular meetings and top executives from the parent companies joining only in the very final stage. The pre-negotiation atmosphere may be rather positive and seemingly integrative, especially at the pure information exchange in the face-to-face negotiation stage. However, more distributive issues will emerge later, such as the funding of the venture, the distribution of key positions, the evaluation of assets, and the way to compensate equity and asset contributions (e.g., royalties, dividends, and/or reinvestment of profits in the venture). The **second stage** is permanent negotiation during the international joint venture's life. Contracts, even well prepared, cannot foresee all implementation details, unforeseen events, and minor conflicts arising throughout the duration of the venture. Interdependence, which is often low at the start, becomes quite high when implementing the venture, requiring a strong relational orientation in many non-Western perspectives. Even with only two parties, deal complexity can be high, because the venture is embedded in a complex series of side-agreements (e.g., a buy-back agreement for the venture's output, a license agreement where the international joint venture is the licensee, and the licensor is a patent-holding firm depending on the global parent company, a management contract, etc.). An international joint venture agreement may be integrated in a more complex scheme of arrangements designed to control the local partner in an unstable environment.

After the basic agreement is orally settled, negotiation will continue in drawing up a contract and related contractual agreements. The presence of lawyers is necessary at this stage to draft clauses related to the venture and in case of possible litigation between its parent companies (e.g., arbitration, laws governing the contract, etc.). An international joint venture is a sort of marital relationship. As in any marriage, divorce is also possible. However unpleasant it may seem, the ways and means to organise a divorce negotiation should be envisaged from the start; for instance, the venture's dissolution or a possible transformation into a company entirely owned and managed by one of the initial partners.

4.6 Controlling foreign operations

There are different basic ways of controlling foreign operations, with two main avenues: (1) control through proprietary know-how and marketing/management knowledge (vertical axis on **Figure 4.7**. below) and/or (2) control through the property (equity stake; cash investment (the horizontal axis on **Figure 4.7**. below)).

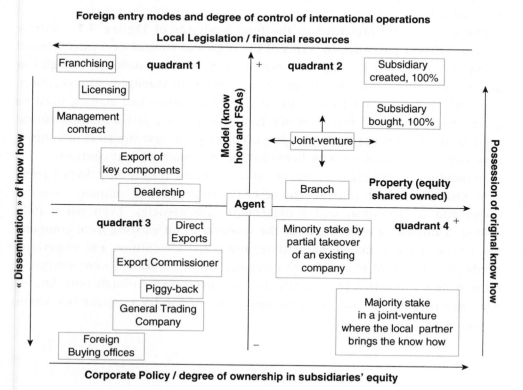

Figure 4.7   Foreign entry modes and control of international operations

The vertical axis corresponds to controlling by proprietary knowledge, based on know-how and firm-specific advantages (FSAs), comprising not only knowledge protected by industrial property rights, but also other forms of knowledge, including what has been learned throughout the internationalisation process. Possession or ownership of original knowledge (see positive arrow on the vertical right side) may increase the degree of control over particular foreign operations. However, the risk exists that proprietary knowledge is copied, or imitated by competitors and, therefore, stops being exclusive knowledge to the firm (see negative arrow on the vertical left side, 'dissemination').

The horizontal axis in Figure 4.7 corresponds to the degree of ownership in property, cash, and equity investment, where a high level of control is associated with full ownership. However, foreign legislation (e.g., by limiting foreign direct investment, imposing a local partner, etc.) may be a limitation to full ownership; also, financial resources may be a constraint for controlling through the property (see negative arrow over horizontal axis). Conversely, corporate policy may play in favour of a high degree of ownership in FDI projects by, for instance, prescribing a controlling share in any foreign subsidiary (see positive arrow over horizontal axis).

The entry modes presented in the four quadrants of **Figure 4.7** illustrate quite a different potential, in terms of the degree of control over international operations. Quadrant 1 is high in control by proprietary knowledge, though low in control by ownership. In this case, compliance with management procedures, payment of royalties for patents and brands, and contractual clauses, must be quite strictly enforced. Export of key components (e.g., active pharmaceutical ingredients that cannot be locally produced) may increase the level of control, especially when combined with licensing and/or a management contract.

In quadrant 2, the highest level of control is brought by a fully owned *greenfield investment,* which provides the best fit with the parent company's ways of doing and its technical and management competencies. Even when fully owned, a subsidiary resulting from the takeover of an existing local company has its own history, management style, and corporate culture, and sometimes needs years to adjust to the parent company. An international joint venture is more or less controlled (e.g., arrows in four directions) through both knowledge and property according to the provisions of the IJV contract (see above section 4.5).

Quadrant 3 corresponds to entry modes in which the degree of control of foreign operations is low both on knowledge and property; the lowest levels are for exporting through buying offices and general trading companies. It is important to be aware that this entails not only transferring knowledge but also learning from foreign operations, which in Quadrant 3 is quite low because there is little, if any, contact with foreign markets and consumers. Direct exports are best placed in this quadrant, especially when a B2B exporter has direct contact with a few customers in local markets.

Quadrant 4 is low in control through knowledge and high in control through the property; here, we have envisioned two archetypal situations. The first (bottom-right) is that of investing a majority stake in a joint venture, where the local partner brings both the know-how and people competencies (e.g., a high-tech start-up with brilliant potential but no cash for growth) and the foreign investor brings money and a capacity to reach the global market. This is quite defensible because of the complementarity of the assets brought by each partner, provided that they are able to manage their relationship, despite asymmetric resources, and are able to overcome possible conflicts of interest.

4.7 Chapter summary

As argued in this chapter, globalisation is a process that occurs at the competition level. Regional agreements worldwide and the GATT framework pave the way for artificial entry barriers, mostly tariff and non-tariff, to be progressively replaced by natural entry barriers related to culture, scale, and experience. As far as consumer behaviour and marketing environments are concerned, natural entry barriers related to culture will diminish gradually and only in the long term: there are still many very different marketing 'villages' rather than a single global village. Global markets work as a set of coherent opportunities, the internationalisation phenomenon comprising, for the most part, a learning and experiential process. Since the cultural variable is fundamental to this learning process, some markets may be used almost purely as learning opportunities. Global markets may also be seen as partnership opportunities with local consumers, with distributors, and (why not?) with competitors.

Appendix 4.1. Checklist of criteria for deciding about target markets (country)

1 – General economic criteria

- GNP / GDP/ National income/ Inflation
- Level of unemployment: declared / real
- Income per capita, private consumption per capita
- Growth rate and evolution of main economic indicators

2 – Balance of payments criteria

- Evolution of the balance of payments over the last years
- Dependence of the country on particular export receipts
- Exchange rate: perspectives
- Foreign exchange rate control / currency convertibility
- Level of official resources in foreign currencies

3 – Political risks criteria

- Ethnic divisions
- Ethnic conflicts
- Linguistic and religious divisions
- Gaps in living standards within the local population
- Type of political regime (dictatorship, democracy, elections, etc.)
- Number of coups and revolutions in past years

4 – Standard of living criteria

- Income per capita, GDP per capita
- Number of cars, phones, TVs, radios, household appliances /1000 inhabitants
- Road and transportation infrastructure
- Private consumption per capita
- Existence of a social security system

5 – Cost criteria

- Cost and availability of energy sources (oil, coal, gas, electricity, other available energy sources)
- Main supplies' costs
- Real estate costs (ground and building)
- Level of custom duties, non-tariff barriers
- Cost and availability of the main industrial products (cement, steel, etc.)
- Cost of expatriation in the country

6 – Social criteria

- Manpower cost (schedule / level of qualification)
- Level of social charges and social protection
- Unionisation, the existence of clauses like 'Union Shop' or 'Closed Shop'
- Work attitude (job stability, behaviour toward hierarchy…)
- Productivity / General level of qualification

7 – Tax and legal criteria

- Corporate income tax
- Indirect taxes
- Regulations on dividends, interests, and royalty repatriation (transfer of funds to home country)
- Non-tariff barriers
- Regulation of foreign investments. Possibly, obligation of having a local partner and/or of a minimal percentage of local participation or a maximum equity share of foreign capital - Existence of bilateral conventions for non-double taxation (tax treaties)
- Local law (Common law, Code law, Islamic law…) and attitudes of local jurisdictions toward legal disputes with foreign physical and moral persons

REFERENCES

1. Wichmann, J. R., Uppal, A., Sharma, A., & Dekimpe, M. G. (2022). A global perspective on the marketing mix across time and space. *International Journal of Research in Marketing, 39*(2), 502–521.

2. Vahlne, J. E., & Johanson, J. (2017). From internationalization to evolution: The Uppsala model at 40 years. *Journal of International Business Studies, 48*(9), 1087–1102.

3. World Trade Organization website, The General Agreement on Tariffs and Trade (GATT, 1947) www.wto.org/english/docs_e/legal_e/gatt47_01_e.htm

4. Australian Broadcasting Network (2 June 2022) 'Will the change of Australian government end the trade war with China?' by Samual Yang, retrieved 8 August 2022 from www.abc.net.au/news/2022-06-02/trade-war-between-australia-china-labor-government/101109164

5. Porter, M. E. P. M. (1986). *Competition in Global Industries.* Harvard Business Press.

6. Vernon, R. P. (1966). International investment and international trade in the product life cycle. *Quarterly Journal of Economics*, vol. LXXX, no. 2, 191–207.

7. Dunning, J. H. (1980). Toward an eclectic theory of international production: Some empirical tests. *Journal of International Business Studies, 11*(1), 9–31.

8. Vahlne, J. E., & Johanson, J. (2017). From internationalization to evolution: The Uppsala model at 40 years. *Journal of International Business Studies, 48*(9), 1087–1102.

9. Oviatt, B. M., & McDougall, P. P. (2005). Defining international entrepreneurship and modeling the speed of internationalization. *Entrepreneurship Theory and Practice, 29*(5), 537–553.

10. Detailed and practical advice on the SWOT approach can be found on Google. For instance:

    https://coschedule.com/marketing-strategy/swot-analysis/
    www.google.com/search?client=firefox-b-d&q=swot+analysis
    www.liveplan.com/blog/what-is-a-swot-analysis-and-how-to-do-it-right-with-examples/

11. Brouthers, Lance E., & Nakos, George (2005). The role of systematic international market selection on small firms' export performance. *Journal of Small Business Management, 43*(4), 363–381.

12. Li, S. (2004), Why is property rights protection lacking in China? An international explanation. *California Management Review, 46*(3), 100–115.

13. The TRIPS (Trade Related Industrial Property Rights) negotiated in the WTO has imposed minimal standards for protection of Industrial Property Rights (IPR) worldwide (see www.wto.org/english/tratop_e/trips_e/intel2_e.htm). IPRs are still an important negotiation matter within the WTO with heated debates, especially for pharmaceutical patents and trademarks.

14. The acceptability of a particular brand name for trademark registration must be proven (in terms of originality and anteriority) and covers only particular product or service categories. Brand names are different from shop signs, models or designs: different legal responses exist according to country. Despite the existence of international conventions and an international organization (WIPO), trademark registration largely remains a matter to be treated at national level, except at EU level. Note that Trademarks, as industrial property rights, are different from intellectual property rights (copyright for books, records, movie films, etc.).

15. *Patents* protect the inventor's rights (issues with originality, precedence, and applicability). Patents are still largely on a national basis, despite some international patent conventions (e.g., Paris Union of 1899, precedence right). Patent registration has the drawback of 'informing' competitors. What is technically original is not necessarily patentable. There is much diversity in registration and patent prolongation procedures according to countries, despite the TRIPS agreement, international treaties (e.g., Patent Cooperation Treaty), and international organizations such as the WIPO (World Intellectual Property Organization) and the European Patent Office.

16. A store or outlet location study defines the best possible location by evaluating the demographic characteristics of an area, the transportation constraints, and the potential clientele if a particular place is chosen.

17. The relationship of manufacturers to wholesalers and retailers in the Japanese distribution Keiretsu system is examined in full detail in Usunier, J.-C. & Lee, J. L. (2013). *Marketing Across Cultures*, 6th edn. Harlow: Pearson.

18. See Fainshmidt, S., White, G. O., & Cangioni, C. (2014). Legal distance, cognitive distance, and conflict resolution in international business intellectual property disputes. *Journal of International Management, 20*(2), 188–200.

19. Kumar, P., Deodhar, S. J., & Zaheer, S. (2022). Cognitive sources of liability of foreignness in crowdsourcing creative work. *Journal of International Business Studies*, 1–31.

20. Kogut, B. & and Singh, H. (1988) (p. 422). The effect of national culture on the choice of entry mode. *Journal of International Business Studies, 19* (3) (Autumn, 1988), pp. 411–432.

21. Cultural distance is often confused with psychic distance. *Psychic distance* is subjective, referring to an individual perception of dissimilarities between its home cultural and institutional context and that of the foreign country. Psychic distance is generally asymmetric. Conversely, *Cultural distance* is symmetric because the distance is assessed at the national, societal, and cultural level and is measured objectively.

22. See Parker, V. (2003). Negotiating licensing agreements. In P. N. Ghauri and J.-C. Usunier (Eds.), *International Business Negotiations* (pp. 243–273). Oxford: Pergamon/Elsevier.

5
CROSS-CULTURAL MARKETING STRATEGY AND IMPLEMENTATION

After reading this chapter and completing the activities, you should be able to:

- Develop a cross-cultural marketing strategy.
- Understand how culture influences consumer behaviour.
- Assess when product and brand adaptations are necessary.
- Explain how market conditions impact pricing decisions.
- Evaluate communication transferability.

Introduction

Global drivers, such as socio-economic trends, geopolitical shifts, environmental challenges, and technological advances, create challenges and opportunities in local markets that can lead to dramatic changes in the balance between the need for more local adaptation or global uniformity. Global convergence in consumer needs and consumption patterns has long been argued on the basis of relatively universal aspirations for world-standard goods and services; however, *the meaning attributed to products and consumption experiences* remains to a large extent embedded in local contexts and shared habits within cultural and linguistic groupings. Increasingly, global products (e.g., smartphones, beer, and coffee), are locally reinterpreted and invested with specific meanings, which needs to be considered when designing marketing strategies. In some cases, local consumer cultures are strong enough to develop resistance to globalised consumption, especially if it is perceived as detrimental to local cultural and economic interests. An example is the strong regional labelling of French wine varieties, such as Champagne, only allowed for wines produced in the Champagne region. In most cases, however, the emergent pattern is a mix of local and global consumer behaviour based on kaleidoscopic ways of assembling diverse consumption experiences and making sense of them in everyday life.

Chapter Overview

In this chapter, we discuss the development and implementation of cross-cultural marketing strategies, drawing on basic marketing concepts, such as the '4Ps' model: *product, price, place,* and *promotion.* We describe the unique cross-cultural challenges for each element and provide potential frameworks that offer solutions to these challenges.

- **Section 1** focuses on the **cross-cultural marketing strategy**, including how to identify market opportunities and examine cultural differences in consumer behaviour that may necessitate adaptation in marketing strategies and implementation.
- **Section 2** deals with **product and branding decisions across cultures**. We discuss how adaptation decisions are likely to differ depending on the type of product attribute (physical, service, and symbolic) being considered.
- **Section 3** deals with **distribution decisions across cultures,** including the retail context, salesforce, online and direct marketing and sales promotions.
- **Section 4** deals with **international pricing decisions** and the impact of widely varying normative practices and differing regulatory environments.
- **Section 5** deals with the **influence of culture on marketing communication**, including attitudes toward advertising, communication strategy and execution, the use of advertising appeals, availability of media, and personal selling, which deserve special attention in an international context.

5.1 Cross-cultural marketing strategy

The American Marketing Association defines marketing as 'the activity, set of institutions, and processes for creating, communicating, delivering, and exchanging offerings that have value for customers, clients, partners, and society at large'[1]. This definition focuses on the concept of 'value exchange', which is far more complex in cross-cultural environments.

All firms should have a set of objectives in terms of targets for growth in sales, revenue, or profit. These targets can be achieved in many ways, including consolidation, acquisition, diversification, vertical integration, and geographical expansion (as discussed in Chapter 4). The choice of geographical expansion to new international markets may seem like a natural progression that is often prompted by saturation in the domestic market and/or the appearance of attractive growth opportunities. However, the success of this strategy depends on the level of understanding of the new market and the ability to plan and execute an effective targeted marketing strategy. While the process of developing marketing strategies usually follows 'generic' concepts (see **Figure 5.1**), in that firm objectives (e.g., profit growth) should systematically drive marketing objectives (e.g., target high-worth customers), which then drive the marketing mix objectives (e.g., project a high-quality image through product differentiation, supported by quality advertising, distribution through high-end stores, and pricing at the high-end of the market), there are many additional external factors that need to be carefully considered when expanding into new international markets.

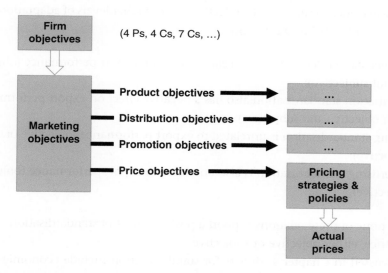

Figure 5.1 A 'generic' process for developing marketing strategies

Developing a culturally sensitive marketing strategy

Firms often begin international expansion by entering culturally similar, geographically neighbouring markets to build their experience and minimise costs/risks. However, these markets may not have the greatest potential. A systematic review of potential market opportunities should be undertaken. Special attention should be paid to differences in environmental (i.e., market and competitive structure, political, legal, and economic systems) and demand characteristics (i.e., customer interests, preferences, purchasing patterns, and price sensitivity) between the home country and the new potential market(s). Depending on the extent of these differences, it may be necessary to develop cross-culturally sensitive strategies geared to different customer needs, different competitive markets, and more broadly, different market conditions.

Taking a culturally sensitive approach, however, does not mean that everything needs to be tailored to each specific market. This approach is compatible with the concept of *glocalisation (think global, act local)*, a term originating in Japan (i.e., *dochakuka*, meaning global localisation). Glocalisation emphasises standardising when true cost reductions can be achieved, and localising when the market demands it. The strategic dilemma for international marketers is to achieve both cost reduction *and* differentiation in the minds of consumers vis-à-vis competitors. While differentiation may result in cost increases, there *are* possible compromises. For instance, cost efficiency can be attained through standardising production, transportation, and some, but not usually all, elements of the marketing mix.

Empirical evidence supports the effectiveness of higher levels of adaptation, at least for product and distribution strategy[2]:

- Product standardisation has a negative effect on export performance (objective but not subjective);
- Distribution standardisation also has a negative effect on export performance (both objective and subjective);
- Pricing standardisation is unrelated to export performance (objective or subjective);
- Advertising standardisation is also unrelated to export performance (objective or subjective).

Notably, none of these relations support a positive effect of standardisation on export performance, either objective or subjective.

As discussed in Chapter 4, drivers for standardisation include economies of scale and the development and maintenance of a consistent worldwide image; however, these drivers are countered by differences between consumers, managers, and countries. Decisions to standardise the marketing mix will be more effective when relatively homogeneous customer segments (i.e., groups of customers with similar characteristics, interests, preferences and purchasing patterns) exist across cultures: potentially some youth, international traveller, and business segments. However, the evidence does not support arguments that markets are generally converging worldwide, and some have argued that developed markets may actually be diverging.

Culture and consumer behaviour

In Chapter 1, we described culture as comprising normative systems, whose influence can be seen in *predictable patterns of consumption behaviour*. Cultural norms reflect *shared knowledge* about *expected normative beliefs, values, and behaviours* that people who grow up in a particular culture implicitly know, but outsiders might find difficult to recognise and understand. Individuals within most societies can choose whether to adhere to, or ignore, prevailing norms. However, those in tighter cultures are more likely to adhere to cultural norms, whereas those in looser cultures are more likely to be driven by their personal preferences and values[3]. There are also contextual differences within most societies, some decisions being tighter and others being looser. For instance, behaviour at job interviews and funerals is more normatively constrained than behaviour in private spaces. Similarly, purchasing gifts for an important event, or items to be shared by others, is more normatively constrained than buying personal and privately consumed products. **Thus, it is important that *specific* and *relevant* patterns of consumer behaviour are carefully examined prior to developing marketing strategies for new markets.**

We also learned, in Chapter 1, that how we view the world is likely to change our understanding of it. Specifically, differences between etic (universal) and emic (culturally specific) views of the world generally lead to different assumptions that guide our perception of reality. This distinction can also be applied to the ways we view (1) consumers and (2) theories about consumer behaviour, leading to four different cross-cultural perspectives, as shown in Table 5.1.

Table 5.1   Consumer behaviour in a cross-cultural perspective

		Consumer behaviour theories	
		Universal (etic)	**Specific (emic)**
Consumers	**Universal**	(1) Global perspective	(3) Ethnic consumption perspective
	Specific	(2) Imported perspective	(4) Cultural meaning perspective

The ***global perspective*** is the most purely etic view, as it assumes that consumer behaviour theories and consumers' beliefs, motivations and behaviours are universal. This view leads businesses to standardise their strategies and the way in which they implement them. However, the *global perspective* is rarely supported by empirical evidence and may only make sense for specific segments of consumers, such as businesspeople who travel worldwide, and their families ('the global nomads').

The ***imported perspective*** is a more reasonable etic application, where consumer behaviour theories are assumed to be universal, but consumers' beliefs, motivations and behaviours are not. This view allows businesses to discover significant differences in consumer behaviour that may require marketing adaptations. For instance, behavioural intention models are often assumed to be universally applicable. At a basic level, the Theory of Reasoned Action posits that people's attitudes and their perceptions of the expectations of important others influence their intentions to perform a behaviour[4]. Taking the imported perspective, researchers have consistently found that, in individualist cultures, the intentions of consumers are more strongly influenced by their own attitudes than they are by the expectations of important others, whereas the reverse is more likely for consumers in collectivist cultures. However, many theories cannot be assumed to be universal. Further insight can be gained from the emic theory viewpoint (***ethnic consumption perspective*** or ***cultural meaning perspective)***, which can uncover new constructs and new relations between these constructs.

The ***ethnic consumption perspective*** assumes that people are fundamentally the same worldwide, but that commonly accepted theories may not be universal. For instance, people have similar basic needs, but they prioritise the fulfilment of these needs differently across cultures. Maslow's hierarchy of needs[5] posits a fixed order of basic universal needs that shape demand across product categories. In this theory, people are assumed to seek satisfaction of *physiological* needs (food, water, clothing, sex, and shelter), followed by *safety* needs (personal, financial, and physical safety), then *social* needs (friendship, intimacy, family and community interaction and belonging), then *esteem* needs (self-esteem and respect), and finally *self-actualisation* needs (achieving one's fullest and greatest potential). However, culture influences this hierarchy on at least two levels:

1. A basic axiom of Maslow's theory is not true in every culture; namely, that needs at a definite level must be satisfied in order for higher order needs to appear.
2. Similar kinds of needs may be satisfied in very different ways (products and consumption types).

In some cultures (e.g., Hindu), the pursuit of self-actualisation is encouraged over the satisfaction of physiological needs, whereas in other cultures, esteem is emphasised over lower-level needs. An example is the Indian potlach ceremony, where extravagant presents are given to guests and possessions are sometimes destroyed to display wealth, whether or not this can be afforded, to improve social standing. This can also be seen in conspicuous consumption, where consumers are willing to forego basic needs (sometimes depriving themselves of food or shelter) to buy products that satisfy social esteem needs.

Finally, the ***cultural meaning perspective*** assumes that everything can differ, where underlying theories are challenged and differences between consumers are assumed. This perspective privileges local meaning at the expense of comparability across cultures, which is likely to lead to full, and often costly adaptation.

It is important to keep an open mind and assume that what you know to be true in your own culture may not be true for those in other cultures. Ask questions about differences you see, but also ask questions about what you consider to be similarities. From an etic view, people in most cultures drink coffee, but *why* they drink coffee and *what they expect from it* may vary dramatically. The consumption of food and drinks is fraught with cultural conventions, as you will see when you do Activity 5.1.

─Activity 5.1─

Exploring eating habits

Of all the cultural conventions that structure daily life in the consumption domain, the most important is probably eating habits. Food is not only a tangible product that provides nourishment, but it is also a symbol that can carry very different meanings. Investigating how these habits might differ across cultures can provide insight into how consumers and concepts may differ in unexpected ways.

TASK: Choose a country that you don't know very much about and investigate norms around eating habits in that country by interviewing someone who grew up there and/or searching for information on the internet. Try to find answers to the following questions, as eating habits should be considered as the whole process of purchasing food and beverages, cooking, tasting, and even commenting on them.

- How many main and smaller meals (e.g., morning tea) are usually consumed each day?
- When does each meal occur in the daily schedule, how many people are involved, and how long does the meal last?
- What types of foods (local ingredients/cooking style) and proportions comprise each meal?
- What is the primary function associated with each meal (e.g., to fuel the body or as a daily social event)?
- What type of beverage accompanies each meal (e.g., water, coffee, tea, wine, beer, and so on) and what type of function does it have (e.g., as a refresher, energiser, coolant, or relaxer)?
- How are the meals put together (e.g., pre-prepared or prepared from basic ingredients) and by whom (i.e., paid help or specific member(s) of the family), and whether it is always the same people?
- What aspects of the meal process are most likely to be commented upon or complimented?

Compare these findings with those from your own and other cultures. Think about which of the four perspectives in Table 5.1 *is more strongly supported by your findings. How would this influence the ability to standardise advertising messages across these cultures?*

The influence of culture on selected aspects of consumer behaviour

Table 5.2 presents selected aspects of consumer behaviour that have been found to differ across cultures. This table is designed to be indicative, rather than exhaustive. Any aspect, preferably the most relevant to the product/service and the markets being entered, can be examined in more detail. In Activity 5.2, we suggest that you explore one or more aspects of consumer behaviour that are likely to be important when taking a specific product or service into specific new markets.

Table 5.2   Possible cultural differences in selected aspects of consumer behaviour

Consumer behaviour	Cultural differences
Perception	Perception of shapes, colours and space differ.
Motivation	Motivation to own, buy, spend, consume, show, share, and/or give differs.
Learning & memory	Literacy levels differ. Memory emphasis differs.
Age	Value of younger and older people in the society differs. Influences across age groups differ. Distribution of purchasing power across generations differ.
Group influence	The extent to which the individual is embedded in their groups differ. The extent the group influences individuals' attitudes and behaviour.
Social class	The extent to which social classes are locally important differs. Whether consumption demonstrates social class belonging differs. The type of goods that social status-minded consumers buy differs.
Gender roles	The division of labour across genders differs, as does who makes the decisions, who shops, and whether they are the same person.
Attitudes to change	Resistance to change in consumer behaviour (possibly related to strong uncertainty avoidance, past orientation, and fatalism), especially when change could clash with local values and behaviour (e.g., resistance to fast food restaurants in France) differs.
Decision-making	The influence of group involvement differs. Impulsive and compulsive buying differs.
Purchase	The concept of loyalty and to whom it is given differs. Environmental factors, especially legal and economic factors, differ. The influence of others, including salespeople, differs.
Post-purchase	Perceptions of product quality and (dis)satisfaction differs. Consumer complaining behaviour differs.

Activity 5.2

Differences in consumer behaviour

Choose a product or service to be introduced into a new country market. From Table 5.2, consider which aspects of consumer behaviour are most relevant to that product and the country you intend to introduce the product or service into.

- Which aspects of consumer behaviour are likely to be most crucial to success of the product?
- What potential cultural differences in this aspect of consumer behaviour need to be accommodated?
- Identify the potential issues and possible solutions that should be considered.

To illustrate, we take the example of group involvement in decision making. To understand how consumers are likely to react to new products, we first need to think about who is most likely to make purchase decisions. Most academic literature depicts individual consumers who make their own decisions, but there is also recognition that our decisions are strongly influenced by social factors. Research into family decision making and industrial (business-to-business) buying recognises that different people exert more, or less, influence, depending on the importance of the decision to individuals and groups. And it is important to recognise that the final decision-maker is not the only one to influence the decision; the roles of different stakeholders needs to be examined across cultures.

In traditional, masculine cultures, where people have more clearly defined roles (e.g., most Latin American countries), purchase decisions for everyday goods are likely to be made by women, whereas in more egalitarian cultures (e.g., Northern Europe), these decisions are likely to be shared between men and women, and children may also have a significant influence on these everyday household purchases. However, other factors should also be considered, such as the prevalence of hired help. The Hong Kong Immigration Department reported that there were almost 340,000 foreign domestic helpers in Hong Kong[6], which, divided by the number of households, indicates that about 1 in 7 households in Hong Kong employs a foreign domestic helper. These helpers often do household shopping, cooking, and cleaning, as well as caring for the elderly, children, and pets. These roles are likely to mean that they are the primary decision-makers for many everyday household purchase decisions. To complicate matters further, these helpers are from very different cultures: around 56% of foreign domestic helpers are originally from the Philippines, with another 41% from

Indonesia[7]. In this case, advertising everyday purchase items in Cantonese may not successfully reach the decision-maker. Needless to say, targeting the wrong decision-maker could be disastrous for a business.

CONDUCTING PRIMARY RESEARCH

Well-planned primary market research can be extremely insightful; however, poorly planned research can not only be a waste of time, but extremely detrimental to a firm, if they act on it. For instance, a European syrup maker ordered a survey of the Swedish syrup market from a large international market research company. Unfortunately, syrup, a solution of sugar dissolved in water and flavoured with fruit juice, was incorrectly translated as *blandsaft*, a Swedish term for concentrated fruit juice, a local substitute for syrup with much less sugar. When the results came in, they were of no use because it was a local product rather than the product category at large that consumers responded to. This simple translation mistake may have cost the company the money and time allocated to the research, but had they not discovered the mistake and acted on an answer to the wrong question, it could have cost them dearly in market share as well.

While primary research is needed, it is often time-consuming and can be quite costly. Careful consideration needs to be given to the research aims, questions, and methods of data collection (e.g., surveys, focus groups, experiments, observation, diaries, and journals).

Consider the following dilemmas when designing primary research across cultures.

1. How should a survey about instant coffee preferences be designed for a traditionally tea-drinking country (e.g., the United Kingdom or Japan)? What information should be sought? How should the data be collected?
2. Which method should be used for personal care products in a country where potential respondents resent interviews as an intrusion into their privacy or some members (e.g., females) of a household are not permitted to talk to strangers?
3. How should a questionnaire be translated and adapted to suit other countries, when the starting point is a questionnaire that was originally designed for a specific country?

This process is more difficult when comparing countries or cultural regions, as the research questions cannot simply be the same as those for domestic market research. Differences in cultural assumptions complicate the questions we need to ask, the methods we need to use to answer the questions, and potentially our interpretation of the answers. In this case, market research expertise may be required to establish the quality of research instruments, consistency of behavioural/attitudinal constructs, and equivalence of samples. Even when commissioning market research expertise, it is important to understand how consumer behaviour is likely to be influenced by culture, to ensure that the right questions are asked.

5.2 Brand and Product decisions: Adaptation versus standardisation

A product can be defined as a set of attributes that provide the purchaser or user with *actual or perceived benefits*. In some cases, these benefits may be universally relevant. For instance, consumers appear to appreciate similar product attributes from IKEA (i.e., low cost, reasonable quality, and Swedish aesthetics), regardless of whether the furniture buyers are in China, Australia, or Saudi Arabia. IKEA is one of the strongest proponents of product standardisation in the global marketplace. You can find the same 'Boksel' coffee table in their Australian stores as you can in China, Saudi Arabia, and basically everywhere else IKEA has a presence.

There are three layers of product attributes that are more or less applicable to standardisation across cultures:

1. *The physical attributes* (e.g., size, weight, colour). Standardisation of these attributes provides the greatest potential for cost benefits, given that economies of scale are mostly gained at the manufacturing stage. As such, any customisation of physical attributes must be carefully weighed up against the cost efficiencies.
2. *Service attributes* (e.g., maintenance, after-sales service, spare parts availability). These attributes are fairly difficult to standardise, as expectations and circumstances for service delivery differ widely from one country to another. Furthermore, most services are performed in direct relation to local customers, which means service attributes are more dependent on culture.

3. *Symbolic attributes.* These often comprise the interpretive element of the physical attributes. A colour is technically a chemical formula, but it can also convey significant symbolic meaning. However, it is not always clear whether symbolic attributes need to be adapted or not. For instance, it can be quite confusing when consumers show a strong liking for domestic goods based on nationalism and also show a fascination for foreign cultures and their goods. Therefore, when adapting or standardising symbolic attributes, the requirements for national identity symbols will sometimes intermingle with those for symbols of exoticism.

Physical attributes

Empirical evidence suggests that neither standardisation nor adaptation of physical attributes is inherently superior. When making decisions, firms should consider the following factors:

- *the type of market* (e.g., similarity in culture, the physical environment, level of economic development, legal system, marketing infrastructure, competition, technology, and the type of customer and their preferences);
- *the type of product* (e.g., the potential for standardisation is clearly lower for cheese or books than for electronics or computers); and
- *compatibility with the firms' strategic direction.*

As a general rule, physical attributes should be standardised where possible, and localised where necessary. There are usually more opportunities for standardisation across developed nations, as more of the market factors (e.g., the market infrastructure) will be similar. When firms from developed nations enter emerging economies, the opportunities for standardisation are likely to be fewer. Necessary product modifications may include the use of cheaper components, simpler packaging, and fewer product features, which enable the product to be sold at a lower price. On the plus side, this type of adaptation may be transferable to other emerging markets, which can compensate for a loss of sales volume for the original version. For instance, Japanese pick-up trucks were successful in emerging countries after product simplifications in their suspension, engine, and gearbox, which lowered their cost. However, product simplifications often fail to achieve their goals.

While standardisation seems desirable, there is rarely a positive relationship between the level of product standardisation and performance. Generally, studies have found that product adaptation has a positive effect on export marketing performance[8]. Further, there are some conditions in which adaptation of physical attributes is necessary, due to factors such as differences in national regulations and standards, as well as in the physical environment:

1. *Industrial standards for the supply of electricity* (e.g., voltage, frequency of alternating current (50 versus 60 Hz), the shape of plugs) differ by region, if not by country. Apple and many other firms have offset the voltage issue by producing most of their products with dual-voltage capabilities.
2. *Safety standards* (e.g., automotive industry standards focusing on lighting and visibility, brake systems, and other safety requirements) often differ by country. If a vehicle needs to be modified physically (e.g., to improve visibility, suspension, brakes, or emission) to meet local standards, not only will production costs increase, but there will also be added costs in terms of documentation and country-specific spare parts.
3. *Hygiene regulations* (e.g., relating to the processing of food, chemicals, and pharmaceutical products) also differ by country. For instance, French *foie gras* producers set up laboratories in the USA, where the product is prepared according to USA hygiene standards. While this inevitably affects the taste and conflicts with the traditional image of a home-made quality product, modifications to hygiene standards are essential for this product to be sold in this market. Even a product as common as Coca-Cola faces different regulations, including specific requirements around the use of artificial sweeteners (e.g., consumer information on potential side-effects) and the necessity to include a product expiry date in some countries, but not others.

Countless regulations influence the need for adaptation, including those that affect packaging, labelling, sizes, advertising, sales promotion, and so on. Firms also need to scan the environment for new regulations that may be imposed in the future. For instance, in 2022, the European Union ruled that all smartphones will require the same charger from 2024. This will be a costly modification for Apple and some Android-based manufacturers, but it is likely to benefit consumers and reduce waste in the long run. However, many businesses fail to consider the issue of adapting products to foreign markets, for ethnocentric reasons. Guidance is available in many countries from public bodies that offer to assist businesses in examining the issues of conforming to the technical aspects of foreign standards.

Perhaps surprisingly, compulsory adaptations are often minor when compared to essential adaptations to differences in consumer behaviour or in the national marketing environment, across countries. Three main issues need to be considered:

1. *Consumption patterns* (e.g., consumer tastes, frequency of consumption, and the amount consumed per helping) differ across cultures. For instance, the size of a cereal box and the style of packaging that preserves the product depend in part on whether consumers eat 50 grams of cereal a day, or larger amounts less frequently. Even products that are considered to be global often need to be customised for

local tastes. Not only does Coca-Cola add different levels and types of sweeteners in different countries (e.g., cane sugar in Australia, corn syrup in the USA, and beet sugar in Europe) to account for differences in taste, but consumers also treat the product differently. For instance, Coca-Cola is served with a lot of ice in the USA and often without any ice in Europe. In contrast, high-end brands, such as Louis Vuitton and Gucci, typically make few (if any) concessions to cultural differences in terms of product design. This is because the main utility of their products is not in their use, but in the image associated with possession of the product.

2. *Physical environment* (e.g., climate, geography, population density) is an important, although sometimes neglected factor, that may necessitate adaptation. In terms of climate, motor vehicles must be specifically designed to withstand the harsh northern European winters or the warmth and humidity of the Middle East. Population density can also influence product and packaging design. Japan, which has a high population density (i.e., 350 people/sq. km), has one of the most advanced packaging technology industries in the world. There are many smaller stores that have limited shelf space that is frequently stocked, often several times a day, with products packaged to fit the available space (e.g., taller with a narrow footprint).

3. *Adapting products to local product usage.* Product usage can vary subtly from country to country, in ways that might not be evident to the ethnocentric marketer. For example, Indian consumers do not typically freeze leftovers for the next-day's consumption, and as such, they prefer smaller freezer sections at the bottom of the fridge where it is out of the way. In Northern Europe, the rising costs of fuel and extremely cold winters, combined with environmental consciousness, have led to a strong preference for extremely energy-efficient designs.

It is relatively easy to observe differences in products and product usage across cultures, but it is more difficult and perhaps important to understand why these differences exist. Understanding why the differences exist is key to deciding whether adaptation is necessary.

Service attributes

The standardisation of service attributes may offer fewer benefits, in terms of economies of scale, than the standardisation of physical attributes; however, there can be substantial learning effects with service attributes (e.g., management procedures around stocking spare parts or product return policies) that make a standardised service more efficient. Examples of service attributes include the following:

- Repair and maintenance, after-sales service.
- Demonstrations, installations, and technical assistance.

- Instruction manuals and guidance on how to use items.
- Guarantees for repair or replacement of goods.
- Protocols around waiting times, delivery dates, and respect for them.
- Spare parts availability.
- Return policy for goods, whether defective or not.

These attributes are often influenced by environmental factors that can lead to differences in service requirements and expectations:

- Climatic differences, which may increase the difficulty of performing maintenance operations because of temperature, humidity, etc.
- The population density and geographical remoteness of locations, which may render services difficult and costly to perform.
- The level of technical expertise in the population, which may be related to literacy and education, but also to the roles different people in society are expected to adhere to (e.g., defined gender roles).
- The level of labour costs, which may influence the balance between durability and repairability (e.g., emerging countries often have greater expertise in repairing worn-out cars and making creative use of waste; see **Figure 5.2**).
- Cultural differences in ways of performing a seemingly identical service, which may relate to differences in time and relationship orientation.

Figure 5.2   African shoemaker expertise in recycling old tyres

Source: Fabian Plock / Shutterstock.com

We need to be careful not to assume that the way services are delivered in our home culture is the best way. For instance, there is no lack of technical expertise and craftsmanship in many emerging countries; however, it is often expressed differently and relates to the prevailing economic conditions. A lot of maintenance may be done by small mechanical workshops, which succeed in repairing cars, but take a long time to do so; although their repair methods may not be orthodox, they do work. As such, service instructions issued by car manufacturers will need some adaptation. It may be more effective to show mechanics how to do a job than to send them a free 800-page book on maintenance operations. Where services are delegated to distribution channels, adaptation may be needed when the size of distribution outlets and the strength of their relationship with customers differs.

Symbolic attributes

Symbolic aspects of consumption convey significant meaning. For some products, this meaning can be even more important than their functional utility. Given the potential diversity in interpretations and associations of symbolic meaning across cultures, it is recommended that market research be carried out in each national market using local informants prior to a product launch.

Standardisation across markets will rely on using symbols and packaging with universal or near-universal appeal. While tech and electronic products may not be standardised in terms of physical attributes, due to differences in socio-economic and regulatory environments, they may still have similar symbolic appeals. Tech companies, such as Apple, Google and Microsoft, are consistently in the most valuable brand rankings worldwide (e.g., Forbes). However, Coca-Cola, Disney and McDonald's also regularly feature in the top 10 brands. Coca-Cola has successfully avoided being associated too strongly with an American image by creating a strong brand association with youth, sports and leisure situations, all universal themes. Coca-Cola uses the same red and white logo in each country, and its bottle design is consistent across markets. Similarly, McDonald's never strays from its yellow arches. The symbolic interpretation then shifts from the parts to the whole: rather than relating to interpretations of yellow and arches in particular cultures, it diffuses a message about McDonald's worldwide.

Branding

Branding is an important tool used to differentiate between products. Despite the potential benefits of corporate branding (e.g., increased market efficiency, reduced advertising and inventory costs), there may be limited benefits from global standardisation. Thus, the potential benefits of differentiation of branding should be examined (e.g., the potential for expanding sales, increased profits, and the ability to survive adverse economic conditions).

Brands are largely symbolic attributes that are often linked to a complex interplay of images, which warrants close analysis when consideration is being given to extending into new markets. Although it is possible to choose favourable images that transfer across cultures and are suitable for both the product category and for the chosen target segments, this process is often more difficult when there are restraints on choices due to the existence of established branding materials.

If a brand name already exists, it may need to be simplified, or a new name may need to be developed independently of the company name. For example, Procter & Gamble simplified their company name to Procter or P & G, with the aim of making the name more memorable and easier to pronounce. They also developed new brand names for their products, independent of the company name (e.g., Vicks, Oral-B, and Gillette). These brand names follow relatively simple rules, in that a brand name should not exceed three syllables, each including only one vowel sound. Adherence to this rule is simpler in some languages than in others. Chinese languages often include simple successions of one consonant and one or two vowels, whereas German and Dutch languages often have many successive consonants (up to seven in a row in German), and French sometimes has long strings of vowels.

Whether a brand name exists or is newly created, it is important to assess whether the name is transferable across countries. First, consider whether the brand name can be easily pronounced in multiple languages. Examples of common brand names that are often mispronounced in English include Hermès (AIR-mez), Porsche (POOR-sha), Givenchy (Zhee-Vahn-shee), Chevrolet (Shev-Ro-Lay), Louis Vuitton (LOO-ee Vwee-Than). These names are all derived from European languages, such as French, which are considerably closer to English than non-Latin-based languages; however, French sounds can be difficult for English speakers. A few examples include the following:

- The throaty French 'CR' sound hardly exists in English.
- 'EU' is a typically French diphthong, which is difficult to pronounce.
- 'O' is a very open sound.
- 'OI' is also a French diphthong that is largely unknown in English.

Languages that rely on tonal variations to indicate meaning create even more difficulties for transferability. For instance, Mandarin Chinese has different tones with distinctive pitch contours that completely change the meaning of the word, as illustrated in Figure 5.3.

mā	Má	Mǎ	Mà	ma
媽	麻	馬	罵	嗎
Mother	Hemp	Horse	Scold	Question mark

Figure 5.3   Some tonal meanings of 'ma'

What are the options? There are two basic methods for extending existing brand names to international markets:

1. *Simple translation*, which is rarely used as it may result in profound differences in meaning, scattered brand image, and inability to create international brand recognition.
2. *Transliteration*, which is more often used, as it attempts to carry over the connotative meaning in the target language that exists in the source language. For example, the American hair care product Silkience (Gillette) is sold under the same brand name in Germany, under the brand name Soyance in France and under the brand name Sientel in Italy. All of these names have phonetic similarities and also convey similar connotations of softness.

There are many linguistic devices that can be considered in creating new brand names, as shown in **Table 5.3**. Whether by accident or design, advertisers and marketers strive to give some *punch* and *evocative* capacity to their brand names. Of course, this needs to be in line with the symbolic connotations that they intend to communicate in relation to product positioning. There are four main categories of linguistic devices: *phonetic devices* (sound, perceived orally), *orthographic devices* (relating to writing, perceived visually), *morphological devices* (adding morphemes to the brand name root) and *semantic devices* (where the figure produces meaning, perceived through culture-based interpretations), as described in **Table 5.3**.

Table 5.3   Linguistic characteristics of brands

Characteristics	Definitions and/or examples
I Phonetic devices	
1. Alliteration	Consonant repetition (Coca-Cola, Cocoon)
2. Assonance	Vowel repetition (Kal Kan, Omo)
3. Consonance	Consonant repetition with intervening vowel changes (Weight Watchers, Tic Tac)

Characteristics	Definitions and/or examples
4. Masculine rhyme	Rhyme with end of syllable stress (Max Pax)
5. Feminine rhyme	Unaccented syllable followed by accented syllable (American Airlines)
6. Weak/imperfect/ slant rhyme	Vowels differ or consonants similar, not identical (Black & Decker)
7. Onomatopoeia	Use of syllable phonetics to resemble the object sound (Wisk, Cif, Jif)
8. Clipping	Product names shortened (Chevy for a Chevrolet)
9. Blending	Morphemic combination, usually with elision (Duracell)
10. Initial plosives*	/b/, /c-hard/, /d/, /g-hard/, /k/, /q/, /t/, (Bic, Pim's)
II Orthographic device	
1. Unusual or incorrect spellings	Kool-Aid, Froot Loops cereal
2. Abbreviations	7-Up for Seven-Up
3. Acronyms	AT&T, M&M, SPAM
III Morphological device	
1. Affixation	Jell-O, PayPal, 7-Eleven
2. Compounding	Airbnb, SnapChat
IV Semantic device	
1. Metaphor	Safari, Pandora
2. Metonymy	Apple, Bounty, Crunch
3. Synecdoche	Band-aid, Styrofoam
4. Personification/ pathetic fallacy	Kinder, Alfa Romeo
5. Oxymoron	Easy-Off, Krispy Kreme, IcyHot
6. Paranomasia	Hawaiian Punch, Raid – insecticide
7. Semantic appositeness	Bufferin, Nutella

*An initial is said to be plosive if, to produce this sound, one needs first to stop the flow of air completely, then audibly release the air previously compressed.

Despite the best intentions, the intended meaning of a brand name can be lost when it crosses borders. For instance, the meaning of Nestlé (*Nestele*: 'little nest' in the Alemannic dialects of the southern German-speaking area) is lost in many of the world's languages, which can cause some confusion as to why the logo represents a bird in a nest. More importantly, the brand name should not have an unfortunate meaning in a different linguistic/cultural context. The failure to adequately check the translinguistic capacity of a brand name is by no means uncommon, even today. There is no shortage of examples. Kellogg's renamed its Bran Buds brand name in

Sweden, so that Swedish people did not read that they were to be served 'grilled farmer' in their breakfast bowls. In contrast, Volkswagen avoided the mistake in the USA when it rolled out the next generation of its popular model, Jetta. In Europe, it was rebranded as 'Bora', but focus group tests revealed that the name 'Bora' did not invoke the right feelings among English-speaking customers, so the decision was made to keep the name 'Jetta' for the US market.

The type of research that should be carried out is straightforward: it is necessary to interview a group of consumers from the target culture about the perceptual effects of the intended names. Sometimes it is necessary to interview several different sub-cultural groups, depending on the number of dialects with the potential for unintended meanings.

Country of origin effects

Another important symbolic attribute is the perception of a product's country of origin (COO). Consumers tend to rely on the COO to infer product attributes (e.g., quality), especially when they have limited product information or knowledge. It is useful to think about how much more you might be willing to pay for a similar product that was designed and made in two very different countries, such as an Italian versus Vietnamese leather dress shoes, or a Japanese versus Chinese-made camera. If you think deeply about this, you might find that you have beliefs about the competency of an industry in a specific country, as well as some more general feelings or emotions about specific countries. COO perceptions influence consumer decision making through both performance-related country cognitions (i.e., competency of the industry) and performance-unrelated country emotions (i.e., country-specific affinity or animosity)[9]. If a product is from a country with a positive or negative cognitive competency perception or a general affinity or animosity, it would be a mistake to ignore the symbolic message that may be communicated to potential customers.

Communicating COO is complicated by brands often having complex 'made in...' labels, with components from multiple countries that generate different COO images. Multinational production causes a 'blurring effect' of the COO. However, there are many ways to claim COO without using a 'made in...' label, including adding COO to the company name (e.g., L'Oreal Paris, France), naming the COO (e.g., Original de Brasil, Brazil), referring to the COO (e.g., Australian Ginseng, Australia), using a famous person from the COO (e.g., Kate Moss UK), using typical COO words (e.g., Kangaroo, Australia), using typical landscapes or buildings from the COO (e.g., Skyscrapers of New York, USA) or using COO flags/symbols (e.g., Swiss flag, Switzerland); see **Figure 5.4** for the prevalence of COO markers found in *Cosmopolitan* magazine across the Netherlands, Spain, and the United Kingdom)[10]. Notably, the 'made in...' label was almost never used.

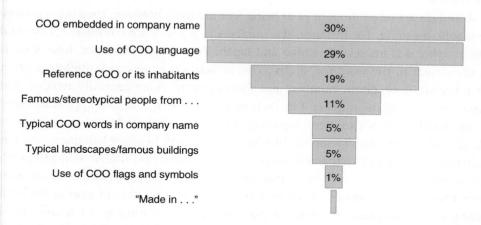

Figure 5.4 contents:

Marker	Percentage
COO embedded in company name	30%
Use of COO language	29%
Reference COO or its inhabitants	19%
Famous/stereotypical people from . . .	11%
Typical COO words in company name	5%
Typical landscapes/famous buildings	5%
Use of COO flags and symbols	1%
"Made in . . ."	

Figure 5.4 Occurrence of COO markers across 750 ads in *Cosmopolitan* (Adapted – used data – from Hornikx, J., van Meurs, F., van den Heuvel, J., & Janssen, A. (2020). How brands highlight country of origin in magazine advertising: A content analysis. *Journal of Global Marketing, 33*(1), 34–45.

Further, standardisation may be easier when there is a positive association with the country of origin (i.e., perfume from France, electronic products from Japan, coffee from Brazil). Many people feel a touch of French romance when they buy Chanel N°5 perfume or a sense of fun when they have a margarita or a shot of tequila from Mexico. In these consumption experiences, ethnic product symbolism is associated with exotic appeal for the consumer; thus, symbolic attributes should be kept standardised, even though the product or its surrounding services are, to a certain extent, adapted to local markets. Standardisation may also be facilitated when the market has favourable perceptions of imported products. However, an adaptation of symbolic attributes may be necessary when there is potential for divergent symbolic associations.

Differences in symbolic interpretations across cultures

The interpretation of symbolic messages conveyed by symbolic attributes, such as shapes, colours, and numbers, may differ significantly between the marketer's culture and the consumer's culture. It is a natural tendency to rely on our own interpretations, taking an ethnocentric view of symbolic meaning. Inappropriate use of symbolic images that are not adapted to the local consumer presents a danger for international marketers. Cultural values, traditions, and often superstitions must be considered.

Numbers are often thought of as being 'culture free'; however, they often convey symbolic meaning. For instance, the numbers 2, 8 and 9 are considered lucky and the number 4 is unlucky in China and Japan. The Chinese word for 'four' sounds quite similar to the word for 'death'. This association is pervasive. Buildings often skip the 4th floor, phone numbers and addresses with 4s are generally avoided, and firms avoid using the number 4 in their model numbers. This also applies to many larger numbers with 4 in them, especially 14 and 74. The number 14 sounds like 'is dead' and the number 74 sounds like 'is already dead'. In other languages, such as Japanese, Korean and Vietnamese, words for 'four' also sound similar to 'death'; with the number 4 being avoided in apartments and hospitals in Japan and housing numbers that end in 4 being skipped in Taiwan. In fact, this type of association with numbers is widespread. In most Western countries, the number 13 is considered unlucky, based on Biblical Christianity, with many high-rise buildings in the USA skipping the 13th floor.

Colours can also have different associations across cultures. Behind each symbolic meaning of a colour is an element of reality. Red, for example, is the colour of blood: it can evoke and suggest meanings that differ widely depending on the culture. However, the colour red can be linked to substances other than blood – certain flowers, for instance. The use of red as the dominant colour on a product or its packaging must therefore be very carefully considered beforehand. A few examples of potential differences in colour associations include the following:

- Red is associated with power, love or danger in most Western countries, but in India, it is associated with purity (Hindu brides often wear red), and in China with luck, happiness and prosperity (Chinese New Year).
- Orange is associated with warmth and fun (clowns wear orange wigs) in most Western countries, but in much of Southeast Asia, it is associated with the sacred and holy (the colour of monks' robes) and in India orange on the flag stands for strength, courage, and sacrifice.
- White is associated with purity or innocence in most Western countries (often worn by brides), but in many Asian countries it represents death and mourning (often worn at funerals) and reflects bad luck.
- Purple is associated with magic and mystery in most Western countries, but in many Asian countries it is associated with royalty, wealth, and fame.

While differences in colour associations may not be as important as other symbolic attributes, they can influence the overall impression or image of a product. For instance, purple packaging may more effectively convey the impression of being luxurious and expensive in Asian cultures than in most Western cultures. Thus, it is important to examine how potential customers are likely to perceive the full spectrum of symbolic attributes of a product before it is introduced into a new market.

Unintended consequences of symbolic misrepresentation can be disastrous. For example, Nike Air Max designed its logo in a way that is reminiscent of how the word Allah is written in Arabic, when the logo is upside down (see **Figure 5.5**). Needless to say, placing this symbol on the soles of shoes was not taken well in the Arabic world.

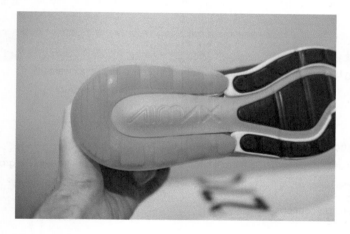

Figure 5.5 Nike Air Max logo

Source valerii eidlin / Shutterstock.com

5.3 Distribution decisions

There is no doubt that in today's business climate, getting the right product to the right place at the right time is crucial to success. The dramatic changes in the growth of e-commerce sales and issues with the global supply chain during the pandemic and with heightened geopolitical conflict have created both opportunities for and constraints upon getting products to the end consumer. While Chapter 4 focuses on market entry and different types of channel structures that offer more or less direct access to customers, this section discusses issues that arise from channel management from a cross-cultural perspective.

The role of the distribution system as a 'cultural filter'

Distribution channels allow the formation of subtle relationships with consumers through direct contact. People get into the habit of buying certain products, which are backed by fixed services, at clearly defined times, in particular shops. Despite the development of e-commerce, many differences in shopping behaviour continue to exist across countries and cultures. **Table 5.4** presents selected aspects of consumer and retail behaviour that continue to be influenced by culture.

Table 5.4 Influence of culture on some aspects of consumer and retail behaviour that influence distribution.

Selected aspects of distribution	Practices that *may* differ according to country/culture
(1) Shopping behaviour	Is time spent shopping experienced as wasted?
	Is the return of goods standard behaviour?
	Who is the shopper?
	How important is personal contact?
(2) Opening hours	How restricted are opening hours?
(3) Product range	Is there limited access or product bans for specific groups?
(4) Willingness to serve consumers and consumers' perceptions of the service	Is there a positive or negative view of serving others?
(5) Waiting lines	How willing are people to comply with rules?
(6) Thefts by consumers or personnel/sales staff	What are the moral norms?

Examples of cultural differences in purchasing from Table 5.4:

1. **Shopping behaviour** is influenced by many cultural factors, including the extent of economicity of time, masculinity/femininity, uncertainty avoidance, and individualism/collectivism. For instance, whether the shopping experience is seen as a cost or a benefit is related to the economicity of time. If time is precious and seen as a resource that is 'spent', time-saving conveniences will be more highly valued (e.g., online shopping, delivery services and self-checkout). Refund, return and exchange policies in China, India, and Mexico are much more restrictive

than in the USA, and consumers in these countries are less likely to seek redress, as retailers do not allow returns or exchanges; however, they still spread negative word of mouth and/or exit[11]. In masculine, as compared with feminine cultures, gender roles are more distinct, which influences who does what shopping. While Saudi women were granted the right to drive in 2018, they are still subject to strict guardianship laws that require the permission of a male relative before than can drive, resulting in mostly high-income professional women driving[12]. The importance of personal contact and trustworthy relationships also impacts the move to online shopping. People from more individualist and less uncertainty-avoidant countries in Europe are less likely to adopt online reselling than those from more collectivist and uncertainty-avoidant cultures[13].

2. Religious practices also impact when people shop and place constraints on **opening hours**: Judaism designates the Sabbath as a non-workday, including household work, such as shopping, cooking and cleaning, whereas Friday is the day for worship in the Islamic religion.

3. Religious and social beliefs may also **restrict the use of products**: Muslims should not consume alcohol, pig meat, or any products from animals that were not slaughtered according to Islamic practices, even those that have only trace amounts (e.g., lard, gelatine, or enzymes), including cosmetics.

4. Whether we see human nature as basically good or bad influences our **treatment of others**: in cultures where the assumption is that people are basically *good* (e.g., Australia, the USA), people tend to be more friendly and open to strangers, but where the assumption is that people are basically *bad* (e.g., most South American and Latin European countries), trust and kindness should only be given to those that prove they are worthy of it.

5. Rules, such as those around **waiting and queuing**, help to create order and reduce uncertainty, but whether people obey the rules can be related to power distance. In high power distance cultures (e.g., Malaysia and most Arab countries), rules are mostly directed at the population from the top, without 'instructions for use', and people are expected to investigate the extent to which rules can be transgressed, whereas in low power distance cultures (e.g., Israel and most northern European countries) people are expected to automatically comply.

6. **Theft by customers or store employees** is another important consideration in distribution channels that differs by country. Naturally, economic constraints play a role, where, for some, theft can be implicitly understood as a legitimate way of social redistribution, but theft is also related to a strong in-group orientation, so that theft from retailers who are foreigners may not always be considered evil, but rather as recovering one's own goods from the outsider.

Naturally, culture explains only part of the variance in behaviours around distribution systems; the prevailing socio-economic and macroeconomic factors also play a major role in the distribution system.

CORRUPTION PERCEPTION INDEX

Transparency International has a mission to cease corruption and promote better transparency, accountability, and integrity at all levels of society, worldwide. They research corruption and rank countries by the perceived level of public sector corruption, from 100 'very clean' to 0 'highly corrupt'. In general, countries with well-protected civil liberties score high, but the COVID-19 pandemic has seen many countries curtail basic human freedom.

Explore the Corruption Perception Index www.transparency.org/en/cpi/2021 for any country you might consider entering to see how they compare with your home country. Click on the country to see the trend over time and read about the latest updates on corruption in that country.

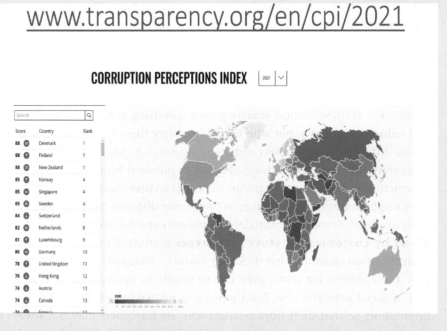

Figure 5.6   Country differences in the Corruption Perceptions Index

Roles, goals, and rewards of the sales force

Sales forces are an essential element of the distribution system, even in the online environment. The primary role of the sales force is to generate revenue for a firm, including demonstrating, promoting, and selling products, answering questions, and providing other services. Further, sales personnel are often required to generate sales leads, negotiate contracts with prospective and existing clients, help to determine quotes, promotions, and pricing, and meet sales goals. Thus, the role of the sales force can range from relatively simple to highly complex, where goals and rewards are crucial.

Goals and Rewards

The idea that sales personnel are evaluated according to merit and that decisions are made on an objective basis is very strong in Western societies. However, in many cultures which have a more fatalistic approach to life, controlling individual performance does not seem to make sense. Such cultures hold that uncontrollable higher-order forces largely shape our acts and our future. In this scenario (e.g., in Saudi Arabia), performance and evaluation control systems often work more informally, without systematic targets and controls based on specific criteria or definite procedures.

Western 'doing' societies that place value on 'affirmative action compliance programmes' ignore criteria that are considered essential to determine *who the person is* in many other societies. However, the birthplace of applicants, their marital status, age, citizenship, or language competencies are standard, non-discriminatory inquiries in most cultures where there is still some *being* orientation.

Who to employ

One of the first questions that face firms that plan to have an international sales force is who to employ and from which country. The most obvious decision is whether to use expatriates (i.e., employees from the firm's home country) or host country locals as sales force representatives. The major advantage of local salespeople is that they are cultural insiders, meaning they understand the nuances of the local culture, and are more similar to their customers. However, local salespeople also typically require more training, and, in some cultures, will be held in lower esteem than expatriates. Conversely, expatriates are usually more embedded in the company culture and have greater product knowledge, but are also more expensive and have less insight into the local cultures. The weights of these factors will depend on the complexity of the product and the distance between the cultures.

Incentives

Organisations often encourage their sales representatives and/or the sales team to attain specific objectives (e.g., turnover target, profit target, promotion of certain products, gaining market share at the expense of competitors) through incentives. Two basic extremes of incentive systems for monitoring sales are presented in **Table 5.5** and described below.

Model 1, based on *formal and realistic evaluation,* is appropriate for a firm belonging to an individualistic society where communication is fairly explicit, power distance is small, and uncertainty avoidance is weak (e.g., the USA). Model 2, based on *internal incentives,* is appropriate for a company in a society where communication is implicit (high context), power distance is high, and uncertainty avoidance is strong (e.g., Japan). The masculinity/femininity dimension also influences the practical implementation of these two models of sales force remuneration in terms of providing more assertive (masculine) or more nurturing (feminine) feedback and corrective action to low-performing salespeople.

Table 5.5 Contrast models

Cultural traits	Model 1	Model 2
Power distance	Low	High
Individualism	High	Low
Uncertainty avoidance	Low	High
Context of communication	Low	High

In **model 1**, *formal and realistic evaluation* is likely, where the sellers must earn their salary. In these societies, relations are depersonalised, and people can be evaluated by sales targets, which are negotiated with the salesperson. Any deviation of actual sales from the target is measured precisely, and rewards, sanctions, and corrective actions may result, as the individual is seen as the source of the performance (individualism). Competition between salespeople, within the sales team, is considered legitimate, even though it may undermine the coherence of collective action in situations where this is needed (e.g., training other salespeople, transfer of experience from senior to junior salespeople, etc.).

In **model 2**, *internal incentives* are likely, where the context is expected to influence the outcome. In these societies, relations are personalised, and objectives are not openly and truly negotiated. In higher power distance societies, it is assumed that the boss knows what the sales staff should achieve, and goals, if provided, are set at excessively high target levels, which serve as an ultimate goal. There is no shame in failing to attain these goals, as they are set significantly higher than a realistic target. In Southeast Asia, the ethics of non-confrontation clearly clash with an objective performance review, as this could cause the subordinate to 'lose face', infringing a societal norm. The motivation theories, which underlie sales force compensation systems, are culturally bound. Generally, staff turnover is low, and closer personal ties exist within a stable workforce (e.g., strong uncertainty avoidance emphasises a high level of job security). The risk is that sellers may seek security and lack personal initiative and drive.

There are different methods to deal with the problem of sellers who are clearly underperforming. In masculine societies (e.g., Australia, Switzerland, the USA), poor results will be called to attention with clear warnings that performance must improve, and if they fail to satisfactorily explain why (based on uncontrollable factors), they will eventually be dismissed. In feminine societies (Sweden, northern European countries, France), a higher value is placed on the quality of life. While these societies also strive for efficiency, a seller is entitled to more understanding. When the reasons for their underperformance have been assessed with them (formally or informally), they receive assistance from colleagues and from the organisation (e.g., additional training). Only after the organisation has done everything within its power to help salespeople to increase their performance is a final decision taken.

The type of product also influences the reward structure in all countries. Large and complex sales (e.g., desalination or nuclear plants) requiring lengthy sales efforts from a team of experts who tend to be rewarded with fixed salaries, in a way preferred by the cultural values of model 2. Smaller and less complex sales (e.g., consumer goods) requiring identifiable sales efforts, tend to be rewarded with salaries that have an element of commission; however, pure commission-based salaries will only be acceptable in model 1.

There are also cultural differences in the emphasis on extrinsic and intrinsic rewards and on whether the reward is attributed to an individual or team. Extrinsic rewards (e.g., variable commissions on sales), are external motivators, whereas intrinsic rewards are related to the satisfaction of inner needs. People may be intrinsically motivated by a job well done, the esteem of their colleagues, or even the securing of a contract per se. Rewards can be centred on the individual (e.g., gifts to sellers or their families, payment of personal expenses), on the group (e.g., a leisure trip for the whole sales team), or mixed. For instance, in Japan, group rewards may take the form of a joint holiday for the sales team, which is both an individual and a group reward and contributes to group bonding. Whereas models 1 and 2 depict extreme characteristics, real-world remuneration systems more often combine intrinsic and extrinsic, individual and collective rewards. However, it is important that the reward structure is appropriate to the cultural values and the product category.

The influence of culture in online and direct marketing

Direct marketing (via email, texts, catalogues, websites, and banner advertising on search engines and apps) allows for customised communication to the consumer, aimed at getting an immediate response. While most companies use their website to provide detailed product information, along with the ability to make online purchases, some companies are entirely internet-based, with no bricks-and-mortar shopfronts at all. Amazon.com is perhaps the most widely recognised of these companies. In 2022, Amazon had dedicated websites for shoppers and sellers in almost 20 countries across five continents, including Australia, Brazil, Canada, China, France, Germany, India, Ireland, Italy, Japan, Mexico, the Netherlands, Poland, Saudi Arabia, Singapore, Spain, Turkey, the United Arab Emirates, the UK, and the USA. In addition, they also export to countries in many different regions (i.e., 31 countries in the Americas, 46 in Europe, 23 in Australia, Asia, and the Pacific, and 30 in Africa and the Middle East). Their website states that they accept seller registrations from residents of over 170 countries, as long as the seller has a valid phone number and an internationally chargeable credit card. Thus, their reach is almost worldwide. However, they are under growing scrutiny in terms of data privacy and rights. Specifically, there are increasing concerns about Amazon's ability to gather data on the shopping habits of millions of people worldwide. These concerns are not just limited to Amazon.

The EU has strict laws on the protection of personal data, including data used for direct marketing activities. The e-Privacy Directive generally requires opt-in consent, which limits the use of the marketing list. The Court of Justice of the EU ruled in late 2021 that advertising messages sent to an electronic inbox constitute direct marketing and are subject to the EU Member States' rules on direct marketing. While most countries lag behind the EU in data privacy law, the landscape is evolving in developed and emerging nations, with substantial penalties and reputational damage for firms that do not comply.

Another important consideration in selling online is deciding where to store and send products from, as goods can be mailed from the home country, from within the target country, or from a third country. Although it may seem easiest to mail from within the target country, because the local language and culture will be understood better, there may be constraints in the local postal service or differences in tax liabilities that make it cheaper to mail from a third country. In most cases, the tax amount that internet-based retailers need to collect from shoppers will depend on where the goods are coming from and where the sales are being made. In most countries, there is a threshold when taxes kick in for those selling into different countries. In the USA, it kicks in when a firm completes over 200 transactions or US$100,000 in sales, whereas in Singapore, a 9% GST needs to be paid on all online sales over SGD$400. These rates are often different from goods sold within the country, which can influence competitive pricing.

Sales promotions, customs, and legal issues

Sales promotions can provide the consumer with an extra incentive to purchase. They are usually designed to create short-term action, via in-store, online, or direct marketing (e.g., price discounts, rebates, coupons, competitions, and free samples or gifts). Some sales promotion techniques are fairly consistent cross-culturally. For instance, (a) free samples as a way to induce people to try the product, (b) discount on the next purchase as a way to induce consumers to repeat their purchase, (c) point-of-purchase materials and product demonstrations as a way to increase consumer knowledge of the product, (d) free food tasting to induce trial, (e) loyalty reward systems, etc. However, some countries object to sales promotion techniques in general because of the risk of consumers being misled. These countries generally have less confidence in the capacities of individuals to make free and responsible choices (e.g., Latin-European and northern European countries), whereas other countries believe in personal responsibility and trust consumers to seek and evaluate information (e.g., Australia, the UK, and the USA).

In countries where consumer bargaining is common and basic prices are not displayed, rebates have little meaning. In such cases, it may be better to target channel members (wholesalers or retailers), rather than the end user. Sales promotions may include the payment of *slotting fees* to encourage a product to be stocked or *display allowances* for prominent placement at the cash register or at the end of aisles. They might also involve cooperative advertising of in-store specials and temporary sale prices (e.g., discounts, two-for-one offers, etc.) or incentives for sales (e.g., gifts). Trade promotions may be especially relevant to commodity-type products that consumers need reminding to buy, such as batteries. Directing promotions at the store may be more effective in less developed countries, where stores are smaller and consumers are limited to the choices offered within the store.

Sales promotion regulations differ cross-nationally according to assumptions about what is moral or immoral, and what is fair or unfair in the relationship between a seller and a customer. The areas in which ethical issues are mostly raised involve competitions, gifts, and cross-product offers. Sales promotions are prevalent in the UK and the USA. Anglo-Saxon countries are generally more liberal than other countries, especially for competitions (e.g., most kinds of lotteries, free draws and sweepstakes are legally permitted). However, in Islam, lotteries are considered gambling, which is forbidden. It is immoral for private individuals to benefit from organising lotteries and betting games. While the European Court of Justice is working to reduce restrictions on promotional marketing in the European Union, many countries differ in their regulation of these lotteries and sweepstakes. This makes it difficult to run international sweepstakes. For instance, in Italy, a public official who is located in Italy must select the winners, and in France, entrants can ask you to reimburse them for the cost of postage or internet to enter the sweepstake or contest. Many national regulations also prohibit gifts or limit their value. In France, the value of a promotional gift can not be higher than 7% of the retail price. The idea behind this prohibition is that consumers should buy products, not gifts. Collectors' items, such as gifts, are subject to the same kind of regulatory ceiling: the value of the collector's item associated with the purchase is often legally limited, especially those targeted at children. Further, sales promotions that encourage an initial trial, such as cross-product offers and purchase-with-purchase offers, are often controlled by national legislation. It is more difficult for consumers to judge value when they pay for two products at the same time.

Marketing infrastructure and sophistication also differ across countries. Retailer sophistication is required when promotional techniques need follow-up, such as redeeming coupons, loyalty reward programmes, or dealing with stamps that need to be collected and redeemed. Further, employees can opportunistically remove samples, gifts, or premiums for themselves, decide to sell what were supposed to be free samples, or pocket money-off offers by increasing prices. Strict control of the retailers involved in promotion is required wherever such opportunistic attitudes are foreseeable.

Redeeming sales promotions can be associated with social status. In Hong Kong, the response to coupons is generally positive, whereas the use of stamps is more popular in Thailand; however, both of these locally popular techniques are associated with middle-class status. In other countries, coupons or discounts can be associated with lower-class status (e.g., in Australia), because the implied price consciousness suggests an image of low purchasing power.

5.4 Pricing decisions

At first sight, price, as a figure, a number, or a unit, appears to be universally understandable and hardly susceptible at all to cultural influences. Firms that view price as an objective, culture-free element will often want to set their prices in the same way as they do in their home market. If their objective in the home market is to maximise profit, they will tend to set the price at a relatively high level to make the most profit per unit. Alternatively, if their objective in the home market is to maximise sales, they will tend to set the price at a relatively low level to achieve the highest number of units sold.

There are three main pricing methods that are commonly used in business:

- **Cost-based pricing, where a set markup is added to the cost of producing a product unit.** This pricing method is relatively simple and easily justifiable, as basic cost data is available within the firm, and this method is often seen as being fair by customers. However, it neglects competitors' pricing and customer needs, which leads to sub-optimal prices that are either too high or too low.
- **Competition-based pricing, where specific or average competitors' prices are used as a basis for determining a target price.** This pricing method is relatively simple for firms, as competitive prices can usually be attained to consider the competitive situation. However, it neglects customer needs, and can lead to price wars.
- **Value-based pricing, where the perceived value of a product is determined as the amount customers are willing to pay.** This pricing method is more complex, but it takes into account the competitive situation and will usually maximise profit. However, it is also more costly to determine, and customers may see this method as unfair or discriminatory if different customer groups are charged different prices.

Each of these pricing methods has its advantages and disadvantages, but together they show how the characteristics of the market, including differences in the cost of getting products to market, the competitive situation, and the perceived value of the product to the new customers, influence effective pricing. However, pricing in the international environment is significantly more complicated than it is in a domestic market.

Cross-cultural considerations

Price is often assumed to be an objective element of exchange, based on rational economic factors. But price also has a more subjective element. It is a signal that conveys meaning and, as such, is perceived in quite different ways across cultures, and also between individuals.

Where goods are sold in mass distribution outlets that allow price comparison between products and/or stores, price is likely to be more objective than when the relationship between a buyer and seller is more important. In the former case, the meaning conveyed by the price revolves mostly around the value of the good and the money transfer. In the latter case, price is more likely to be a negotiation between the buyer and seller, and as such is more central to the relationship.

Relationships between buyers and sellers will be more important in the process of negotiating a price, under the following circumstances:

1.   Price is not displayed.
2.   It is not necessarily the seller who announces the first price.
3.   There is no clear market reference for what would be a 'fair price'.
4.   A particular price is understood by both sellers and buyers as taking place within a series of transactions (i.e., past, present, and future).
5.   Prices for particular transactions are not necessarily meant to cover even marginal costs.
6.   Total price is a combination of direct and indirect costs (e.g., product price plus costs of maintenance, spare parts, updates, etc.).
7.   Prices may be distorted by inflation and government price regulation.

From this list, it is clear that characteristics of the environment, as well as cultural and personal norms and preferences, determine whether or not bargaining takes place. The connection between bargaining and price display is obvious. Wherever the law demands the vendor display prices clearly, the practice of bargaining will diminish. However, clearly displaying prices is nearly impossible in countries where there is extremely high inflation. For instance, in Venezuela, where the inflation rate was estimated at over 1,000% in early 2022, prices, if they were to be displayed, would need to be changed on a daily basis. Even at an inflation rate of over 60%, as was estimated for Turkey in early 2022, price setting is a real challenge[14].

Bargaining

The importance of bargaining is often underestimated because in many developed countries, it is normal experience for consumers to prices that are clearly displayed. If the price is not right, the product will not be bought. In most cases, people no longer bargain – or at least they appear not to. Bargaining is either legally prohibited or strictly controlled. Prices are unilaterally set by vendors and are largely non-negotiable. Bargaining at the supermarket checkout is rare, and liable to result in confusion or embarrassment. However, once the price reaches a substantial level, people, even in developed countries, often return to bargaining. Bargaining is common when purchasing new and second-hand cars, property, or large quantities of a product. Bargaining is also common in informal retail contexts, such as garage sales or flea markets, where the value of the transaction is often insignificant to both vendor and consumer. Bargaining in these contexts is not just motivated by rational economics, as it can provide a sense of enjoyment and empowerment when consumers have the ability to influence the price of goods through their knowledge and skill.

Bargaining is very common, if not the rule, in most emerging economies (e.g., Thailand, India, the Philippines, and the Middle East). Moreover, in certain African markets (e.g., Mauritania), where sugar can be sold by the 'lump' and carrots by the 'slice', and island economies (e.g., The Marshall Islands), where cigarettes are sold by the 'stick', bargaining is essential for survival. People may also be less pressed for time, making the rewards of bargaining greater than the costs. Great satisfaction can also be obtained from what is perceived to be a 'good' bargaining exchange.

Bargaining can differ substantially between cultures and people within those cultures. Some important questions that should be considered include the following: Who should set the initial price point? Who should be the first to make concessions? Who will be more likely to compromise?

At least four factors play a major role in answering these questions:

1. The initial power position of each party.
2. The degree of urgency for either buyer or seller to close the deal.
3. The importance of negotiation margin from the initial price.
4. The type of social process by which buyer and seller progressively adjust their price.

Some of these factors are illustrated in the scenarios described in the following box.

PRICE LEVELS AND BUYER–SELLER RELATIONSHIP

Scenario 1: The seller wishes to offer a fair price from the start, close to the final price, expecting it will win the customer's loyalty. This should convince the buyer of the vendor's honesty, openness, and genuine desire to do business. If the customer shares this view, as might be expected in Western Europe, the USA, or Australia, and decides to cooperate, an agreement is quickly reached, and each party is satisfied.

(Continued)

Scenario 2: The same vendor suggests the same price, close to the final price, as a sign of goodwill towards the buyer. However, in this case, the buyer, who comes from a different culture (e.g., India or Pakistan), sees their role as centring on the price rebate rather than on the price level. The buyer's boss expects them to obtain the greatest possible discount from the seller. The announced price, being close to the final price, leaves buyer and seller with little satisfactory negotiating room; therefore, no deal is made.

Scenario 3: The vendor announces a much higher initial price than they expect to obtain, leaving room for negotiation from the start. This allows the buyer to demonstrate skill in a mutually beneficial bargaining exercise and enables both parties to increase the long-term value of their social relationship. The final agreed price is very close to that in Scenario 1. With the buyer interested mostly in the rebate and the seller in the price level, both can achieve greater satisfaction than in Scenario 1.

Price and consumer evaluations

Consumers tend to use price as a proxy or cue for quality, especially when specific quality criteria are absent or difficult to evaluate objectively. While it is expected that price and quality should be strongly correlated, in reality the correlation is weak, perhaps because consumers are imperfectly informed about the price and quality of competing products. Further, consumers' perceptions of the price of a product include more than the ticket price. Put simply, the price of a nail is not easily separable from the non-monetary price involved in driving it in, including the risk of hitting one's finger in the process. Non-monetary price reflects costs related to time spent, the search itself, psychological risk, etc. These costs shape the consumer's perception of the sacrifice involved in the consumption experience in exchange for the satisfaction to be derived from it. Perceptions of non-monetary price vary a great deal across cultures. A trip to buy a product, or the preparation of meals, may be perceived as enjoyable in some cultures, reflecting no perception of sacrifice; however, the same tasks may be perceived as being tedious in other cultures. In the USA, where there is an economic view of time, perceptions of the non-monetary price will be higher.

Obviously, there are differences in the price–quality relationship across product categories, as some products are more difficult to assess prior to purchase than others. For instance, it is not possible for consumers to assess whether a German Miele washing machine, which is three times more expensive than a machine branded by Zanussi (the Italian arm of the Swedish Electrolux group), lasts three times longer before they purchase one. Consumers often need to use other cues to make inferences, such as associating attractive, elaborate packaging with a higher price–quality relationship.

In the absence of information based on actual product use, consumers may be forced to simplify the information they use. Cues, such as brand, packaging, and price, are examples of simplified information that influences what consumers perceive. For instance, in Western countries sellers often use prices ending in 99c, which are perceived as being significantly cheaper than if the amount was rounded up to the nearest dollar; however, studies have found that this practice can negatively influence perceptions of quality, especially for those who are not driven by price. As such, higher-priced products may do better if they avoid 99c endings. Further, it should not be assumed that the 99c ending is transferable across cultures. In Asian cultures, particularly Chinese-speaking communities, prices ending in 8 are more common, as the pronunciation of 8 is similar to the word for 'luck,' and seen as a cue for good value.

International price tactics

Price is more than a number. It is a tactical tool in local markets and a strategic tool in the face of global competition. While price can be used to increase profits or sales, it can also be used to support market objectives, such as developing new markets, eliminating competition, or promoting the product image (see **Table 5.6**).

Table 5.6 Pricing objectives

	Objectives	
Profit	(1)	Maximise company profits
	(2)	Reach target profits
Sales	(3)	Increase unit volume
	(4)	Attain sales figures
	(5)	Increase cash flows
Market	(6)	Develop new markets
	(7)	Maintain customer loyalty
	(8)	Achieve greater market stability
	(9)	Attain price parity with competitors
	(10)	Eliminate competitors
	(11)	Promote the image of the company and/or its products and/or brands

Price can be relatively consistent across markets, with a single global price using the cost-based method, including production costs, insurance, freight and customs/tax costs, etc. This is often termed a *price extension or ethnocentric position*. Alternatively, the price can be adapted to local market conditions using value-based and/or competition-based pricing. This is often termed a *polycentric adaptation position*. Finally, the price can be adapted to be relatively consistent across a region, where the local market conditions are coordinated into an *intermediate geocentric position*.

Price discrimination occurs when the price is adapted to different local or regional market conditions. For instance, a firm may sell products at a discount to a country or region where local consumers cannot afford the price paid in other regions. In this case, the price manipulation distorts the price of goods in different markets, as long as opportunistic behaviour from customers and distributors can be avoided (e.g., buying where it is cheapest, either for consumption or for resale at a higher price in another market).

The question of who gets the lowest price depends on market conditions and the positions of the respective markets on the firm's cost curve. For a firm to maximise profit, it must sell its products at a price greater than or equal to the marginal cost of producing one extra unit. In practice, firms usually consider the cost-price to include total costs, which include both marginal and fixed costs. In industries where overheads are high and/or significant research underlies product development (e.g., aerospace, pharmaceuticals, etc.), direct costing (i.e., variable costs directly related to production) may be used. Here, the question is whether the domestic market or the export market is supposed to 'pay' for the depreciation of these sunk costs.

If a firm exports at a lower price than what it normally charges in its home market, it is called *dumping*. While the WTO does not regulate firms' behaviour, it works with governments on how to react to dumping. Specifically, Article VI of the General Agreement on Tariffs and Trade (GATT) prohibits dumping where it prejudices the production of one of the contracting parties[15]. Firms are more likely to engage in dumping if they see the role of the domestic market as recovering sunk costs and/or they see foreign markets as a way of increasing market share, with the intention of raising prices once a sizable share has been secured. However, while slashing the price in the short term may appear to be an attractive strategy for obtaining new clients, building customer loyalty, and increasing market share, it could result in a longer-term loss of profit, especially where competitors engage in a price war to maintain or regain their previous share.

Price discrimination also sets up the potential for parallel imports and grey markets, where consumers and even distributors can seek cheaper supplies across borders, making the manufacturer compete with its own products. If the price differential is large enough to offset transaction costs, unauthorised intermediaries may compete with sole agents or exclusive dealers in national markets where a specific marketing strategy has been implemented. In this case, unofficial intermediaries can benefit from advertising and marketing strategies carried out by the company and its regular dealers, without having to contribute to these costs.

Firms usually try to minimise the conditions that create grey markets. Possible solutions to counter grey markets and parallel imports are as follows:

1. **Reduce the price differentials** between markets, so that there is little profit in parallel importing. This, however, may be at the expense of the global coherence of the marketing strategy in either one or both countries.

2. **Materially alter the product** to favourably differentiate the official product from the parallel imported product. To reduce adaptation costs this could be limited to minor product attributes (e.g., extended warranties may be granted only to authorised dealers, a label 'not for export' or 'for domestic sale only' may be attached to the packaging to prevent some dealers from re-exporting, although the effectiveness of these labels is limited).

3. **Educate the dealer** to explain why such price differentials are important, as weaker dealers may be prime targets for grey market attacks.

4. **Terminate the dealer agreements** (or threaten to do so) when the dealer buys from unauthorised parallel sources.

5. **Buy back the grey market goods**, which will be seen positively by authorised dealers, who feel actively protected by the brand owner. However, this solution is only possible when a permanent solution to parallel imports has been found and is quickly implemented after a short – and costly – buy-back period.

6. **Sell products under a different name**, leaving the foreign distributors to promote the products, or develop a unique trademark in each country. The danger here is loss of benefits from a global trademark.

7. **Target different consumer segments**, determined on the basis of the degree of risk aversion.

Depending on the distribution channel chosen, firms will have more or less influence over their product price positioning. In some countries, legislators prohibit producers from dictating resale prices to agents, whereas this is allowed in other countries. Firms try to manoeuvre around these laws through recommended retail price labelling, thus controlling an agent's discretionary margin. Even so, the agent could still sell the product at a discount price (e.g., to promote the agent's store), in conflict with the producer's pricing strategy.

Market situations, competition, and price agreements

Competition in new markets is difficult to assess, and even more difficult to predict the reaction of competitors to new market entrants. In some cases, firms might battle fiercely to hold their market share or to eliminate new entrants entirely, whereas others may implicitly agree to divide territory to avoid price wars. However, it is unlikely to be this simple. Firms may compete for market share in some segments, brands, and national markets, whereas in other segments and for other brands, a compromise may be implicitly reached. Competitive patterns should therefore be analysed on a per-case basis, as competition and alliances between firms will always occur.

The competitive code that constrains new entrants into a market is even more complex, as it determines how they should behave towards already established players. Large new entrants frequently face a combined attack from all firms (domestic and foreign) in a national market. Existing competitors may, for instance, lower their prices or spread rumours about the new entrant's product or service policies and their lack of long-term commitment to local customers. This results in poor competition, which may be detrimental to customers.

The dynamics of competition may lead to the concentration of supply amongst a limited number of companies, decreasing the competition. Decreasing competition is attractive to firms, as it is often associated with the ability to charge higher prices to customers. This is why antitrust legislation (e.g., the US antitrust legislation and the Sherman Act) has been introduced to oversee the proper functioning of competition, discourage dominant positions, and deter the establishment of monopolies through mergers and acquisitions. However, every country has a few monopolies, as well as some markets where pure and perfect competition reigns. In addition, there is usually a large number of oligopolies that are usually producers of large-scale consumables or durable consumer goods, as well as bilateral oligopolies that are usually producers of industrial input goods, such as steel, chemicals, rubber, and capital goods (see **Table 5.7**). What varies, as a function of culture, is the social approval or disapproval of these different market forms. Local decision-makers need to determine whether monopolies may be desirable or dangerous for the community. Foreign intruders may be seen positively from the consumer's point of view, or negatively from the local competitor's point of view. However, it must be remembered that consumers are often also employees whose employment may be put at risk by the competition.

Table 5.7   Basic forms of markets[16]

Buyers		Sellers		
		One	**Some**	**Many**
	One	Bilateral monopoly	Contradicted monopsony	Monopsony
	Some	Contradicted monopoly	Bilateral oligopoly	Oligopsony
	Many	Monopoly	Oligopoly	Pure competition

Protection of local firms from the government also needs to be considered on a country-by-country basis. Americans are often shocked by the amount of protection European governments provide to their flagship firms. The Airbus–Boeing saga is typical of conceptual differences that partly derive their roots from culture. Europeans consider that government loans – often viewed as sunk costs – were used wisely in view of the success of the Airbus aircraft, the number of jobs created, the positive effects on the trade balance, and the preservation of a previously threatened European civil aeronautics industry. However, for the Americans, it was a costly mess that helped no one: Boeing's success was challenged by disloyal competition, European taxpayers were burdened, and international trade rules were distorted.

Managing prices in highly regulated environments

Countries differ widely in how they control their economic environment, ranging from free markets, which are controlled by market forces of supply and demand, to planned economies, which are fully controlled by the government.

- In free markets, products are exchanged voluntarily between sellers and buyers, where sellers don't face any barriers to selling products at any price that a buyer is willing to pay.
- In planned economies, the government controls the market, including the pricing of products, distribution channels and even the producers.

However, most economies are somewhere in between, keeping at least some controls over the types of products sold and to whom they are sold (e.g., selling alcohol to children) and over tariffs on imports and/or exports.

Planned economies are a feature of Communist nations. For instance, in North Korea, the state controls all production. It rejects foreign investment but has had some economic exchanges with a limited number of countries (e.g., China and South Korea). In contrast, China and Russia moved from planned economies to mixed economies; however, since the invasion of Ukraine in 2022, the Russian economy has been largely closed to international markets due to sanctions and government controls. For example, the EU sanctioned specific individuals with travel bans and asset freezes, placed export restrictions on certain products (e.g., technology, transportation, aviation and space, energy, and luxury goods), as well as import restrictions on fuels, some metals and seafood and liquor (caviar, vodka). Further, Russian banks were prevented from making or receiving international payments using SWIFT, meaning they cannot get foreign currency or transfer assets abroad without incurring substantial costs. This means the Russian ruble is no longer a convertible currency, cutting Russia off from the global financial system. This has forced multinational organisations with operations in Russia to suspend trade (e.g., Ikea, Nestlé, American Express), temporarily close stores (e.g., Nike, Starbucks), withdraw, and, where possible, sell off assets (McDonald's, PepsiCo, Shell), often at great cost to the companies.

Exchange controls, high inflation, and price stability

At the national level, price stability is based on macroeconomic policies, as well as cultural values. The requisite discipline is based on: (1) future time orientation, which provides the monetary authorities with a perspective of continuity in fighting inflation; (2) control of the creation of money and credit; and (3) a belief in free market forces that may keep price increases under control because of active competition. Such a belief is, in general, related to individualism and low power distance.

Venezuela, which has an extremely high inflation rate (more than 1000% in early 2022), is a high power distant, uncertainty-avoidant, masculine, collectivist culture. The country is in a protracted major crisis, which many economists blame on their currency control system that promoted a dysfunctional market.

High inflation rates cause non-convertible currencies to weaken systematically against stable and convertible foreign currencies, because of constantly decreasing nominal purchasing power. When the exchange rate is maintained at unrealistic levels, it can create a parallel foreign exchange market, which is illegal, but generally tolerated by the authorities. In comparison with official exchange rates, parallel rates are favourable to foreign currency sellers and unfavourable to buyers. In such situations, foreign exchange controls serve the purpose of enriching the most powerful, who can buy foreign currencies at the favourable official rate, while restricting the capacity of local exporters to receive a real price, because exporters are obliged to sell export receipts in hard currencies at the usually over-valued official rate.

In these situations, high inflation is combatted by price control, an expression of the power of regulatory authorities over companies. Where there is high power distance, there tends to be oppressive rules. Price increases, so vital for a company's survival, may be delayed by public authorities, even though last month's inflation rate may have caused the entire industry to go into the red, as costs soar while sales stagnate because of controlled prices. Consumers and companies adapt to high inflation by stocking up with items during favourable periods, and becoming very price conscious. Companies rely on negotiated price increases with public authorities, rather than depending on consumer demand in defining prices. They overestimate cost prices and exaggerate losses to obtain a favourable new price, so they have a reserve before the next increase. Naturally, this process fosters inflation rather than slowing it down.

In Venezuela, USD is commonly being used by private companies, increasing inequality, as State employees are paid in Bolivars (average of US$30–$100 a month), whereas most of the private sector are paid in USD (average of $106–$247 per month)[17]. It is estimated that the average cost of basic family food needs is $300 per month, which is fuelling further crises.

5.5 Communication decisions

Integrated advertising and promotional strategies are designed to ensure that the target audience receives consistent, persuasive messaging through a range of marketing channels to help move potential buyers through the decision-making process. Their development would usually incorporate strategic and communication objectives, market research, audience segmentation, media channel selection, creative briefs, campaign messaging, budgeting, return on investment analysis, and systems for measuring and evaluating performance.

While communication decisions are considered to be the most culture-bound element of the marketing mix, the general process for forming a communication strategy is relatively 'generic', as shown in **Figure 5.7**.

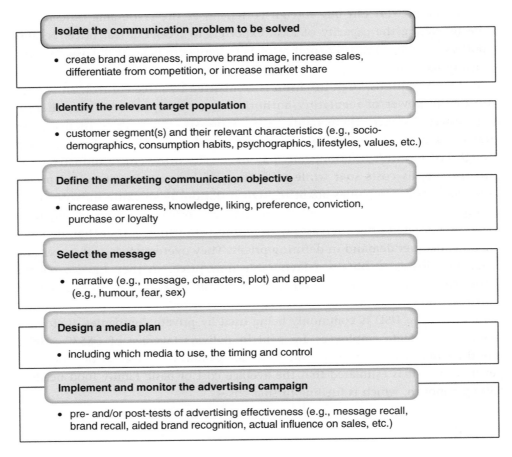

Isolate the communication problem to be solved

- create brand awareness, improve brand image, increase sales, differentiate from competition, or increase market share

Identify the relevant target population

- customer segment(s) and their relevant characteristics (e.g., socio-demographics, consumption habits, psychographics, lifestyles, values, etc.)

Define the marketing communication objective

- increase awareness, knowledge, liking, preference, conviction, purchase or loyalty

Select the message

- narrative (e.g., message, characters, plot) and appeal (e.g., humour, fear, sex)

Design a media plan

- including which media to use, the timing and control

Implement and monitor the advertising campaign

- pre- and/or post-tests of advertising effectiveness (e.g., message recall, brand recall, aided brand recognition, actual influence on sales, etc.)

Figure 5.7 Steps in developing a communication strategy

These steps can be broken down into strategic elements or 'what is said' (i.e., the communication problem, identification of target segment(s) and defining the communication objective) and execution elements or 'how it is said' (i.e., designing the message and the media plan). The **strategic elements** tend to follow similar approaches; however, the emphasis and outcome will likely differ across countries. For instance, a new product will naturally lack brand awareness; however, aiming to increase brand awareness may not be enough in a market, especially if the product cannot be evaluated without trial. It might be necessary to encourage the trial of the product to emphasise differentiation from existing competition. Thus, identifying the communication problem may still be complex. Identifying target segments may also be complicated. For instance, a base model product in one country might be considered a high-end product in another. The **execution elements** are likely to be more strongly influenced by culture and existing marketing infrastructure. Messages are interpreted in relation to context, especially local culture. The media plan will be strongly influenced by local idiosyncrasies, including media availability, viewing habits and media regulations, which still differ greatly across countries.

Influence of culture on attitudes towards advertising

Before a specific message can be crafted, it is important to understand the role of advertising and how people may differ in their attitudes towards, and perceptions of, advertising across cultures. The role of advertising can be perceived as positive (e.g., informative, entertaining) or negative (e.g., misleading, irritating). While there was evidence that people in many emerging economies had more positive evaluations of advertising than those in developed economies, the gap is closing. Recent studies of Chinese consumers show quite negative feelings toward advertising in general, even more so than in the USA[18].

More attention is being given to the idea that advertising, though undeniably useful to society, can also have negative results, such as encouraging conspicuous consumption, harmful consumption, and the creation of wants that cannot be satisfied. Some countries (e.g., Norway, Quebec [Canada], and Sweden) have bans on all advertisements during children's television programming, whereas other countries (e.g., most of Europe, Australia, Canada, Malaysia, and Korea) have laws that set some limits (e.g., advertising times and marketing techniques – bans on the use of cartoon characters). For instance, advertising junk food to children is recognised as harmful, especially in countries with growing obesity levels. To address this, the UK announced a ban on junk-food advertising online, and before 9 pm on TV, as well as a ban on specific promotions, such as 'buy one get one free', and soft drink refills.

Aside from advertising to vulnerable segments and advertising vice products (e.g., gambling, alcohol, and tobacco), another major area of contention across cultures is the use of *comparative advertising*, which depends on societal views towards the following questions:

1. What is the social function of comparative advertising?
2. What are the prevailing arguments concerning the legitimacy of comparative advertising?
3. How should competition between brands be facilitated?
4. Does comparative advertising result in misleading consumers by using questionable information to praise one's own brand and disparage others?

Socially dominant responses to these questions directly influence comparative advertising regulations in a given country. In some countries, comparative advertising is held in low esteem. For instance, comparative advertising is banned by law in France, where it has traditionally been considered a denigration of competing brands. In order for the advertisement to be considered comparative, and, therefore, illegal, it needs only to be a comparison of two competing products, even if the information is basically correct. In other countries, comparative advertising is permitted. However, it can draw undesirable attention from the competition, potentially sparking an advertising war. While basic arguments in favour of comparative advertising seem to make sense, in that it facilitates consumer information, choice and competition between brands, opponents of comparative advertising argue that truly objective comparisons would need to be handled by completely independent testing organisations. Where legislation allows comparative advertising, comparisons should be objective and not discredit competitors or their brands. False or misleading comparative advertising is illegal in most countries, with rather harsh penalties.

How societies perceive the role of advertising has led to many differences in advertising rules and regulations, generally and specific to product categories. For example, in the USA, sellers of food do not need to prominently note on the packaging that the product contains genetically modified plants or meats, whereas in most EU countries, this is a requirement. This example illustrates the importance of the issue of genetic modification and the role of advertising in accurately informing consumers.

Communication strategy

Once the communication problem and target market have been identified, a communication objective needs to be chosen. The ***hierarchy of effects model***[19] identifies the steps in a consumer's journey toward purchasing a product:

1. Awareness
2. Knowledge
3. Liking
4. Preference
5. Conviction
6. Purchase

This model can be used to help define the communication objectives. While these steps were originally depicted as a hierarchy of progressive steps, the ordering of these steps can vary depending on the consumer, product, and even purchase occasion.

That is, some consumer journeys may begin with emotions (e.g., impulse purchasing where liking may be the first step), whereas others may begin with product trials (e.g., a taste test in a store). Regardless of where the process starts, it is important to understand where consumers are in their purchase journey, as this will likely differ across countries and segments.

Another important consideration in setting communication objectives is whether the communication should be aimed directly at consumers or at members of the distribution channel who sell to consumers. **Pull strategies** target the end consumer to pull the products through the channel, whereas **push strategies** target the channel members to motivate them to sell the product to consumers. Pull strategies are influenced by differences in consumer behaviour, and push strategies are influenced by differences in channel members and the available marketing infrastructure across countries. In new international markets, firms will likely need to include both push and pull elements.

Communication execution

Communication execution is about translating the strategy into a story that enhances consumers' understanding of the brand's value and positioning: What does the brand uniquely offer to the selected target market segment? Why should consumers buy it? This stage serves as a significant cross-cultural 'filter', since the meaning transfer is fine-tuned through the executional details, most of which are strongly culture-bound.

Firms often hire professional advertising consultants or agencies who have creative directors, copywriters, graphic and digital designers, photographers, art directors, film producers, etc., to help transform the communication strategy into compelling narratives and appealing visual imagery. International advertising often includes less text and more reliance on visual elements, due to issues around translation, but conveying the correct meaning may be just as difficult with visual elements, as discussed in Section 5.2 under symbolic attributes. For instance, rain may either evoke freshness or coldness, depending on where you are from. This is problematic for global advertising.

Where television advertisements must be easily transferable across countries, there should be a heavy emphasis on visual elements with voice-overs in the local language. Television advertisements aimed at a European audience often use a script where the characters do not speak to the audience or to each other; a voice-over message is added to the image track. This cleverly avoids the drawbacks associated with dubbing. Most people lip-read unconsciously, and when watching a dubbed commercial, they may feel uneasy about the incongruity between lip movements and sounds.

The basic narrative structure used in most advertising includes the following elements:

1. a message that conveys the essential elements of a brand's value or positioning;
2. a conflict that creates a desire or motivation to resolve it (e.g., good versus evil, new versus traditional concepts or products);
3. characters that are identifiable to the consumer and meaningful to the story (e.g., a hero, villain, expert, rebel, the brand, consumers);
4. a plot that is a sequence of events that sets the scene and triggers our interest and involvement, with the opening and closing moments being most memorable and often including the brand; and
5. a meme (e.g., an image, video, or catchphrase) that captures a cultural norm or behaviour that attracts consumer attention and prompts them to share it with others.

Crafting the main communication message

Given that it is estimated that people are exposed to thousands of advertisements per day, it is important that the main message in advertising is memorable and meaningful for consumers. There should be a key takeaway, often highlighted in a tagline, as a user-friendly version of the product positioning. For instance, American Express uses different forms of its *Don't leave home without it* tagline (e.g., *Don't live life without it; Don't do business without it*) to warn of the dangers of being caught without the safety of their credit card. However, messages often need to be adjusted to be locally meaningful. For instance, McDonald's Happy Meal advertisements focus on themes of 'socialising' and 'bonding' in Asia, whereas they highlight individuality and self-expression in the USA[20].

An important decision is whether to state the main message directly, or allow consumers to derive their own conclusions by thinking about the advertisement. The latter adds complexity to message development, but research has shown that when consumers elaborate on a message and draw their own conclusions, the message can be more memorable and more persuasive. However, in international and cross-cultural advertising this process must be carefully tested. Research has found that consumers interpret advertisements differently from experts. For example, traditional content analysis of advertisements (i.e., coding advertisements on a pre-set list of characteristics) differs from coding consumer interpretations of the same advertisements (see Activity 5.3)[21]. Unless managers have a strong understanding of local consumers and their culture, it may be more effective to state the key message explicitly, in order to minimise the possibility that it is missed or misinterpreted.

Activity 5.3

Consumer interpretation of advertising messages

Studies have found differences between direct content coding of advertisements and coding of consumers' interpretations of the same advertisements. Advertisements are often coded by the values embedded in them to understand whether there are differences between people in different countries. The following table shows differences in the frequency of values in liquor and car ads in the USA and Spain, highlighting cultural and method effects:

Coding scheme	Advertisements	Consumer narratives about the ads
Tradition	More in the USA	
Modern		
Productivity		
Enjoyment		
Independence		More in Spain
Status	More in the USA	
Affiliation		
Family	More in Spain	More in Spain
Morality		

Activity: Design a tagline and message for a product being introduced into a new market. Check target consumers' interpretation of your message by asking them the following questions:
   In your own words, please describe the advertisement.

1. Describe your opinions and feelings about the advertising message.
2. What do you think the advertiser was trying to communicate with the ad?
3. How do you know what the advertiser was trying to communicate with this ad? What makes you think so?

Activities adapted from Lerman, D., & Callow, M. (2004). Content analysis in cross-cultural advertising research: insightful or superficial? International Journal of Advertising, 23 (4), 507–521.

Message appeals

Messages are often communicated using more rational or more emotional appeals. **Rational appeals** persuade with logical arguments (e.g., scientific and technical evidence) from believable sources (e.g., authorities, celebrities, and credible consumers). However, information cues and the quantity of information are culture-bound. **Emotional appeals** persuade by evoking positive or negative feelings, often using humour, fear, or sex.

- **Humour** is enjoyable and can put the consumer in a good mood, which may increase purchase intentions, as long as the humour is appropriate. Most humour has an incongruity-resolution structure; however, the type of humour may need to be culturally adapted to be effective.
- **Fear** can be a powerful motivation as it can tap into the instinctual fight-or-flight response, as long as it is not too distressing for consumers. The intensity of the fear may have to be adjusted for cultures, as people may have less tolerance for fear in high uncertainty avoidance countries.
- **Sexual** innuendo and imagery can be memorable; however, religious and moral codes and practices need to be carefully examined.

Characters and roles represented in advertisements

Advertising is often accused of perpetuating traditional social roles; however, it can also be an agent of change. Traditional social roles are often conveyed in advertising through the depiction of characters; however, traditional roles are more likely in masculine, traditional and religious cultures. In contrast, advertising can be an agent of change, serving to normalise non-traditional roles (e.g., depicting women in science and men as carers). Cross-cultural differences also exist in how the elderly are portrayed. Countries with stronger traditional values generally portray the elderly respectfully.

An especially sensitive area is around religious and moral codes and practices that act as filters of advertising messages, transforming factual information into culturally interpreted meaning. For instance, a naked woman washing her hair in her bathroom may be designed to communicate factual information about a product, but may also be seen as scandalous. Even the relationship between men and women depicted in advertising can be problematic. This highlights the importance of investigating local attitudes, even when two countries are ostensibly very similar, such as the USA and Australia. It should be remembered that the role of advertising has never (at least officially) been to change a society's mores, but rather to sell a product. Respect for the existing social conventions in the target society remains a prerequisite for the localisation of advertising messages.

Language

Advertisements usually have text elements (e.g., catchphrase, product description, slogan), often using colloquial language which is subtle, yet precise in meaning. Consumers understand messages all the more readily when colloquial language expresses the nuanced messages of daily life (e.g., sentiments, sensations, family relations, friendships, love affairs) reflected in advertising. However, we need to be careful of colloquial words or slang that are particular to local people and, as such, are difficult to find in dictionaries.

Translating colloquial language is difficult, since it often includes idiomatic expressions, which have a meaning that is different from the literal meaning of the words. These can change from one language to another and even across cultural regions that use the same language. Tourism Australia launched its 'So where the bloody hell are you!' campaign, but soon discovered that the slang Australian term 'bloody hell' evoked different reactions around the world. In the UK, they were forced to air the ad only after 9pm due to 'bloody' being deemed an expletive. Meanwhile, in the USA, the conservative lobby group, The American Family Association, launched a boycott action based on the use of the 'bloody hell' phrase, despite no official concerns from the US government. Finally, in Singapore, the words were removed from the ad altogether.

As explained in Chapter 2, English is the most frequently spoken language; however, for most, it is not their native language. It cannot be assumed that they fully comprehend a nuanced message. However, the use of English in primarily non-English speaking countries might be adequate for simple or factual messages or to convey a worldly or cosmopolitan image. As such, only certain elements (e.g., the brand name) are likely to be in English, whereas the body copy is more often in the local language. Further, the growing number of bilingual people adds a layer of complexity to language presentation. Generally, bilinguals have been found to interpret information differently when they read in one or the other language. Language tends to cue the salience of a self-concept related to one or the other culture and their interpretation and behaviour changes.

Checklist for cross-national transferability of advertising materials

If advertising is to be transferred from one country to another, the following elements should always be carefully checked:

1. Is the problem being solved the same?
2. Is the target market similar?

3. Are the communication objectives the same?
4. Is the main message similar?
5. Is the type and style of information meaningful?
6. Are the copy themes appropriate for the local mores and customs?
7. Are the background themes, colour, use of words (puns, suggestive words), use of humour, use of symbols, types of characters and roles (age, sex, status), situations and types of relationship depicted appropriate?
8. Are there relevant local regulations around this type of advertising?
9. Are there constraints in the availability and use of different media?

Media worldwide

Worldwide differences in advertising expenditure

There are dramatic differences in advertising expenses across countries, even though these countries may have comparable levels of economic development. The total advertising spending worldwide is projected to be almost US$885,000 million in 2024, with the USA being the highest advertising spender, at almost three times that of its closest competitor, China, in 2021, followed by Japan[22]. This can be partially attributed to media availability and prevalence (e.g., radio, television, newspapers, magazines, film, billboards, social media). Where some media have limited or no presence, expenses are automatically restricted.

Cross-cultural differences in media availability and use

The availability of advertising media is influenced by the level of a country's economic development, and also by its view of the appropriate mix between commercial activities and cultural/recreational activities. For instance, cinemas were banned in Saudi Arabia for over 30 years, until the first one opened in Riyadh in 2018. Many countries limit access to the world wide web and impose limits on social media. For example, China and North Korea block website content, prohibit the use of personal VPNs and monitor internet access. Since the start of Russia's war on Ukraine in 2022, Russia has also blocked websites and controlled the media. Further, ethical debates about whether certain products (e.g., vice products) can be advertised, especially to vulnerable populations (e.g., children), have an influence on regulations.

The availability of the media is also influenced by social representations concerning the relationship between the media and its audience. First, there are differences in what local audiences consider to be reasonable ratios between advertising and entertainment (e.g., news, sport, programmes) and also what local audiences consider to be appropriate sequencing, in terms of television movies being sliced up by advertising. Second, there are differences in how entertaining advertising is considered to be. If entertaining the target audience is a necessary condition for capturing their interest, creative effort may have to be devoted to entertainment rather than communicating the core messages. This may reduce the effectiveness of the advertisement because the viewers' attention is attracted by the creative side of the message and diverted from the product that is being presented.

Most countries have instituted rules that place limits on television advertising. Many countries (e.g., Australia, Sweden, the UK) also have national channels that prohibit commercial advertising. Some countries (e.g., Saudi Arabia) closely monitor advertising to ensure that they conform to moral and religious standards. Even where little or no advertising regulation exists, there can sometimes be such an invasion by advertising that viewing television programmes becomes little more than watching advertisements.

A paradoxical situation is that as the number of media channels increases, it becomes more difficult to reach and monitor a target audience, since viewers' saturation with advertisements reduces their ability to listen to advertising and encourages skipping or muting. The assumption that the audience has no saturation threshold suggests the absolute legitimacy of mass advertising.

Advertising standardisation: feasibility and desirability

After a review of arguments for and against advertising standardisation worldwide, a more meaningful question is whether standardised advertising should be used or not, even if it is feasible. The arguments in favour of standardised advertising focus on the provision of a consistent image worldwide, decreased cost of preparing campaign themes, copy and materials, and more control over the planning and execution of campaigns across countries. However, markets differ in many ways that inhibit standardisation, including differences in competition, media infrastructure, regulations, and market/societal variables. While it may be possible to standardise some elements (e.g., theme), other elements (e.g., creative executions and the media mix) are less suitable for standardisation, due to differences in language, preference for humour types, education, and consumer tastes, as well as media infrastructure, consumer media and product habits, and competition.

Personal selling and public relations

In Ghana, there is a saying: 'Mouth smiles, money smiles better'. Although money is always at the very centre of personal selling, so are the intricacies of human relationships. Personal selling involves a salesperson meeting face-to-face with a potential buyer to actively promote a product or provide expert advice. They may also help to diagnose a problem, customise a product, or answer questions. **Table 5.8** provides a summary of the influence of culture on buyer–seller relationships that should be considered in different cultural contexts.

Table 5.8 A summary of the influence of culture on buyer–seller relationships

Cultural value	Influence on seller and buyer
Inferior status for trade	Poor status for sales; selling is reserved to a minority group
Being/doing	More personal relationship orientated; more impersonal deal orientated
Money	Price bargaining as friendship ritual
In-group orientation	Only people from a certain in-group are considered as adequate for sales roles; transactions are preferably made with in-group members
Family orientation	Buyer–seller relationships are viewed as an element of a larger family network
Short-term orientation	Achieving the sale is the ultimate goal
Long-term orientation	Keeping the client is the ultimate goal
Low/high power distance	Equality/inequality between buyer and seller
Listening versus talking	Soft sell versus hard sell

Public relations (PR) involves managing how information about a firm, or individual, is communicated to the public. PR activities involve the production and dissemination of information designed to encourage media and other influencers to spread the word. PR can also be generated though special events for reporters, bloggers, etc., to test products or by offering free samples to celebrities. Given that the firm cannot fully control the message that is disseminated, it is important that they build strong and positive relationships with these parties. This is the case in normal situations, where PR aims to create and enhance a favourable corporate image, but it is even more important in crisis situations, such as boycotts, accidents, strikes, product recalls, and so on, to maintain goodwill by responding to criticism, explaining remedial action to overcome the problem, and anticipating and countering messages that may damage the corporate image.

Cross-cultural differences have been noted in the way companies react to disasters, such as plane crashes, major pollution, etc. They reflect the prevailing sense of responsibility vis-à-vis the community, but also the companies' sense of privacy and the view of what is culturally appropriate for dealing with these events. For instance, a company may choose to adopt a very low profile and wait for the storm to calm, or conversely, adopt a high profile, pleading either guilty or not guilty. In some countries, such as Japan, formal apologies and explanations are expected. If the company does not step forward to do this, the government will. In other countries, where there is an emphasis on privacy and a dislike for public display (e.g., Switzerland), a company is likely to adopt an extremely low profile and engage in very little communication, even if it is clearly in the wrong.

5.6 Chapter summary

In this chapter, we discuss cross-cultural influences on the development and implementation of marketing strategies. We describe the unique cross-cultural challenges for each element of the marketing mix – product, price, place, and promotion – and provide frameworks and tools to help address these challenges. Naturally, some elements of the marketing mix are more heavily culture-bound than others and some elements are more cost-effective for adaptation than others. In general, evidence supports the effectiveness of higher levels of adaptation to the local market.

References

1. American Marketing Association (2017). Definition of Marketing, retrieved from www.ama.org/the-definition-of-marketing-what-is-marketing/ accessed July 17, 2022.

2. Shoham, A. (2021). Standardization of international strategy and export performance: a meta-analysis. In *Strategic Global Marketing: Issues and Trends* (pp. 97–120). Routledge.

3. Elster, A., & Gelfand, M. J. (2021). When guiding principles do not guide: The moderating effects of cultural tightness on value-behavior links. *Journal of Personality*, 89(2), 325–337.

4. Ajzen, I., & Fishbein, M. (1975). Belief, Attitude, Intention, and Behavior: An Introduction to Theory and Research. Reading, MA: Addison-Wesley.

5. Maslow, A. (1943). A theory of human motivation. *Psychological Review*, 50 (4), 370–396.

6. Hong Kong Immigration Department (2022). Statistics on the number of Foreign Domestic Helpers in Hong Kong, retrieved from www.immd.gov.hk/opendata/eng/law-and-security/visas/statistics_FDH.csv accessed July 25, 2022.

7. Hong Kong Immigration Department (2022). Statistics on the number of Foreign Domestic Helpers in Hong Kong, retrieved from www.immd.gov.hk/opendata/eng/law-and-security/visas/statistics_FDH.csv accessed July 25, 2022.

8. Mandler, T., Sezen, B., Chen, J., & Özsomer, A. (2021). Performance consequences of marketing standardization/adaptation: A systematic literature review and future research agenda. *Journal of Business Research*, *125*, 416–435.

9. Kock, F., Josiassen, A., & Assaf, A. G. (2019). Toward a universal account of country-induced predispositions: Integrative framework and measurement of country-of-origin images and country emotions. *Journal of International Marketing*, *27*(3), 43–59.

10. Hornikx, J., van Meurs, F., van den Heuvel, J., & Janssen, A. (2020). How brands highlight country of origin in magazine advertising: A content analysis. *Journal of Global Marketing, 33*(1), 34–45.

11. Blodgett, J. G., Bakir, A., Mattila, A. S., Trujillo, A., Quintanilla, C., & Elmadağ, A. B. (2018). Cross-national differences in complaint behavior: Cultural or situational? *Journal of Services Marketing*, 3(7), 913–924.

12. Saleh, W., & Malibari, A. (2021). Saudi women and vision 2030: Bridging the gap? *Behavioral Sciences*, *11*(10), 132.

13. Lucia-Palacios, L., Bordonoba-Juste, V., & Pérez-López, R. (2021). Consumer-to-consumer reselling adoption among European countries: differences between old and young millennials. *Service Business*, *15*(2), 253–279.

14. The World Bank in Turkiye www.worldbank.org/en/country/turkey/overview (retrieved 28 August, 2022)

15. WTO Anti-dumping information www.wto.org/english/tratop_e/adp_e/adp_e.htm (retrieved 28 August, 2022)

16. Von Stackelberg, H. (1940). *Die Grundlagen Der Nationalökonomie*. Berlin: Springer Verlag.

17. Armas, M. & Polanco, A. (May 9, 2022). In Venezuela, inflation and dollarization deepen schism between private and state employees www.reuters.com/world/americas/venezuela-inflation-dollarization-deepen-schism-between-private-state-employees-2022-05-09/ (retrieved 29 August, 2022)

18. Haytko, D. L., Clark, R. A., Hermans, C. M., & Parker, R. S. (2018). Examining the dimensionality in global attitudes toward advertising: A comparison of perceptions of Chinese and United States consumers. *Journal of International Consumer Marketing, 30*(2), 85–97.

19. Lavidge, R. J., & Steiner, G. A. (1961). A model for predictive measurements of advertising effectiveness. *Journal of Marketing*, 25, 59–62.

20. Happy Meal advertisements in the U.S. www.dropbox.com/s/zo50reck8ug4pa9/McDonald_s_Happy_Meal_US.mp4?dl=0
And in the Philippines:
www.dropbox.com/s/1n3nz9rp60dish3/Mcdonalds_Happy_Mean_Philippines.mp4?dl=0

21. Lerman, D., & Callow, M. (2004). Content analysis in cross-cultural advertising research: Insightful or superficial?. *International Journal of Advertising, 23*(4), 507–521.

22. Guttmann, A. Advertising spending in the world's largest ad markets 2021 (July 12, 2022) statistica.com

6
DESIGNING A CULTURALLY SENSITIVE BUSINESS PLAN

After reading this chapter, you should be able to:

- Design a well-structured and coherent business plan.
- Understand what should be included in each section of the plan.
- Explain the purpose of different analytical tools.
- Know which figures and tables best present different types of information.
- Understand the importance of presentation.

Introduction

It is important to understand that relatively few firms succeed in entering new international markets. As an example, a large study of 20,000 companies in 30 countries that expanded internationally found that the average Return of Assets (ROA) after five years was minus 1% and after 10 years was just +1%, as compared with those that expanded domestically with an average ROA of +1% after five years and +2% after 10 years.[1] This illustrates how important it is for a firm to carefully plan for international expansion before embarking on this potentially costly move.

International expansion is much more complicated than domestic growth. Many more factors come into play at the macro level (e.g., political, economic, socio-cultural, technological, ecological, and legal factors), meso level (e.g., industry norms, competitors, supplies, and substitute products), and micro level (e.g., consumer segments and groups) that need to be carefully scanned and considered, especially if they are significantly different from the domestic market. Failure to consider the potential impact of these factors on the plan to extend to one or more international market will at best limit potential and, at worst be fatal to the firm.

Writing a business plan seems very far from culture, cultural analysis, and cultural dimensions as described in Chapter 1. *A priori,* a business plan and the analytic process to prepare it seem rather culture-free. However, this is truer for the concept of a business plan itself and for the general process of drafting the plan than when dealing with the intricacies of markets, strategies, and implementation. Whereas the concept of a business plan is *etic,* the planning, analysis, and implementation details are not (e.g., due dates, schedules, tasks, deadlines, and penalties associated with not meeting them have a lot to do with the doing orientation and cultural understanding of the concept of time, presented in earlier chapters). As discussed in prior chapters, it is important to be aware of your own cultural biases and be ready to accept new ways of seeing the world.

Whenever intercultural teams are involved in business planning, cultural biases and ethnocentrism must be carefully monitored. Sometimes, as in the case of the X-Culture project, team members have to work interculturally with people whom they have not chosen. Personality and individual character, personal affinities, and the like may ease or hinder the collaborative process, but the key asset, if managed in a sensitive way, is cultural diversity. Cultural diversity is a vital strength for discussing together what is and what is not culturally relative. All opinions should be considered, but the assessment should be based on consensus. There is a need to be reflective and self-critical, and this is always more effective as a team rather than as an isolated individual. Even when work is divided among individual team members, team discussion should be an active part of the process.

Chapter Overview

In this chapter, we discuss the design and development of a business plan, including the types of analytical tools that are commonly used to help solve business problems and ways to present information and format a report that add value to the reader.

- Section 1 describes the essential elements of a business plan in detail. In this section, we present a range of important analytical tools that can be used to explore potential solutions to a different business problem(s) or question(s) being answered in the report. We also offer insights in how to present your analyses and in an impactful manner.

- Section 2 presents information that will help you develop a clear and pragmatic business plan. We emphasise the need to ask the right question and how to make your points clear. We also include a brief introduction to inductive and deductive reasoning, either or both of which are often used in presenting observations of evidence and drawing conclusions from it.
- Section 3 offers a range of tips for writing a business report, including effective use of figures and tables and a final list of dos and don'ts in report writing.

6.1 Elements of a business plan

The purpose of a business plan is to communicate your business analysis efficiently and effectively. Behind every good business plan is a great deal of background work, which includes identifying the key problems and issues, gathering and analysing the required data, and thinking critically about solutions and recommendations. You cannot include all your work in the report, but it will be clear from a well-written report that a great deal of work underlies it.

The following describes what goes into each section of a business plan:

- Title page
- Executive summary
- Introduction
  - Current situation and problem statement
- Market analysis
  - Internal analysis (to demonstrate that you understand the firm)
  - New market selection analysis (to provide clear criteria and credible research)
  - Industry and competition analysis (to identify key competitive advantages)
  - Customer analysis (to identify segments)
  - Market entry strategy (to provide direction and options)
  - Analysis of important trade regulations, certification, logistics, etc.
- Marketing strategy and implementation
  - Product, promotion, pricing and distribution strategy and implementation
- Conclusion, including future opportunities and threats

Each of these elements is described in the following sections in detail, including how to present the information in a clear and coherent manner.

Title page

People often judge a book by its cover. The title page of a business report should look professional and be informative. It creates a first impression, not only in terms of visual appeal, but also in showing your ability to select and present relevant information. At a minimum, it should include the (a) name of the firm, (b) title of the report, (c) date of completion or submission, (d) author information, and, if necessary, a confidentiality statement. Additional elements, such as a relevant graphic, professional formatting, and judicious use of colour and font choices, can add interest.

- **Firm name and logo**: In addition to adding the name of the firm, you might consider adding a high-resolution thumbnail of the logo. All graphics throughout the report should be high-resolution so that they are clear and look professional.
- **Title**: A title should convey important information about the report, rather than simply stating a generic topic like a 'Business Plan'. The title should clearly reflect the content of the report. The more specific this is, the better. Often the problem or question being addressed in the report is part of the report title.
- The **date** the report was completed or submitted is also important. It should at least include the month and year.
- The **author information** should give prominence to the firm you are working for, if the report was commissioned, but it should also provide enough detail for interested parties to be able to contact the key author(s). Usually, an email address is enough.
- A **confidentiality statement** may also be included at the bottom of the page. For example: *This report provides confidential and proprietary information, intended for informational purposes only and should not be reproduced without consent of [name].*

In the end, the title page should look professional. Plan the layout, fonts, and colours to be balanced and visually pleasing, and then carry these choices throughout the report.

An excellent X-Culture report title page should be *informative* and *impressive*. To be *informative* it should include the relevant information:

- company name and (optional) logo
- the problem or question being answered
- the date of submission
- the team's name and number
- a list of team members and their roles in developing the business plan

To be *impressive* it should look professional. There are many ways to make a report title page impressive. Some simple ideas are as follows:

- use different sized fonts to convey the importance of the information
- add a relevant graphic to pique the interest of the reader
- use bullet points or columns when information is a list (e.g., author names, roles, and emails)
- author pictures can also add interest, as long as they depict the team as professionals

Executive summary

An executive summary is usually written after a report has been completed. It should be a stand-alone section that briefly conveys the highlights of the entire report. In many cases, the reader will start with, and perhaps only read, the executive summary. If the ideas are compelling, they will go to the rest of the report to find the relevant information. *It is essentially a sales pitch for the report.* Think about the substance that needs to be included and only include most important highlights and recommendations. The length is often just one page, although it can be up to 5–10% of an entire report.

Commonly, executive summaries of a business plan will introduce the purpose of the report (i.e., the problem or question being addressed) and provide the most important information about the firm and market analyses, the proposed marketing plan, and the financial implications. Remember that it is a summary; no new information should be introduced in this section.

The executive summary should be well laid out to capture the reader's attention and convey the information succinctly. The use of subtitles, bullet points, bold text, etc., help to convey information clearly. If subtitles are used, they should convey the essential information in just a word or two.

Example outline for an X-Culture Executive Summary (1 page maximum)

- Company analysis:
  - Key strengths
  - Key weaknesses
  - Great opportunities
  - Substantial threats

(Continued)

- **Market analysis**: State the recommended new market and the reasons why.
- **Entry mode**: State the recommended mode of entry and the reasons why.
- **Distribution partners**: Identify the partners (contact details should be in the report).
- **Promotion**: Provide the main promotional recommendation and brief key points on how to organise it (i.e., with contact information, and costs provided).
- **Staffing**: List any positions that need to be recruited, and how they can be recruited.
- **Pricing and payment information**: State the recommended pricing and any factors that need to be considered in receiving payment for goods sold, including regulations.
- **Shipping**: State the shipping recommendation, the cost and timing, as well as the cost of any taxes and tariffs that might be incurred.

Introduction and business description

The introduction of a business plan usually begins with a short description of the firm and industry they currently operate in, to show you understand the business. It should briefly outline the issues, to identify what led to the problem at hand, and then clearly state the problem(s) or question(s) that the report will address.

Important information in the introduction will come from your analysis, which makes it difficult to write prior to any analysis. For instance, the significance of the problem(s) being addressed may only be clear after an analysis of the firm's strengths and weaknesses and the opportunities and threats in the environment (SWOT analysis).

A 'generic' example of a brief introduction

Business Y is a successful small to medium enterprise that is the market leader in the manufacture of *gold widgets* in Australia. However, sales have stagnated, and the home market is expected to slowly decline over the next 10 years. *Business Y* is looking to expand internationally to counter this trend and wants to know which market(s) have the most potential for their *gold widgets*, or a modified version, given their limited international experience.

Market analysis

The market analysis should be designed to answer the main problem(s) or question(s) being address in the report. As discussed in Chapter 4, if a firm plans to expand internationally, your analysis should clearly show evidence that suggests where the firm is most likely to be successful. The research will likely be multi-staged, first focusing on prospective regions, then countries, then segments within and/or across countries, at each stage becoming more detailed. It is important to clearly state (a) what market characteristics are necessary for the firm to succeed, (b) which markets meet the criteria for success, and (c) where the demand is likely to be highest and the supply (competition) lowest. Tables or figures are often useful to highlight the more relevant evidence.

The type of analyses that goes into business planning depends on the problem(s) or question(s) that need to be answered. It is extremely rare that clear answers can be easily found without any real analysis. But, once the problem(s) or question(s) being asked is clear, primary and secondary information (including proxy information) can be gathered that will help to develop an effective strategy for the firm. The type of information that can be gathered is limitless, which is why it is important to (1) have a clear problem(s) or question(s), (2) find one or more tools, concepts or theories that can help to direct the type of information needed, and (3) understand how this information can be communicated to support your recommendations.

Analytic tools

There are many helpful analytical tools available that can be used for market analysis. Some are broader and more likely to be helpful when considering new international markets (e.g., SWOT, PESTLE, Porter's Five Forces), whereas others are more focused on the firm's product portfolio (e.g., Boston Matrix, Product life cycle, Ansoff's Matrix). **Table 6.1** provides a brief description of the purpose and information needed for some commonly used analytic tools. It is important to think about which analytic tool(s) you intend to use before you begin analysis. Choose carefully, as only those analytical tools that are directly related to *both* the *question* and the *solution* should be presented in the report.

Detailed descriptions and how-to videos can easily be found for the full range of market analysis tools on the internet. Here, we provide brief descriptions (see also images in **Figure 6.1**) of the more common tools, to help you think about which tools will best address the business problem(s) or question(s) you need to address in the report:

Table 6.1 Example of analytic tools and their utility

Analytic Tool	Purpose	Information analysed
SWOT	Identify strategic opportunities that a firm is well placed to take advantage of, while understanding weaknesses and threats.	• Firm's internal strengths and weaknesses • External opportunities and threats
PESTLE	Identify the impact of external factors that may affect business operations, especially when expanding to new markets.	• Political, Economic, Social, Technological, Legal and Ecological factors
Porter's Five Forces	Assesses industry attractiveness to examine how a firm can increase their competitive advantage and profitability.	• Competitors, new market entrants, supplies, customers, and substitute products
Competitive Advantage Model	Assesses the firm's relative position within an industry to establish a profitable and sustainable position.	• Competitive scope and source of the firm's competitive advantage
Boston Matrix	Identify where to invest to generate the most value.	• Company competitiveness (share of market) and market attractiveness (growth)
Product life cycle	Identifies which products should be invested in.	• Sales over time
Ansoff's Matrix	Identifies business strategies that inform the marketing mix tactics.	• Product growth and market growth

- **SWOT[2] analyses** can help a firm better understand their **weaknesses**, take advantage of their **strengths**, deter **threats**, and capitalise on **opportunities** to develop their business goals and strategies. It is usually a good start, but complex issues will require more in-depth research. SWOT analysis can produce a lot of information, not all of it being useful. It will be necessary to take additional steps to prioritise and interpret the information before it can be used to generate viable solutions. A PESTLE analysis can often help identify the important external factors in a more structured way.
- **PESTLE (or PEST, PESTEL, …)[3] analyses** can help firms better understand the complex external environment that might impact new business. This model identifies key risk factors in the environment that need to be considered, including **political, economic, social, technological, legal,** and **environmental** factors. This tool provides a comprehensive but relatively simple framework to analyse external issues.
- **Porter's Five Forces[4]** examines the competitive structure and profitability of an industry with the aim of increasing the firm's competitive advantage and profitability. The five forces analysed include the power of **buyers** and of **suppliers**, the threat of **new entrants** and of **substitutes** and **competitive**

rivalry (rated low, medium, or high). It helps firms understand competitive factors more broadly to help mitigate these forces through product development and marketing strategies. This analysis can be combined with SWOT or PESTLE to better understand the external factors in a new market.

- **Competitive Advantage** model[5] examines the firm's competitive advantage and the type of markets it competes in to identify four generic marketing strategies: ***Cost Leadership*** (cost advantage in a broad market), ***Cost Focus*** (cost advantage in a narrow market), ***Differentiation Leadership*** (differentiation advantage in a broad market), and ***Differentiation Focus*** (differentiation advantage in a narrow market). It might also be useful to consider the Five Forces analysis to consider supplier and buyer power for cost leadership or a product portfolio model (e.g., Ansoff Matrix) for the differentiation strategy.

- **The Boston Matrix**[6] examines each of the firm's products' share of the market and the rate of growth of their markets, to identify which of four growth categories their products are currently in: ***stars*** (high market share in a high growth market – invest), ***question marks*** (low market share in a high growth market – invest or divest), ***cash cows*** (high market share in a low growth market – milk to invest elsewhere) and ***dogs*** (lower market share in a low growth market – liquidate, divest or reposition). This analysis can be a quick and easy way to make product development decisions, but the understanding of market share should also take into consideration the size of the market and how profitable the product is. This type of portfolio analysis helps firms to understand how their existing product sales might support the development of a new international market.

- **Product life cycle** depicts the sales of products over time. It is expected that initial product investment will have a negative cash flow until the ***product introduction*** *phase*. In this phase, pricing is crucial. Either a penetration strategy should be used to drive sales, or a price skimming strategy should be used to drive profit. Through the ***growth phase,*** sales rapidly increase (advertising is crucial here to support this growth) until the ***maturity phase,*** where sales growth slows but profits are often high (promotional offers are crucial here to encourage purchase). At the ***saturation phase***, sales begin to drop until the ***decline phase*** begins. This type of portfolio analysis can help firms to know when to introduce new products or product modifications. The main caution here is that there are no guarantees in forecasting and consumer tastes can change rapidly, altering their trajectory.

- **Ansoff's Matrix** examines product growth and market growth in sales to suggest which of four strategic growth options should be prioritised. The lowest risk option is a ***penetration strategy***, selling more existing products to existing markets. The ***product development strategy*** has more risk, as it involves the adaptation of at least the product and promotion elements of the marketing mix, which should be based on customer research and firm capabilities. The ***market development strategy*** has more risk again, as it looks to adapt distribution channels, supported by promotions, to target new market segments. Finally, the ***diversification strategy*** is the riskiest, as it develops new products for new markets.

a)

SWOT

	Helpful	**Harmful**
Internal	**Strengths** Advantages over competition	**Weaknesses** Disadvantages relative to competition
External	**Opportunities** Advantageous conditions	**Threats** Disadvantageous conditions

SWOT

b)

PESTLE

- Political
- Economic
- Social
- Technological
- Legal
- Environmental

c)

Porter's Five Forces

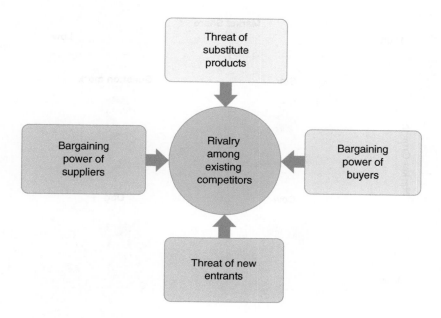

d)

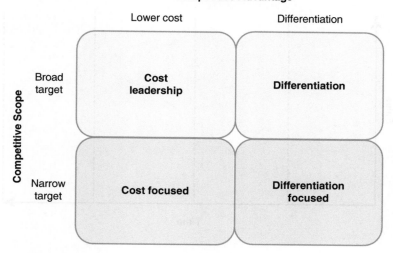

e)　　　　　　　　　The Boston Matrix

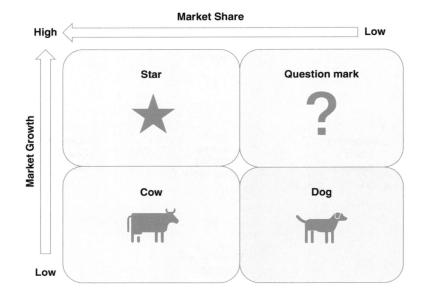

f)　　　　　　　　The Product Life Cycle

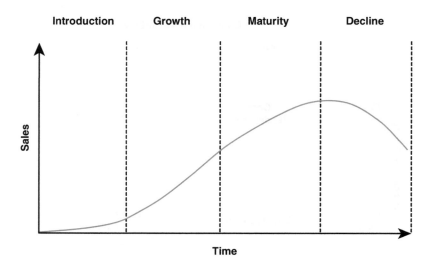

g)

Ansoff's Matrix

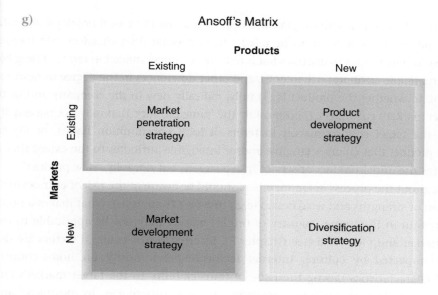

Figure 6.1   Pictorial examples of market analytical tools

As previously mentioned, it is likely that a combination of analytic tools will be used in any international marketing analysis. The more culturally distant the country being entered is from the home country, the more accommodations and adaptations are likely to need to be made, to maximise the opportunities. The market analysis should be in-depth, allowing firms to understand the key differences in cultural, economic, political, legal/regulatory, business environments. It should identify differences in consumer tastes, preferences, buying criteria, highlighting differences from consumers in their home country. As discussed in Chapter 4, this information can often be found online if the budget does not allow for primary market research.

Gathering information for the business plan also needs collective cultural sensitivity. Generally, collecting secondary data seems to be more culture-free than gathering primary data. However, one needs to be prudent when interpreting comparisons of secondary data especially in a PESTLE analysis as figures may not be directly comparable across cultural/national contexts. Collection of primary data is much more culture-bound – interviews, samples, respondents are carriers of their own culture – and subject to possible response biases (see Chapter 2).

For firms new to international markets, the Ansoff Matrix is more likely to indicate market development. However, this is often combined with product development to adapt and fine-tune the products or services to the new target market. For smaller firms, it is very unlikely that a business plan will deal with a case of vertical or lateral diversification, and much more likely to be related to horizontal diversification into foreign market(s). You may want to discuss what is new for the target market in terms of tangible and/or intangible attributes (Chapter 5), and other differences in the degree of newness according to whether the product is (1) fully, radically new to the company and/or to the target market's customers, (2) ostensibly the 'same product' that may not necessarily fit with the target country-market in terms of local consumption habits, or (3) an adapted product that changes tangible and/or intangible attributes to the extent that it transforms the initial product or service into a largely, but not fully, 'new product'.

Throughout the process, team members should be aware of the risk of ethnocentric extension of strengths and weaknesses (e.g., in a SWOT analysis): what makes a product successful in the home (country of origin) market may not be applicable to the target market and vice-versa (see Chapter 5). Internal versus external factors are differently impacted by culture. Internal factors depend mostly on home-country cultural characteristics raising the issue of transferability to the target market's culture. External factors include knowledge of any differences in business, and management practices are likely to be essential to success.

Marketing objectives, strategies, and implementation

The marketing objectives, strategies, and implementation need to be realistic and coherent. Specifically, marketing strategies are long-term plans designed to achieve marketing objectives (e.g., increased sales, market share, brand awareness, etc.) that are linked to the firm's objectives (e.g., profitability, growth, etc.). As such, the long-term objectives of the company will have a significant impact on both the marketing objectives and marketing strategy adopted. For instance, a firm with longer-term objectives that include both profitability and goals around social responsibility may want to adopt social marketing that raises the profile of a cause in addition to being profitable. Thus, marketing objectives should reflect the aims of the firm and provide a path to achieve these aims. They should also provide a clear vision of what needs to be done, as well as a way to monitor and measure progress.

In Chapter 5, cross-cultural implications on the four elements of the marketing mix were considered in detail (product, price, promotion, and place), but other elements, including people, process, and physical environment should be considered, especially if the product is a service. All of these elements need to be coordinated with each other to form a coherent strategy. For example, if the marketing strategy calls for Cost Leadership, then all of the marketing mix elements need to focus on ensuring the longevity of maintaining the low-cost position.

Details about how to implement the strategy are also important.

- Any product or service modification should be justified and detailed.
- Any required product or safety certification should be identified, as well as information on how it can be obtained.
- Price ranges should be suggested, as well as any potential issues with payments and regulations listed.
- If the distribution strategy calls for the products to be sold through high-end stores, potential distributors should be listed, along with contact information.
- If advertisements or promotional materials are recommended, a step-by-step guide for how to place the advertisement, as well as estimates of costs, frequency and tips for effectiveness, will be important. A mock-up of a locally tailored marketing flyer, brochure, email, social media post or webpage may also be included.
- If the products need to be shipped to the market, options should be included, along with price, time, and reliability information. Any import tariffs, custom duties, and other feeds that the buyer or seller will need to pay should also be listed.

Presentation of the market analysis

While the content of the report is the most important feature, the presentation of content is almost as important if you want a busy executive to read it. Since the market analysis section of the report will contain most of the evidence and interpretation that supports the conclusions and recommendations, it is good practice to use subheadings that clearly identify the purpose of each analysis. Also consider adding the conclusions and/or highlights immediately following the subtitle, prior to the more detailed analyses. Business writing usually presents the conclusion before the evidence, so this is good practice. **Figure 6.2** provides an example of how this might be done.

Summary
- Recommendation(s)
- Observations of evidence
- Conclusion

Figure 6.2 Example structure for highlighting the main conclusions

When presenting your main analysis, ensure that complex information is presented in an easily digestible manner, including the use of bullet points, tables, graphs, and diagrams (see Section 6.3 for tips on developing effective figures and tables). Finally, each section should end with a conclusion that summarises how the main findings help to solve the problem.

The conclusion

The conclusion should start with the solution to the problem(s) or question(s) being answered. It should then briefly summarise the observation of evidence that led to this answer. It is acceptable to use bullet points for this. At the end, the conclusion should consider not only the next step, but also the longer-term future. Any potential threats or limitations should be briefly noted and addressed.

The aim of the conclusion is to provide a clear answer to the problem(s) or question(s) being addressed that is consistent with the evidence presented, and provides actionable solutions for the firm. Readers should come away with the impression that the report has achieved its purpose and offers significant insight into the problem(s) at hand. Given that it is a conclusion, no new information should be included in this section.

> After careful consideration of all the options, *Firm A* should begin its international expansion by entering *Country B*, as it has a similar market, but is at an earlier stage in the product life cycle, with good potential for growing sales and generally weaker competition than what is in the home market. Given that the firm is new to international marketing, it is recommended that they partner with *Retailer C* who has significant local capabilities. In terms of adaptation to the local market, some modification of the gold widget may be required, given homes are generally smaller and people shop more frequently in smaller stores. However, continual monitoring of the international environment is warranted as similar products have attracted tariffs due to geopolitical tension in recent years. In summary, the benefits of international expansion into *Country B* partnering with *Retailer C* outweigh the costs, and will help the firm to gain experience in an international market before they expand further.

The referencing

Sources of information should be referenced to allow readers to seek more information and acknowledge the copyrights of other authors. Any official reference style (e.g., APA, Chicago, Harvard) can be used, as long as it is consistent throughout the report.

The X-culture project uses APA (American Psychological Association) style. In-text citations always include the authors' last name(s) and the year of publication. If you use Google Scholar to search for a paper, you can click on the "**Cite** tab to get the reference already in APA format. At the end, the complete references should be provided.

In-text citation examples:

- Culture influences consumer behaviour (Davaei et al., 2001; Usunier, van Herk, and Lee, 2005)
- Davaei and colleagues (2001) state that culture influence consumer behaviour.

References

Newspaper article

- Backer., N., & Whitfeld, A. (2022, September 2). 'What is Japanese humour and why is it so misunderstood?'. ABC News: www.abc.net.au/news/2022-09-02/what-is-japanese-humour-and-why-is-it-so-misunderstood/101352386

Journal article

- Davaei, M., Gunkel, M., Veglio, V., & Taras, V. (2022). The influence of cultural intelligence and emotional intelligence on conflict occurrence and performance in global virtual teams. *Journal of International Management*, 100969.

Book

- Usunier, J. C., Van Herk, H., & Lee, J. A. (2017). *International and Cross-cultural Business Research*. Sage.

6.2 Developing a clear and pragmatic business plan

To state the obvious, a business plan should deliver insight, rather than generic descriptions or naïve opinions. The problem(s) or question(s) you are answering should be clear, and everything in the report should be focused on solving the problem. To start with, you need to answer the right question.

Answering the right question

As part of your analyses, you will have developed a clear understanding of the situation and complications that lead to the main problem that needs to be solved. Understanding this will help to ensure that you are asking and answering the *right* question in your report. Even slight differences in the question may require the use of different analytical tools and market research methods to uncover the required answers.

Analysing the firm's current situation will usually provide insight into the question and sub-questions that need to be answered. For example, **Firm A** *has experienced declining sales growth in their domestic market over the last 3 years and it is looking for growth opportunities in a new international market to extend the product life cycle and gain international experience*. The initial question is: which country market should they enter? However, it is worth considering what information is needed to know the answer to the main question. Brainstorming sub-questions will help your analyses: for example, what made the product successful in the domestic market? Why are sales declining? What segment have they been, and are they currently, serving? What criteria would make a new international market attractive? How willing are they to learn and understand markets that have different macro and meso environments? Does the firm have the necessary capabilities? Once the question and sub-questions have been defined, the information needed and potential broad solutions will be easier to arrive at.

It is important to consider that in international markets the problems and solutions will likely be different. The objectives cannot simply be the same as those for domestic market research. Differences in cultural assumptions complicate the questions we need to ask, the methods we need to use to answer the questions, and potentially our interpretation of the answers.

How to make a clear point

In business writing, the norm is to start with a conclusion that is subsequently supported with evidence (i.e., main point =>arguments/reason/evidence). It keeps attention and ensures the most important information is read first. For example, early in the report, you might present a clear, actionable question, followed by a concise recommendation or statement that answers the question, followed by support for the recommendation (e.g., specific sub-issues and or causes of the problem). In the body of the report, there will likely be more detailed recommendations, followed by their supporting arguments.

The basic types of reasoning that are used to reach a logical conclusion are deductive and inductive reasoning. By correctly using these two techniques, your points will be clear, logical, and well-supported.

- **Deductive reasoning** is theory-based. It begins with a proposition or hypothesis and then examines the relevant evidence to reach a specific conclusion. Specific observations of the evidence may or may not support the hypothesis, therefore, the conclusion should be drawn from the observations.
- **Inductive reasoning** is observation-based. It begins with specific observations with the aim of identifying a pattern to infer a generalisation or explanation of the data. The reliability of the conclusion depends on the accuracy and completeness of the observations.

In reality, there is often an interplay between inductive and deductive reasoning as we develop our understanding. Inductive reasoning is often used to form hypotheses and theories and deductive reasoning allows the application and testing of theories to particular situations.

6.3 Tips for writing a business report

Presentation, formatting, and proofreading are all essential to effective report writing. The effort is worth it, as even small mistakes can lead to a lack of confidence in the rigor behind the report.

Take the time to be clear and concise

The first, and probably most important, tip is that a report should be clear and concise. A famous quote from Mark Twain is: *'If I had more time, I would have written a shorter letter'*. The message is that it takes longer to write a short, clear communication than a long rambling essay. The challenge in a business report is to write what you have to say in as brief a text as possible. Effective use of bullet points, tables, and figures can help to convey important information clearly and succinctly. However, poorly designed tables or figures can detract from the report (see Table 6.2).

Developing effective lists, figures and tables

Figures and tables can effectively convey complex information. They should be visually appealing and clearly illustrate your point at a glance. Carefully choosing the most appropriate form can assist with this. For instance, the form chosen will change how the data is interpreted or understood:

- A **table best** presents data when precise numbers are important.
- A **pie chart** best presents parts that add up to a meaningful whole.
- A **bar chart** best presents numbers that are independent but comparable.
- A **line graph** best presents change over time.

The title of a figure or table should begin with a number and convey the essential information about what is presented. All tables and figures should be sequentially numbered throughout the report.

Sequences are also important in lists. For instance, think about the ordering of a list of competitors. Is it more useful to sort them from the largest or strongest to the smallest or weakest? The sorting of a list can in itself convey important information and be more memorable.

Which list strikes you as organised and well thought out? Which will be easier to remember? The key is in the organisation, formatting, and presentation.

• Insight 1	Insight 1
• Evidence 1	• Observation 1a
• Descriptor 2	• Observation 1b
• Issue 3	• Observation 1c
• Insight 2	Insight 2
• Timing 1	• Observation 2a
• Risk 2	• Observation 2b
• Benefit 3	• Observation 2c
• Insight 3	Insight 3
• Descriptor 1	• Observation 3a
• Issue 2	• Observation 3b
• Cost 3	• Observation 3c

Table 6.2 Alternative presentation formats

For tables, column and row titles should be clear and precisely convey what the information is, including the units of measurement, if numbers are included (e.g., $, %; if used in the title, there is no need to add these to each number in the row or column). When the numbers in a table include many zeros, they should be reduced by adding a key to the unit of measurement into the column or row title (e.g., use '000 to reflect numbers that are in thousands'). Similarly, decimal places should only be added when necessary, and not to already large numbers. Given that percentages are already at two decimal places, they should not include additional decimals. Make sure the numbers in the table are aligned and the font is readable. If you need to reduce the font size, the table has too much information.

Figures may include a graph, diagram, picture, map, etc. They should be carefully chosen to reflect their purpose and clearly make their point. Figures should be large enough and of high enough resolution to be clearly seen. Centre them on the page and set them apart from the text. Important information can be highlighted by colour, but keep colour use consistent throughout the report. If colours are used in graphs (e.g., bar charts) and diagrams, they should not distract attention from the data. Avoid colours that clash (i.e., those on opposite sides of the colour wheel), instead choose a cool or a warm colour palette. Avoid using a legend that relies on colour alone, as about 1 in 12 men and 1 in 200 women are colour blind.

Most word processors have excellent smart art tools and table formats to create interesting visual images. **Figure 6.3** shows two images of the same information. Which is more professional and easier to read? This figure also shows how referencing as a footnote can declutter figures that necessarily include observations from research activities.

Strengths	Weaknesses
I. Strong reputation for safety and quality II. Dominance in domestic air travel market[1] III. Diversified air services, with domestic and freight services remaining profitable, while international air travel lost money[2] IV. More agile and flexible, reducing operational expenses by 62% in 2020/21 over 2018/19 pre-pandemic[2] V. Strong loyalty programme[2]	I. Cash flow from operations was negative with increasing debt in 2021[2] II. Losing money on international air travel[2] III. More expensive airfares than many other airlines IV. Relatively high labour, aircraft operation and fuel[1] V. Employee layoffs and disputes[2] VI. Reduction in advertising[2]
Opportunities	Threats
I. Demand increasing in some sectors, Interstate travel, freight, [3] leisure travel with price increases on busy routes[1] II. Online shopping growth[2] III. Future partnerships with other airlines	I. Pandemic resurgence[1] and geopolitical crises[4] II. Increased competition[1] III. Increased operating costs[1] IV. Cyber security risks[2] V. Concerns about emissions[5]

Figure 6.3a Standard presentation

Strengths
- Strong reputation for safety and quality
- Dominance in domestic air travel market[1]
- Diversified air services, with domestic and freight services remaining profitable, while international air travel lost money[2]
- More agile and flexible, reducing operational expenses by 62% in 2020/21 over 2018/19 pre-pandemic[2]
- Strong loyalty programme[2]

Weaknesses
- Cash flow from operations was negative with increasing debt in 2021[2]
- Losing money on international air travel[2]
- More expensive airfares than many other airlines
- Relatively high labour, aircraft operation and fuel[1]
- Employee layoffs and disputes[2]
- Reduction in advertising[2]

Opportunities
- Demand increasing in some sectors, Interstate travel, freight, [3] leisure travel with price increases on busy routes[1]
- Online shopping growth[2]
- Future partnerships with other airlines

Threats
- Pandemic resurgence[1] and geopolitical crises[4]
- Increased competition[1]
- Increased operating costs[1]
- Cyber security risks[2]
- Concerns about emissions[5]

1. Australian Competition & Consumer Commission. 'Airline competition in Australia – March 2022 report', 8 March, 2022, www.accc.gov.au/publications/serial-publications/airline-competition-in-australia/airline-competition-in-australia-march-2022-report (accessed April 11, 2022).
2. Qantas Annual Report 2021 https://investor.qantas.com/investors/?page=annual-reports (accessed April 1, 2022)
3. Bouwer, Saxon, Wittkamp, 'Back to the future? Airline sector poised for change post-COVID-19', 2 April 2021, www.mckinsey.com/industries/travel-logistics-and-infrastructure/our-insights/back-to-the-future-airline-sector-poised-for-change-post-covid-19 (accessed February, 4).
4. Baldanza, 'Five Ways Russia's Ukraine Invasion Will Affect Airlines Worldwide', March 1, 2022, www.forbes.com/sites/benbaldanza/2022/03/01/five-ways-the-ukrainian-invasion-will-affect-worldwide-airlines/?sh=3d1b7a4f1e0d (accessed April 11, 2022).
5. Ellis, Guira, Tyers, 'What future do airlines have? Three experts discuss', The Conversation, 22 Apr. 2020, https://theconversation.com/what-future-do-airlines-have-three-experts-discuss-135365 (accessed April 11, 2022).

Figure 6.3b Enhanced presentation

Figure 6.3 Presentation of the same SWOT Analysis: Growth opportunities for Qantas

Proofreading for style and grammar

Once the content has been checked, the copy should be proofread for flow, spelling, punctuation, and grammatical mistakes. Reading a report aloud can be helpful in detecting errors (e.g., Word has a *Read Aloud* function that can be useful). Often reports are written by multiple people, which can cause issues with the internal consistency of the report. Ideally, a proofreader should be someone who writes well, and did not write the bulk of the text; this provides a fresh set of eyes. Always use spell-check and grammar-check, but be aware that these programs will not pick up all mistakes and grammatical errors (e.g., 'has' instead of 'as'). Finally, either British or US spelling conventions are acceptable for English text, as long as they are consistent throughout the report.

A final list of dos and don'ts about the details

- Always carefully proofread the text, figures, and tables. Even one small mistake will make the reader question the quality and accuracy of all your work.
- Formatting should look professional. Carefully choose the layout, fonts, and colours.
- Section titles and summaries (these can be bullet points) are useful at the start of each section.
- Judicious use of figures and graphs can convey important information parsimoniously. They should be high-resolution, easy to read, and centred on the page.
- Check that your graphs actually convey what you are trying to show.
- All fonts, including in figures and tables, should be easily readable and not too small.
- Use short, clear sentences focusing on just one main point. Avoid long and convoluted explanations.
- Repeat the same word when you mean the same thing. Choosing synonyms just for the sake of avoiding repetition can be confusing to the reader.
- Use *they* rather than singular specific *he/she her/his* gender pronouns.
- Some consistent punctuation mistakes found in reports include the following:
  - Misuse of apostrophes is common. For example, a possessive apostrophe should go before the s if the noun that it relates to is singular (*A firm's products*) and after the s if it is plural (*Many firms' products*) .
  - Misuse of colons and semicolons. For example, a semicolon (;) can be used to separate two parts of a sentence that are closely linked in

meaning, whereas a colon (:) can be used to introduce a list or to connect two independent sentences when the second clarifies or explains the first.

- ○ Confusing affect and effect. *Affect* is normally a verb and should be used when it denotes action, whereas the *effect* is normally a noun and should be used when it refers to the end result.
- ○ Past, present, and future tense. Be as consistent as possible in the use of all tenses.
- Finally, always convert a report to a portable document file (pdf) before submission, as word processing software may open in a different format from the one you intended.

Note. Also see the Chapter 2 appendix for further advice for non-native English speakers on how to write in English.

6.4 Chapter summary

In this chapter, we describe the essential elements of a business plan and describe the contents of each section. We provide an overview of commonly used analytic tools that can help to focus the market analysis. While insightful content is essential, so is the way in which it is presented. We offer tips on the presentation of tables and figures and tips for writing the report.

References

1. Stadler, C., Mayer, M., & Hautz, J. (2015). Few companies actually succeed at going global. *Harvard Business Review*. https://hbr.org/2015/03/few-companies-actually-succeed-at-going-global
2. Weihrich, H. (1982). The TOWS matrix—a tool for situational analysis. *Long Range Plan 15*(2), 54–64. https://doi.org/10.1016/0024-6301(82)90120-0
3. Aguilar, F. J. (1967). *Scanning the Business Environment*. London: Cambridge University Press.
4. Porter, M. E. (1979). How competitive forces shape strategy. *Harvard Business Review 57*(2), 137–145.
5. Porter, M. E. (1998). Competitive advantage: Creating and sustaining superior performance. 2nd ed. New York: Free Press.
6. Boston Consulting Group (2022) What is the Growth Share Matrix www.bcg.com/about/overview/our-history/growth-share-matrix

AUTHOR INDEX

SUBJECT INDEX